iPhone® *& iPad*®
Web Design
FOR
DUMMIES®

by Janine Warner, David LaFontaine, and
Lee Andron

WILEY
Wiley Publishing, Inc.

iPhone® & iPad® Web Design For Dummies®

Published by
Wiley Publishing, Inc.
111 River Street
Hoboken, NJ 07030-5774
www.wiley.com

Copyright © 2011 by Wiley Publishing, Inc., Indianapolis, Indiana

Published by Wiley Publishing, Inc., Indianapolis, Indiana

Published simultaneously in Canada

For general information on our other products and services, please contact our Customer Care Department within the U.S. at 877-762-2974, outside the U.S. at 317-572-3993, or fax 317-572-4002.

For technical support, please visit www.wiley.com/techsupport.

Wiley also publishes its books in a variety of electronic formats and by print-on-demand. Not all content that is available in standard print versions of this book may appear or be packaged in all book formats. If you have purchased a version of this book that did not include media that is referenced by or accompanies a standard print version, you may request this media by visiting http://booksupport.wiley.com. For more information about Wiley products, visit us www.wiley.com.

Library of Congress Control Number is available from the publisher.

ISBN 978-1-118-00643-6 (cloth); ISBN 978-1-118-09899-8 (ebk); ISBN 978-1-118-09900-1 (ebk); ISBN 978-1-118-09901-8 (ebk)

Manufactured in the United States of America

10 9 8 7 6 5 4 3 2 1

About the Authors

Janine Warner is an author, a web designer, and the creator of the web training site DigitalFamily.com.

Since 1996, Janine has written more than a dozen books about the Internet, including *Mobile Web Design For Dummies, Web Sites Do-It-Yourself For Dummies*, and *Dreamweaver For Dummies* (all eight editions).

A popular speaker, Janine offers training in techy topics, such as web design, and gives keynotes on Internet trends, the growing importance of the mobile web, social media, and online reputation. Janine is fluent in Spanish and has given many speeches in Latin America and Spain.

Janine is also the host of a growing collection of training videos for Kelbytraining.com in web design, Adobe Dreamweaver, and Cascading Style Sheets.

Janine has worked on large and small websites. From 1998 to 2000, she worked for *The Miami Herald,* first as its Online Managing Editor and later as Director of New Media. She left that position to serve as Director of Latin American Operations for CNET Networks, an international technology media company.

Since 2001, Janine has run her own web design firm and worked as a writer, speaker, and consultant. To find out more about Janine, find free web design training materials, and get answers to common questions, visit www.DigitalFamily.com.

David LaFontaine's first cellphone came in a backpack and weighed about 20 pounds, and the closest he got to using gestures to control the phone came when it fell on his toe. Despite this early mishap, Dave remains fascinated with the promise of these little portable pieces of technology.

He has more than 20 years of experience as a journalist, an editor, and a multimedia producer working on a variety of projects in film, television, print, radio, and the Internet. The Newspaper Association of America commissioned him to write two case studies about the promise of mobile advertising, which gave him a head start at figuring out what kinds of content work best on the mobile web.

He began the shift from writer to multimedia content producer when ABC's *PrimeTime* shipped him a video camera and turned him loose to set up and shoot interviews on his own. Seeing his first shaky efforts on network television was a revelation — a "Hey, I guess I can actually do this after all" moment. Since then, Dave rarely leaves the house without some kind of video recording device on him, although he does occasionally feel nostalgic for days when all he needed was a pencil and notepad. He's also a popular blogger whose work can be found on Sips from the Firehose (`www.sipsfromthefirehose.com`) and the Mobile Web Design blog (`www.mobilewebdesignblog.com`). Dave is a partner in Artesian Media; to learn more, visit his personal site (`www.davidlafontaine.com`).

Dave has spoken to audiences around the world about the promise of mobile and set them loose on GPS-fueled scavenger hunts designed to teach them how to leverage the power of content everywhere, all the time. He continues to worry about what will happen when we're all able to plug digital content directly into our neo-cortexes, but figures that by the time this happens, there'll be an app for that.

Lee Andron began designing websites while still in college in the early 1990s. He was chosen to build the website to promote Ericsson's product placement in a James Bond movie. This led to a career working in all aspects of web development. Soon he advanced to work in information architecture, search engine optimization, usability improvement, site design and development, and web application creation.

As the code that runs the web has changed over the years, Lee has learned six different programing languages. In the new millennium and with the current explosion of the mobile web, he has produced more than a hundred mobile sites and apps working with Fortune 500 brands such as Microsoft, Intel, Sony, HP, Subway, Bose, Ford, GM, Coca-Cola, GE, McDonald's, and many more.

Dedication

To all who venture into the future of the web, and to those who are working to make sure there is beauty and value when they get there.

Authors' Acknowledgments

Janine Warner: Over the years, I've thanked many people in my books — family, friends, teachers, and mentors — but I have been graced by so many wonderful people now that no publisher will give me enough pages to thank them all. In this book, I focus on the people who contributed directly to these pages, starting with the hard-working editorial team at Wiley Publishing: Rebecca Huehls, Becky Whitney, Virginia Sanders, and Bob Woerner.

Thanks to Beth Renneisen for the beautiful design that graces the cover of this book (and all the delicious honey). Thanks to coauthor Lee Andron for his perspective on mobile web design and for his contributions to the examples in this book. And thanks to Dennis Koliris for his careful review of all our work.

Thanks to my partner in all things digital and analog, David LaFontaine, for your unfailing sense of humor in the face of impossible deadlines, your talent for turning a phrase, your ferocious research skills, and your passion. You have made this a better book and made me a better person.

Special thanks to Mark Jenkins (www.mobilynx.net) for his expertise in mobile devices and testing, to Jonathan Thaler (www.whenimmobile.com) for his experience creating multimedia sites, and to Andrew Taylor (www.taopro.com) for his help with e-commerce site research.

Most of all, I want to thank all the people who have read my books or watched my videos over the years. You are my greatest inspiration and I sincerely enjoy it when you send me messages and links to your websites. You can always find me at www.DigitalFamily.com. Thank you, thank you, thank you.

David LaFontaine: I want to thank my parents, Gail and Dave, for making trips to the library such a treat when I was young (and for the lifelong love of the written word that those trips engendered), and my sisters Linda, Beth, and Sara for the lively (ahem) discussions that taught me to always be prepared to examine and logically defend my conclusions.

A big shout-out goes to all the other ink-stained wretches of the fourth estate working at newspapers all over the world, laboring to produce the daily miracle; so many have placed their hopes for the future in tablet-based publishing. May your faith be rewarded. I also want to thank all the mentors I have had over the years; I have come to realize that the best lessons I have learned have not been so much about what to do — but about how to be.

But always and ever, I want to thank my wife and coauthor Janine, for sharing my delight at discovering the new and quirky. Your laughter and smiles are my greatest reward, and they kept me going when the projects we thought were easy (or at least manageable) suddenly sprouted fangs and started trying to eat us alive. We work together, and we work. Together. *Esto si es amor.*

Thanks also to *Mad* magazine, *Monty Python's Flying Circus,* the original cast of *Saturday Night Live,* and George Carlin, for giving me the skewed sense of humor and appreciation of life's little absurdities that have helped my writing so much.

Lee Andron: I want to thank Janine Warner for all she has taught me in writing this book. She helped me appreciate everything that goes into creating a book (and understand at least part of it). Much thanks to Dave LaFontaine and the cats for helping her throughout the process.

As always, my gratitude goes out to Niles Lichtenstein and Paul Cheng for the support, patience, and leeway to complete this project while keeping my day job. Thanks to Mark Riedeman, a good friend who taught me the basics of programming and opened up a new world for me. For inspiration and teamwork in creating examples for this book and others, thanks to Nobu Nakaguchi and Sia Ea.

Finally, thanks to Mom and Dad for all the support throughout the years, and special thanks to my wonderful wife, Trish, and darling daughter, Grace Elizabeth, who keeps me mobile.

Publisher's Acknowledgments

We're proud of this book; please send us your comments at `http://dummies.custhelp.com`. For other comments, please contact our Customer Care Department within the U.S. at 877-762-2974, outside the U.S. at 317-572-3993, or fax 317-572-4002.

Some of the people who helped bring this book to market include the following:

Acquisitions and Editorial

Project Editor: Rebecca Huehls

Executive Editor: Bob Woerner

Copy Editors: Virginia Sauders, Becky Whitney

Technical Editor: Dennis Koliris

Sr. Editorial Manager: Leah P. Cameron

Editorial Assistant: Amanda Graham

Sr. Editorial Assistant: Cherie Case

Cartoons: Rich Tennant (`www.the5thwave.com`)

Composition Services

Project Coordinator: Sheree Montgomery

Layout and Graphics: Joyce Haughey, SDJumper

Proofreaders: Lauren Mandelbaum, Linda Seifert

Indexer: Sharon Shock

Publishing and Editorial for Technology Dummies

Richard Swadley, Vice President and Executive Group Publisher

Andy Cummings, Vice President and Publisher

Mary Bednarek, Executive Acquisitions Director

Mary C. Corder, Editorial Director

Publishing for Consumer Dummies

Kathleen Nebenhaus, Vice President and Executive Publisher

Composition Services

Debbie Stailey, Director of Composition Services

Table of Contents

Introduction

*A*pple's iPhone and iPad have turned the dream of holding "the web in the palm of your hand" into a reality — a reality that has far-reaching implications for the future of web design.

This book has been written to help guide you toward this future, by giving you

- ⮞ **A better understanding of all the new capabilities this new mobile platform offers**: Location awareness, motion sensitivity, and even varying aspect ratios
- ⮞ **Tips on how to handle Apple's restrictions:** No Flash allowed

The Safari browsers on the iPhone and iPad support many of the newest advances in web design (such as HTML5 and CSS 3), technologies that will enable you to create cutting-edge websites and web apps. One benefit of pushing the limits as you learn to design for Safari (for the Mac iOS) is that it also prepares you well to design for most smartphones or tablets that use Android (the mobile Google operating system) and other mobile operating systems. The Mac iOS is the operating system that Apple uses on all its mobile devices, such as the iPhone, the iPad, and the iPod touch.

The debate is ongoing about creating a "native app" (one that you download from iTunes or another App Store like the Cydia App Store for Jailbroken iPhones `http://cydia.saurik.com`, Android Market `https://market.android.com`, or HP's WebOS AppCatalog `http://www.palm.com/us/products/software/mobile-applications.html`) versus a website that's optimized for the screen size and special features of the iPhone and iPad or other devices.

Since the mid-1990s, one ongoing challenge has been making web pages look good on monitors as big as widescreen televisions or as small as 3½-inch smartphone screens.

If you build websites based on the best practices outlined in this book, your site can look good on any screen and you can still create complex designs and full-featured web apps. For this reason, we devote a great deal of time and effort in this book to defining current standards and demonstrating why adhering to them has become even more important on the mobile web.

About This Book

We designed *iPad & iPhone Web Design For Dummies* to help you find the answers you need when you need them. You don't have to read this book from cover to cover, and you certainly don't have to memorize it. Consider it a quick study guide and a reference you can return to. Each section stands alone, giving you easy answers to specific questions and step-by-step instructions for common tasks.

Want to find our top design tips for the iPhone as compared to the iPad? Jump right into Chapter 3. Still trying to figure out where to start? Chapter 2 helps you create a plan to upgrade an existing site or create a new one. Ready to dive right in to the new design possibilities of CSS 3? Chapter 6 is full of examples and easy-to-follow instructions.

We realize that you may be reading this book on an iPad or a Kindle or another type of mobile device, and we promise that this book (and its authors) won't complain if you take it with you.

Foolish Assumptions

The focus of this book is how to design for the iPhone and iPad and similar devices using the latest strategies in HTML5 and CSS 3. If this is your first foray into web design, this book may not be the best place to start. We've written several guides to web design that are designed for beginners, including *Web Sites Do-It-Yourself For Dummies* and *Dreamweaver CS5 For Dummies*.

This book is designed for readers who have at least a basic understanding of web design and are excited to try these new, more advanced options. We include some basic material, such as an overview of XHTML and Cascading Style Sheets (CSS) in Part II, to give you a review and ensure that you have a solid foundation before you move on to more advanced chapters, but we move quickly through the basics in this book.

We don't assume that you're a pro — at least not yet. In keeping with the philosophy behind the *For Dummies* series, this book is an easy-to-use guide designed for readers with a wide range of experience.

Conventions Used in This Book

Keeping things consistent makes them easier to understand. In this book, these consistent elements are *conventions*. (We italicize new terms and then define them so that you know what they mean.)

When we type web addresses (known as *URLs*) or e-mail addresses within regular paragraph text, they look like this: `www.digitalfamily.com`. Sometimes, however, we set a URL on its own line, like this:

```
www.digitalfamily.com
```

Then you can easily spot a URL on a page if you want to type it into your browser to visit a site. You can type domain names with all lowercase letters, all uppercase, or a mix of the two. Domain names aren't case sensitive, but remember that you must match the case exactly for any part of a web address that comes after the extension, such as `.com` or `.net`. So, for an address such as `www.digitalfamily.com/mobile`, you must type *mobile* in all lowercase letters. (Try it out — that's the special address for the website that goes with this book. You can find code samples and many other goodies when you get there.)

We also assume that your web browser doesn't require the introductory characters `http://` for web addresses. If you use a *very* old browser or you're creating a link in HTML code, remember to type `http://` before the address.

We include HTML and CSS code in this book whenever we think it can help you better understand how things work. Anytime you see a lot of code, you'll find a reference reminding you that you can copy the code from our `www.DigitalFamily.com/mobile` website. We don't expect you to type long strings of code, but we want to make sure that you get all the code you need to create the examples in the steps you find throughout this book.

When we provide an example that links a URL to a web page, such as in the following line of code, we set off the HTML in the same monospaced type we use for URLs:

```
<a href="http://www.DigitalFamily.com">Learn more about Web
           Design at DigitalFamily.com</a>
```

Whenever we introduce you to a new set of features, such as options in a dialog box, we set apart these items with bullet lists so that you can see that they're all related. When we want you to follow instructions, we use numbered step lists to walk you through the process. We always try to keep things as easy as 1-2-3.

How This Book Is Organized

To ease you through the learning curve associated with presenting new material, we have organized *iPhone & iPad Web Design For Dummies* as a complete reference. This section provides a breakdown of the five parts of the book and the information you can find in each one.

Part I: Laying the Groundwork

Part I gets you started by giving you an overview of the options, helping you develop a plan to guide your work, and introducing you to the design concepts that will serve you best on the iPhone and iPad.

In Chapter 1, you discover what's possible when you design for these new devices. In Chapter 2, you create a plan and prioritize the features you want in your site. In Chapter 3, you read our review of a series of designs for the iPhone and iPad and share in our top design tips and strategies.

Part II: Using Markup and Programming Languages

Chapter 4 provides an introduction to using HTML with CSS and gets you ready to use the more advanced features covered in Chapters 5 and 6. CSS is *the* way to create web page designs, and HTML5 and CSS 3 build on the strategies that many web designers are already using.

In Chapter 5, you discover how to create the foundation of an HTML5 page, by delving into the specifics of doctypes and tags in HTML5. In Chapter 6, you focus on CSS 3 and all its new design possibilities, including rounded corners and drop shadows and any font you want on your web page. In Chapter 7, you explore more advanced and complex interactive features.

Part III: Adding Multimedia and Web 2.0 Features

In Part III, you explore the best ways to add multimedia and to work around complications from the lack of Flash support in the iPhone and iPad. You also discover the latest in e-commerce services and options. In Chapter 8, you find instructions for optimizing images. Chapter 9 is all about audio and video, including the top online services that can help you host and deliver multimedia. In Chapter 10, you find out what it takes to make e-commerce work on the mobile web and how Google Checkout, PayPal, and other services make it possible for anyone to add a mobile-friendly shopping cart to a site.

Part IV: Publishing Your Site

Part IV helps you ensure that your site is ready to go live and direct site visitors to the best version of your site for the specific devices they're using.

In Chapter 11, it's test, test, test using all our best suggestions and helpful online resources you can use to ensure that your code is crystal-clean.

In Chapter 12, you find advanced tips for optimizing your pages and setting up an autodetect system to manage visitors on your site. In Chapter 13, find out what it takes to make a blog mobile-friendly and discover the best mobile templates for Joomla!, WordPress, and other blogging tools.

Part V: The Part of Tens

Part V features two quick references to help you develop the best sites possible for the iPad and iPhone. In Chapter 14, you find reviews of ten useful web 2.0 services and descriptions of how they can help you deliver everything from interactive maps to slide shows across multiple devices.

In Chapter 15, you find ten ways to market your site. From advertising to social media, mobile offers many new advantages with the ability to reach people based on geographic location, time of day, and other factors.

Icons Used in This Book

This icon reminds you of an important concept or procedure that you should store away in your memory bank for future use.

This icon signals technical information that you may find informative and interesting but not essential for designing a mobile website. Feel free to skip these paragraphs.

This icon indicates a tip or technique that can save you time and money — and a headache — later.

This icon warns you of any serious pitfalls — and gives you the all-important information on how to avoid them. You don't see many Warning icons, but when you do, pay close attention.

Where to Go from Here

If you want to read an overview of this new design landscape and what it means for web design, don't skip Chapter 1. If you're especially interested in e-commerce on the mobile web, jump to Chapter 10. If you're looking for another specific topic or technique, consult the table of contents or the index; you won't miss a beat as you work to make those impossible design deadlines. Most of all, we wish you great success in all your projects for the iPhone and iPad!

Part I
Laying the Groundwork

*1*n Part I, you find an introduction to mobile web design and tips for planning and designing a site for the iPhone or iPad. Chapter 1 explores how designing for the iPad and iPhone is different and why they represent the future of web design. In Chapter 2, you find instructions for planning a great mobile site and tips for managing the unique and fast-changing aspects of mobile designs. In Chapter 3, we explore the best in interface design for the iPad and iPhone and lay the foundation for creating a great design for your website.

Designing for the Future of the Web

*N*ever before has a computer so sophisticated fit into your hands — and responded so well to your touch. On the iPhone, and even more on the iPad, the touchscreen interface makes navigating the web easier than using a television remote control, and far more interactive.

Anyone who has used a touchscreen — from 2-year-olds to great-grandparents — appreciates the ease with which you can tap, point, tilt, swipe, and shake the iPhone, iPad, and iPod touch. From games to art projects, music to movies, recipes to homework, it's more fun to surf the web on a touchscreen.

In this book, we explore how best to design websites for these new touchscreen devices: the iPhone, iPad, and iPod touch. From the challenge to reinvent interface design on the web to the latest techniques in HTML5 and CSS 3, this book is designed to help you appreciate where web design is going and how to make your website look its best along the way.

Smartphones and tablets are changing the way the world shares information and communicates. Our goal in this book is to make sure that your website takes best advantage of all that these new devices have to offer.

Pushing the Limits of Web Design

We've always been skeptical of hype, and HTML5, with its new logo (see Figure 1-1), has certainly gotten more hype than any new markup language in the admittedly short history of the web. In the past, only true web geeks got all excited about refinements to the underlying language of the Internet. (And reading manuals and treatises about this subject is as sure a cure for insomnia as we've been able to find.) However, for good reason, both creative web designers and hard-core "code monkey" developers are excited about HTML5. Visit the innovative sites already adding new interactive features with HTML5 and its companion CSS 3 (the latest version of Cascading Style Sheets) and you can see the web is becoming a truly interactive place.

Using the latest in HTML5 and CSS 3, you can create highly interactive websites that work well on the iPhone and iPad. If upgrading to the latest flavor of web design seems complex and intimidating — relax. Everything you already know about creating web pages should help you; and as in any *For Dummies* book, we don't assume that you know all the answers already. In Chapters 4-7, we take you from the basics of HTML and CSS to the latest in interactive design features that you can create by combining HTML5 and CSS 3 (with just a dash of JavaScript or PHP programming thrown in once in a while).

Logo and website design by Ocupop.com.

Figure 1-1: The new HTML5 logo is designed to help promote the new HTML5 standards.

Bringing high-touch design to the web

One of the biggest trends in web design is kind of a *Back to the Future* movement, where designers are dusting off old design textbooks and rethinking the limits to the web that people have settled on for more than a decade. Because of advances in HTML5 and CSS 3 — including the ability to use any font and to add design features such as drop shadows with ease — you can now design more creative interfaces for the web. Driven by the user experience made possible by the high-touch design space of the iPad, graphic designers are striving to create *rich media* — interactive sites that look as good as anything ever designed for print — and sometimes even better.

In the early days of the web, the Internet was ruled by the geekiest of the geeks. With all due respect to the programmers and system administrators who shaped the early days of the web, we think that most of them would readily admit that design isn't their collective strong point. Most developers wouldn't understand the fuss about choosing just the right font or why color theory is a lost art in the world of code. (If you find yourself relating to this description, you'll find design tips in Chapter 3.)

Figure 1-2: The high-resolution screen on the iPad makes it an ideal device for viewing photos and videos.

The big news in the world of iPad design is precisely that — design. Over the past decade, the web has been dominated by programmers. The result is text-heavy pages, where navigational elements clutter the design space and users of web browsers settle for only a few common fonts.

The best part of the iPhone experience is not just the eye-pleasing and friendly navigation icons, it's the beautiful way photos and videos come alive on the screen. Studies have also shown that iPhone and iPad users love their devices (Janine sometimes sleeps with hers). The intuitive way you touch the screen to navigate, and the ease with which you can curl up with an iPad or iPhone in a comfy chair, makes it an inviting device to browse an online photo gallery, such as the one shown in Figure 1-2, or surf the web.

As the new design possibilities of HTML5 and CSS now begin to transform the web, we think it's safe to say that the next decade on the Internet will be shaped more than ever by designers and that the World Wide Web will become a more beautiful and aesthetically pleasing place as a result.

Web designers are now experimenting with completely new approaches to interface design. In Figure 1-3, you see one of our favorite examples of the first serious use of CSS 3 in an interactive website. At Any Time Zone (www. anytimezone.com), you can drag the bar across the top of the page to compare time zones without reloading the page. The slider is smooth and the clean design helps focus your attention on comparing time zones. This relatively simple site delivers a rich, app-like experience rarely seen on the web.

Reaching the broadest audience

Though the focus of this book is the iPad and iPhone, we don't ignore the desktop web, which, after all, is still where the majority of web browsing occurs. We demonstrate the latest and best design options for the iPhone/iPad, and we also point out how you can gracefully adapt those designs to work on browsers on the desktop web as well.

Figure 1-3: Using HTML5, the Any Time Zone site can provide a rich, app-like experience in the Safari web browser.

If you want to reach out to users on all the other mobile devices flooding the marketplace (such as the Android, BlackBerry, or Windows Phone 7 platforms), check out *Mobile Web Design For Dummies*, by Janine Warner and David LaFontaine. In that book, we explore how to reach the broadest mobile audience by creating extremely limited websites that work on the most basic mobile phone models or by setting up highly complex device-detection scripts and adapting your pages dynamically to fit a variety of screen sizes and other variables.

In this book, we're excited to leave those constraints behind and show you where web design is headed and what you can do when you design for the future of web design on the fastest growing part of the web — the touchscreen.

Pushing the limits of web design is still, well, limiting. Some of the features we cover in these pages don't work in all web browsers or mobile phones. Similarly, not all sites designed with HTML5 work on the iPad. Because HTML5 and CSS 3 aren't equally supported by all web browsers, sites that are designed for one browser may not look the same in another, unless you write special code to address the unique tags supported by each browser. (You learn more about creating code that works well in many browsers in Chapters 4, 5, and 6.)

The most popular app on the iPhone is (surprise!) Safari

The "gold rush" environment of the iTunes App Store includes a growing list of magazines, TV networks, and other businesses scrambling to launch apps for the iPad and iPhone. At the time we wrote this chapter, the most popular app in the App Store was *Angry Birds,* a silly game in which you use a slingshot to shoot birds at pigs. Yeah, we wouldn't have picked it to be the most popular app in the iTunes App Store a year ago, either.

Despite commercials in which users showcase apps by scratching on deejay turntables or slaying dragons or checking traffic reports, the most popular application on the iPhone and iPad doesn't even need to be downloaded from the App Store — it's already on the device when you take it out the box. The Safari web browser beats all other apps in the touchscreen popularity contest — another reason why designing websites for these devices is worthwhile. People surf the web a lot more on the iPhone and iPad than on any other mobile devices.

As professional web designers, we hope that we won't have to create different code for each browser forever, but we love the new features in CSS 3 so much we think they're worth the extra effort. Fortunately, Safari is one of the best browsers when it comes to supporting HTML5 and CSS 3. The rapid adoption of smartphones by consumers and the growing popularity of tablet devices means that the number of people using limited, old-fashioned cell phones web browsers is quickly decreasing, but the mobile web still isn't a perfect place for designers.

Wherever we provide instructions for how to create pages specifically for Safari on the iPhone and iPad, we try to include tips or techniques you can use to ensure that your web pages display well in more limited web browsers, such as Internet Explorer, which has been slow to adopt the new HTML5 and CSS 3 features.

Because we're pushing the limits of web design, we realize that some of the code featured in this book may change over the coming weeks and months. In each example in this book, we show you what we think is the best approach *now,* and we encourage you to visit the website we created to accompany this book at `www.digitalfamily.com/mobile`, where you can find updates, code samples, and other resources to help you continue learning.

To App or Not to App

Apple's compelling marketing campaigns have spread the idea that no matter what you want to do — take your blood pressure, plan your next trek to Kilimanjaro, or buy a new car — "There's an app for that."

An *app* is a small computer program. On the mobile platform, there are *web apps,* which run in a web browser, and there are *native apps,* which run on the operating system on your iPhone or iPad. Native apps must be downloaded from the iTunes App Store, which means that if you create an app, you as the developer have to set up an account with Apple and submit each app to Apple for review before it can be made available to consumers in the App Store. The review process is increasingly controversial because Apple rejects apps it doesn't approve of, and even if your app is approved, the review process can delay the launch of your app by days or weeks.

Although we love the mobile web, and all that you can do when you design websites for Safari on the iPhone and iPad, we're not against apps. We agree that nothing compares with a native app when you want to create the most rich, interactive features possible. If you want a race car game that lets you "drive" the car by tilting your iPhone or iPad back and forth, you'll need to create an app for that. Accessing the accelerometer, location detection, and other advanced features often requires a native app.

Despite our love and respects for apps, we believe that the iTunes App Store has received too much hype. The bottom line is not everyone needs an app, but every website on the Internet should be mobile friendly and designed to look good to the growing audience of web surfers on the iPhone and iPad. Some companies, such as Amazon and American Airlines, have created both. In Figure 1-4, you see the Amazon native app on the left and the highly interactive website at www.amazon.com on the right.

If you choose an app over a mobile website, remember you need to create a different version of your app for every type of device — one for the iPhone, another for the iPad, and then additional versions if you want your app to work on the Android, BlackBerry, Windows Mobile, or another mobile operating system.

Here are just a few reasons that we recommend creating a website instead of an app:

- You can update websites faster and more efficiently. Websites aren't subject to the unpredictable (and sometimes long) iTunes review process.

- You can develop a more direct connection with your audience. Distributing an app through the iTunes App Store means you can't track your customers' actions directly or even keep their contact information for future sales.

- One well-designed mobile website can work well on all popular mobile devices, from the iPad to an Android phone. (You don't have to be a math genius to figure out that creating one website is more cost effective than having to code a series of apps.)

 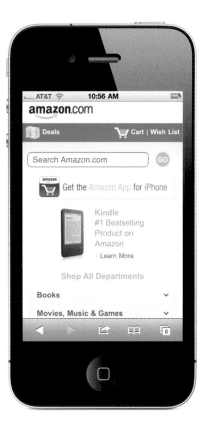

Figure 1-4: Amazon.com created both a native app and a web app for the iPhone.

Setting Records and Changing the Game

According to the mobile phone manufacturer Ericsson, the amount of worldwide mobile data traffic every month now measures 225,000 terabytes (roughly equivalent to 45 million DVDs of data). The iPhone generates about 50 percent of that traffic, according to *ByteMobile,* and studies show that iPad users like to surf the web even more.

Though early usage statistics vary wildly, the bigger screen of the iPad has resulted in users web surfing 2½ times more often than iPhone users. The amount of data traffic generated by the iPhone is even more surprising when you consider that the iPhone still isn't available in many developing countries, and even in the United States it accounted for less than 15 percent of the total number of phones in use.

Mobile web traffic is predicted to grow 4,000 percent by 2015, largely because most of the phones in use by then will be equipped with sophisticated web browsers, along with the expected explosion in tablet devices, sparked by the success of the iPad.

Compared to the clunky navigation of early mobile devices, the iPhone and iPad create a new and delightful user experience. Here are a few of their game-changing features:

- **Multi-touch screen:** The iPhone and iPad "wow" users with interactive features, such as the ability to use your fingers to make pinching or opening motions to shrink or enlarge web pages, photos, and text.

- **Scrolling:** Zipping your finger down a web page or a list makes the page contents spin past like the wheels in a slot machine.

- **Accelerometer:** This tiny gyroscope can tell when the iPhone or iPad is moved, and in which direction, so shaking the device can be used to randomly change the song you're listening to or clear the screen of a game so that you can start fresh, for example. The accelerometer also determines whether the device is being held in portrait or landscape mode.

- **No manual:** Neither the iPad nor the iPhone comes with a manual. The devices are so easy to use (and so inviting) that most people learn to use them by playing around with them.

Appreciating the impact of the iPhone

For years, developers have been talking about the mobile web and all the things that would be possible when the mobile Internet reached the masses. Year after year, pundits declared "the year of mobile," but not until the iPhone came along did the dream become reality.

The iPhone changed *everything* in the mobile world. From the moment Apple CEO Steve Jobs strode on stage to introduce the iPhone (shown in Figure 1-5), a kind of over-the-top technological frenzy enveloped the

Photo courtesy of Apple, Inc.

Figure 1-5: The iPhone deserves credit for driving the popularity of the mobile web.

mobile phone industry. On June 29, 2007, eager Mac fans stood in lines that crawled around city blocks and waited for Apple stores to open and sell the iPhone. Before the iPhone became available outside the United States, enterprising travelers could buy one for $300 and sell it on the streets of Moscow or Bangkok for $2,000 or more.

The iPhone was also the first mobile device that could display web pages almost as well as most desktop computers do (with the notable exception of its inability to play Flash and many video formats).

Understanding the power of the iPad

Initially derided as "an iPhone that can't make phone calls," the iPad's success has been unlike anything ever seen by the electronics industry. Even the DVD player, which was the previous champion at upending established markets, has been buried by the iPad frenzy. The iPad was selling at a rate of 4½ million units per quarter and is already generating more revenue for Apple than its entire desktop and laptop computer lines.

With this information in mind, any forward-thinking web designer must explore what it means to design websites for these new mobile platforms. You can start by considering the difference between creating content and consuming all the text, video, web pages, e-books, music, and other increasingly interactive rich media that's now available.

Whether you're designing a website to be viewed in business settings on the *desktop web,* as traditional browsing is called, or consumed on an iPhone while killing time waiting in line, remember that at the end of the line is a person. And, every member of the digital world is quickly coming to expect to find what they want, when they want it, on whichever device they want it on.

Designing for Two Screens

Throughout this book, you see screen shots taken on the iPhone 4 and the iPad displayed side by side (refer to Figure 1-5). We do this to show you how the landscape and portrait views look side by side. To help you quickly identify designs on an iPhone, such as the one shown on the left in Figure 1-6, from designs on the iPad, such as the one shown on the right of the figure, we used Photoshop to insert each screen shot into a frame so that you can see the surrounding edges of each device.

Figure 1-6: For the best results, create different designs for the iPhone and iPad screens.

We've been careful to preserve the integrity of our screen shots: The proportions and amount of the design you can see in the display area are true to life, though we don't always display the iPhone and iPad to scale when we put them next to each other.

In most figures where both devices appear, the iPhone is larger than actual size in comparison to the iPad. We do this not because we favor the iPhone (although it *is* cute), but, rather, because we believe that all devices should have an equal opportunity to look good: If we printed the iPhone screen to scale next to the iPad screen, the iPhone screen would be too small for you to see clearly the details of the designs.

Reaching Android Users, Too

Although the iPhone has been the subject of all the hype of the past few years, Droid phones, which run on the Google Android operating system, started outselling iPhones in the first quarter of 2010 and are likely to continue to do so. Many predict that Google could beat Apple with the Android operating system on the mobile platform in much the same way that Microsoft won on the desktop.

Because Android phones can be created by many companies (not by just one, such as Apple making the iPhone), they're generally cheaper and available on more networks. A growing list of phones and tablet devices run on the Android operating system, and more are being released all the time.

The good news is that most of what's possible when it comes to web design for Safari (the iOS on the iPhone and iPad) will work just fine on devices that run Android. Consider it a bonus: You aren't simply finding out how to design sites only for Apple's popular consumer devices — you're also finding out how to develop sites that will work well on most of the new mobile devices expected to reach the market in the years to come.

Combining the "Three Screens" into One

Advertisers and TV producers have talked about wanting their content to appear on the "three screens" that tech-savvy consumers use, as described in this list:

- **Television screen:** Though it's the oldest type of screen in most households, it's starting to undergo some radical changes, with Google TV, AppleTV, and various other players attempting to fuse web browsing with viewers' favorite programs.

- **Computer screen:** Many consider this type of screen to be the most powerfully interactive platform because most computers now empower users to write stories, enhance photos, edit video, and compose songs.

- **Mobile phone screen:** This newest competitor for our attention (and money) is the one that people take with them everywhere.

One reason that the iPad is generating so much excitement is that it offers designers and content creators the best of all three types of screens. The iPad matches up well for these reasons, in the same order as in the preceding list:

- Video playback takes place on a screen that is large enough and with a resolution high enough to make watching a full-length movie an enjoyable experience rather than an exercise in eyestrain.

- An iPad has enough processing power, memory, and functionality to allow users to type long messages without blowing up their carpal tunnel muscles while also allowing them to compose music or splice together clips into video sequences.

- An iPad can be detached from the wall outlet and Ethernet cable and taken just about anywhere — and still be able to connect with the Internet.

Admittedly, the iPad isn't better than the three classes of screens we list; it's neither a 50-inch, high-definition plasma screen nor an octo-core video editing workstation; it isn't tiny enough to fit into a shirt pocket. But it comes close, and that makes it handy to have around. It's the Swiss army knife of content platforms.

What this means for designers is that you can play with a lot more screen real estate than you can on a mobile phone, while still building in hot new functions such as location-aware content, fun accelerometer interactions, and intuitive touch screen functionality. Though many early reviews of the iPad dismissed it as "a device in search of a purpose," we couldn't disagree more.

The iPad is a jack-of-all-trades — a platform that will only grow more accepted into all our lives, providing users with an enjoyable web browsing experience, a way to create complex content, and a cool companion whenever they want to curl up on the couch with a good book (or giggle at the latest quirky viral video hit). Much of the quality you insert into that experience for your users depends on how well you're able to understand and employ the latest web technologies: HTML5 and CSS 3, as you discover in Part II.

Planning the Perfect Mobile Experience

When carpenters build a house, they don't show up on the site and just start nailing boards together; they follow a plan — ideally, one created by an experienced architect.

The comparison between building a home and building a website is common — and for a reason. Creating a project plan for your website is as important as creating a blueprint for a house. Of course, the bigger the house, the more complicated the plan.

Whether you're building a simple site or a highly complex, interactive masterpiece, taking the time to develop a solid plan from the beginning saves you from a lot of heartache and desperate, last-minute improvisation. Even if you're simply sketching your idea on the back of a napkin, arriving at a clear and agreed-on vision of your destination increases your chances of getting there on time — and on budget.

In this chapter, we describe how a pro team would develop a site for a customer, in this case the Seattle Asian Art Museum (SAAM). The team needs to create a site plan for the customer to approve before creating the

Start Here:
m.deadphonemuseum.com

Home — Foote of eac page

Signup for Alerts | Exhibition | Image, curato text & comme

Thanks! (Email Capture) | Art Piece Detail | Social Mec Submissic

Visitor Comments | Sub

site to ensure the team creates what SAAM wants. In the sections that follow, you find detailed instructions for how to plan your site before you start building.

Assessing Your Current Web Presence

The first step in developing a plan is to assess what you have (or don't have) in the here and now. If you're creating a completely new website, you need quite a different plan of action than if you're developing a new version of an existing site for the iPhone or iPad. Here are a few common starting places and issues to consider:

- ✓ **Create an iPhone/iPad site from scratch:** If you're creating a new site from scratch, be sure to start your plan from the beginning. In many ways, this option is the simplest because you don't have to accommodate legacy content or features that would be difficult to transfer to these new devices.

- ✓ **You already have a modern site designed with CSS (cascading style sheets):** If your site is already up and running and you created the site following contemporary web standards (which means that you used CSS and HTML to separate the formatting from the content), you're off to a good start. The key point is that separating your design from your content enables you to create your mobile site design from existing content much more easily.

- ✓ **You have a very old website:** If you created your site years ago and the design is integrated within the HTML, you have your work cut out for you. If your site uses the HTML table tag to create the design, you should start by redesigning the old site before you even begin to create the new, mobile version using the latest HTML5 and CSS 3 technologies or choose the first method in this list (to create one from scratch).

   Taking the time to transition to the more modern model using cascading style sheets saves you time. Creating your site with a clear separation of content and design by developing a site that stores the information in HTML and creates the design with CSS is the proper way to develop sites according to the World Wide Web Consortium (W3C), the group that sets the standards for web technology.

Consider this situation a perfect opportunity to redesign your site to put it to work for you. Start your plan with this first step in mind. (In Chapter 4, you find an introduction to HTML and CSS and an explanation of how you design a site by separating content from style.)

Developing a Project Plan

A good project plan is composed of a series of tasks, a budget, a timeline, and a list of needed resources and materials. Taking the time to create a detailed project plan gives you a structure within which you can work with greater confidence and a much better chance of meeting your original goals on time and on budget.

Follow these basic steps to create a site plan:

1. **Define the goals and objectives of your site.**

   See the later section "Defining Goals and Objectives" for details about this step.

2. **Create a wireframe.**

   See the section "Creating a Wireframe," later in this chapter.

3. **Organize your content and create a content list.**

   We discuss the details of this step in three later sections in this chapter: "Sketching out a site map of the major sections," "Determining what goes on the home page," and "Planning the interior pages of a site."

4. **Create a task list.**

   Visualize what you need to do at every stage of the site creation process. Then break that down into tasks that need to be accomplished. Note whether a task is dependent on the completion of an earlier one. This list helps you estimate how long the project will take and the resources needed.

5. **Set a timeline.**

   Using your task list from the previous step, estimate the time it will take to accomplish each task. Keep in mind that the creative process is rarely problem-free; you need to allow a reasonable amount of time for unforeseen problems, such as having your site-rendering technology take longer than you think. Setting a timeline helps you guide the process and enables you to change plans if needed.

6. **Establish a budget.**

   Not surprisingly, the bigger and more complex your mobile site, the more money you'll likely need.

7. **Assemble a team.**

   You may not have all the skills or time to do everything that needs to be done. Here are some common roles:

- *Team Leader:* Every team needs someone who is able to make the final decisions.

- *Designer:* Depending on the scale of the project, besides the familiar graphic designer, the team may need a user experience (UX) designer, creative designer, or interaction designer.

- *Client-side developer:* Also known as a user interface (UI) designer, this developer specializes in creating interfaces that function efficiently on the iPad/iPhone platform.

- *Server-side developer:* If you are building a dynamic site, you will want to have a developer skilled in programming languages like PHP or JavaScript to handle the server side code.

- *Database administrator:* Depending on the complexity of the site, you may also need a database specialist to set up and maintain a database.

8. **Create a site design and navigation structure.**

   Clean and efficient navigation is important on any website, but even more so on devices with smaller screens, such as the iPhone and iPad.

We don't go into exhaustive depth about every step, but we think that keeping these steps in mind can help you impose order on chaos if you start to feel like you're losing focus during the design process.

Defining Goals and Objectives

Take the time to ask yourself why you want a website and what you want it to do for you. Your final site will help you accomplish your goals and provide a better user experience as a result. Remember that you can always start small and develop a website over time; there's no rush to add, as fast as possible, every feature you think you might need. The web isn't going anywhere, and the best uses of the web are the ones that will be around for a long time. Here are some suggested questions to help you achieve clarity in your project:

✔ **Why is it important for you to have a website?**

✔ **What are your objectives?**

As you work through the planning and development process, you should strive to refine all your hopes and dreams down to two (or, at most, three) clear objectives for your site. Write those goals on a sticky note, and keep it in a spot that you're forced to see regularly, such as the edge of your computer monitor or the bathroom mirror. Whenever you have a question about any aspect of the design, content, or development of your site, refer to the list. It will act as your compass needle, pointing the way forward so that you can remain true to your objectives.

- **How will you measure success?**
- **Whom do you envision as your core users?**
- **What do you want those users to gain by visiting your website?**
- **What do you want users to do after or while they're on your website?**
- **How does your idea for a website compare with others?**
- **Do you expect to make money on your website?**

After you have determined your site's goals, you can organize the route users should take to move through your site according to those goals. Strive to construct your site so that your users can reach the places where they can accomplish a goal — whether it's placing an order or learning how to cross-stitch their baby's name on a T-shirt. One of the most useful tools in this next stage is to create what is known as a wireframe.

Creating a Wireframe

A good wireframe is a lot like the set of blueprints for a house. The plans of a building describe its underlying structure, where electrical wires run, how the plumbing will work. It's a plan for building the structure of a home. The plans from an architect don't describe which colors to paint the walls, which furniture to place inside, or which kind of cereal to store on the pantry shelves. Likewise, a *wireframe* describes the structure of your site, without getting bogged down in all the design details.

In Figure 2-1, you see a wireframe on the right and the completed web page created from it on the left. Wireframes are like sketches of a site — they're not always perfect plans. Notice in Figure 2-1 that the elements in the final page design aren't always precisely where they were in the wireframe.

Most website designers who create wireframes agree that design elements should not be added at the initial stages — no images, no color, no fancy fonts. The wireframe is a structural document designed to help the developer (as well as clients) focus on how a site works without being distracted by design details. The details aren't necessarily bad — in fact, having a gorgeous picture or text treatment can make a bad design look good, and blind a designer from seeing that the page they've constructed doesn't function the way it should.

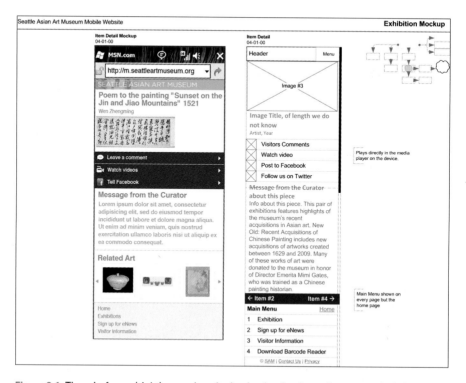

Figure 2-1: The wireframe (right) served as the basic plan for the web page on the left.

Don't be impatient to start adding all the content and design elements to your wireframes. As the development process evolves and the structure is approved, you can add mock-ups to show how the site will look.

Visualizing Your Site's Building Blocks

Think of your site pages as reusable building blocks. For example, the header of your site is usually in the uppermost part of the page, and you usually want to keep it consistent across the site. It's the same concept as a pile of uniformly shaped building blocks that a construction team uses to make sure that all its walls fit together nicely.

Your wireframe helps you visualize and create these consistent building blocks — and this result, in turn, helps your users efficiently navigate your site to find what they're looking for. To help you appreciate how wireframes look and work, we use as a model a fictitious example of how to develop the wireframes for an art museum in Seattle.

Resources and software for creating wireframes

You can create a wireframe document in almost any software program. Some designers use common applications, including Microsoft Word or PowerPoint, but a number of programs and online services are designed specifically for creating wireframes. Here are a few:

✓ **Google Drawings (http://www.google.com/google-d-s/drawings)**: Part of Google Docs, this web-based tool can be used to create great wireframes for free. Visit http://mortenjust.com/2010/05/02/iphone-wireframe-stencils-for-google-docs for Stencils that you can use in Google Drawings.

✓ **Cacoo (www.cacoo.com)**: This online drawing program includes many icons and other features designed for creating wireframes, site maps, and charts. Cacoo has a free level of services as well as a premium paid membership with more options for $4.95 per month.

✓ **iPlotz (www.iplotz.com)**: Use this online tool to create clickable and navigable wireframes and prototypes. iPlotz has a free level of service, as well as a premium paid membership at four different levels of pricing and service.

✓ **Flairbuilder (www.flairbuilder.com)**: This online tool can be used to create complete interactive prototypes and wireframes. Using the service to create wireframes costs $24 per month, but you (and your clients) can use a free viewer to view the wireframes.

✓ **Microsoft Visio (www.microsoft.com/visio)**: Visio, a popular program among professionals who favor Microsoft products, is available only for Windows computers. The program uses vector graphics and features a broad collection of templates and other sophisticated tools designed for developing complex projects. The professional version costs more than $500.

✓ **Omnigraffle (www.omnigroup.com)**: This program, which works on Macintosh computers and iPads, can be used to create diagrams, wireframes, and charts with many useful design features built in. Omnigraffle can also import and export Visio documents. The professional version costs $200.

Sketching out a site map

A site map like the one shown in Figure 2-2 provides a visual overview of the major sections of your website and serves as a guide for how you expect the traffic to flow from one section to the next. Think of the site map in terms of a blueprint, where architects lay out the rooms in a house and show the traffic patterns of how a family will walk around the building.

The initial site map often changes quite a bit by the time designers reach the final version of the wireframe, but the map serves as a guide that can help ensure your project doesn't spiral out of control.

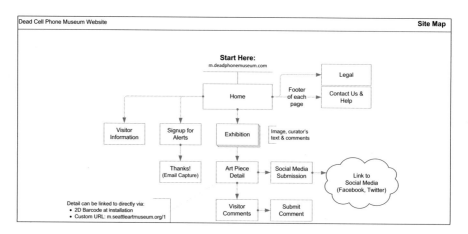

Figure 2-2: The site map shows the website's major sections, and how the pages will link to each other.

When you're ready to decide which content appears on your site's home page, use the goals document you created in the earlier section "Defining Goals and Objectives" to prioritize your content on a wireframe of your home page. As you can see in Figure 2-3, the designers have determined that visitors to the mobile website need to see three elements: the featured exhibition, a sign up for news alerts, and a link to visitor information.

Also, note the diagram in the upper right corner of the wireframe page. The diagram is a graphical expression of your location in the site, which can be quite handy when you're working on a particularly complex site.

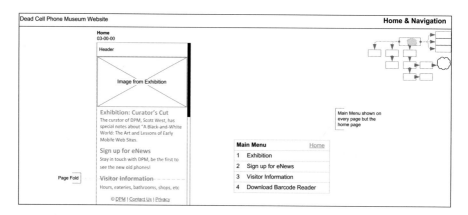

Figure 2-3: The home page wireframe includes the information you want your mobile web users to see first.

Demonstrating the path users will take

As you start the process of designing interior content pages, you should organize the main subsections, and then extend this process to the final destination pages of your site — for example, a transaction page, where your users buy merchandise, or a page with forms where your users can respond to your content.

These pages are the logical ends of the road for your users because the whole point of your site has been to lead them to a place where, after looking at your content, they take the action you want them to take (and have been nudging them toward all along).

In Figure 2-4, you see how the interior content page is designed to entice users into performing various Web 2.0 actions: enabling users to share the museum's content with their friends or prompting users to share their thoughts and feelings about the content by posting a comment. Notice how the wireframe includes elements such as rating stars, where users can vote on how much they like the content, as well as clear links to the form pages.

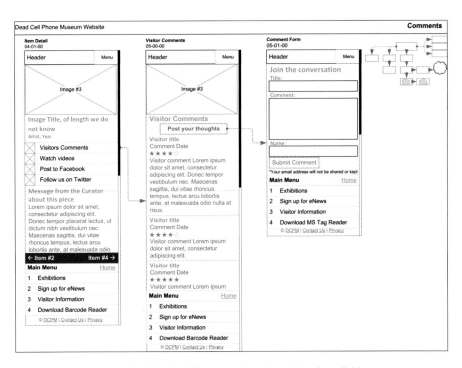

Figure 2-4: Wireframes should include important details, such as form fields.

3

Designing for the iPhone and iPad

*W*eb pages are now viewed on everything from tiny cellphone screens to projectors that can light up the side of a barn. The constraints you face when creating sites for the small iPhone screen leave many designers feeling as though they're being asked to paint Easter eggs in a straitjacket. And even seasoned professionals find it challenging to create websites that look great on screens of every size and dimension used to access the Internet.

One of the most exciting aspects of creating websites for the iPhone, iPad, and iPod touch is that they offer you a chance to completely rethink how you design for the Internet.

Design is highly subjective — you either love pink or you hate it and there's probably not much we can do to change your mind. But beyond the color choices and font preferences (which we leave up to you), we cover a few design principles in this chapter, and we introduce two approaches to web design:

    ✔ Creating multiple designs for optimal display on the iPhone, iPad, and iPod touch.

    ✔ Designing one flexible page layout that can adapt to the differences in size of iPhone, iPad, and even laptops and the monitors people still keep on their desks.

Along the way, we cover these topics:

- ✒ The design features and limitations of the screen sizes, resolutions, and aspect ratios of the iPhone, iPad, and iPod touch
- ✒ How best to help users navigate your pages on a touch screen
- ✒ The best practices for creating icons for the Home screen of the iPhone or iPad

In this chapter, we focus on the visual aspects of design. In Chapters 4, 5, and 6, you find detailed coverage of how to turn any design into a web page using HTML5 and CSS 3.

In most figures where both the iPhone and the iPad appear next to each other, the iPhone is larger than actual size in comparison to the iPad so that you can better see the design differences on the smaller screen.

Creating Device-Specific Designs

If you want to optimize your pages to look their best, you need to consider the screen size and resolution differences between the iPhone and iPad. In Figure 3-1, you find a simplified diagram illustrating a common way designers alter their pages for each device: arranging the layout for the best fit on the different screen sizes.

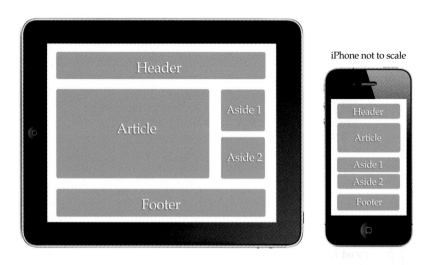

Figure 3-1: For the best results, simplify your designs for the smaller iPhone screen.

On the iPad, shown on the left side of Figure 3-1, you see plenty of room for a second column so that the asides can be aligned to the right of the article. On the right side of Figure 3-1, you see that the best practice is to limit your design to one column on the smaller iPhone and iPod touch screens.

If you look at Figure 3-1 and think, "Wait a minute — the iPad is in landscape mode and the iPhone is in portrait mode, and that makes a big difference," you're right. If you weren't thinking this thought, don't feel badly: This chapter is about helping you appreciate the complexities of optimizing designs for all variables, including the difference between landscape and portrait modes.

Now check out Figure 3-2 to see how the American Airlines site uses only one column for iPhone design, even in landscape mode, and uses multiple columns on the iPad, even when it's in portrait mode.

Figure 3-2: The American Airlines site is designed to display far less information on the smaller iPhone screen.

Notice on the iPhone that the American Airlines team changed not only the design but also the information that's displayed, focusing on the elements most likely to be important to a person on the move, including easy flight check-ins.

Creating different page designs for landscape and portrait views

When you turn on an iPhone or iPad, the orientation of a web page automatically adjusts accordingly. The Safari web browser cleverly enlarges (or reduces) web pages to fit the screen, but it's not perfect. Even if Safari can make your pages fit the space well overall, your designs may suffer because:

- ✔ When the page is enlarged to fit landscape mode on an iPad, optimized images can get blurry.

- ✔ Reducing the size of pages can make text impossible to read.

For years, most people have optimized web pages' width and height for the most commonly used computer monitors:

- ✔ **Width:** In the early days of the web, using this strategy meant that you created designs that were no more than 780 pixels wide so that they would fit within a monitor resolution set to 800 x 600 pixels. Most people chose 780 pixels because that setting left a little room for the scrollbar on each side of the browser window. In more recent years, as larger monitors have become more affordable and more widely used, most web designers updated the target size of 960 to 980 pixels, which fits comfortably on monitors with a resolution of 1024 x 768 pixels.

- ✔ **Height:** Though most designers agree on the width of a design optimized for these screen sizes (give or take 10 or 20 pixels), a debate has raged about whether web page designs should fit within the height of these designs.

   The theory behind limiting the height of web pages is based on studies suggesting that users don't like to scroll down a page and that any content that isn't visible when the page first loads is ignored. We happen to think that scrolling has gotten a bad rap over the years. Whether or not you agree with us, it's time to abandon the notion that web designs should never extend more than 600 pixels down a page.

Figure 3-3 illustrates why the iPad has forever changed the debate about how long a web page should be. In Figure 3-3, you see a screen shot of the ING Direct website as it appears on an iPad in portrait mode. In fairness to the designers at ING Direct, the site fits comfortably within the constraints of a monitor with a resolution of 800 x 600 pixels. By limiting the site's content to the 600-pixel cutoff, however, the design occupies only about a third of the iPad screen in portrait mode. Even if you don't consider yourself a designer, you'll likely agree that the design looks rather odd, especially with the orange area occupying most of the page. Even in landscape mode on the iPad, the design doesn't take up the vertical space, instead filling the bottom quarter of the screen with the bright orange background color.

As you can see later in this chapter, if you want to create just one design for a web site, your best bet is to design its pages to be 980 pixels wide and then extend them at least 980 pixels down the screen. If you do this, both the iPad and the iPhone automatically adjust the design to fill the screen in landscape and portrait modes by adjusting the size to fit. This strategy may be good enough for many sites, but if you truly care about design and want your pages to look their best on the iPad and iPhone, your best bet is to create two different designs.

When you design for the iPhone and iPad, our best advice is to create two versions of each page design (or at least two versions of any page where the design changes significantly from landscape to portrait view). We know that can add a lot of work, so we've included tips and instructions in this book to help you design mobile sites in the most efficient way possible.

Figure 3-3: The ING Direct banking site was designed for best display on a small computer monitor, but the vast area of orange space below the design doesn't look good on the iPad.

The rules for Cascading Style Sheets (CSS) include the option to create multiple style sheets to best take advantage of the size and features of each device. For example, you can create styles targeted to the landscape or portrait orientation of the iPhone or iPad (as we did in the design shown in Figure 3-4). Similarly, you can target different devices with different style sheets by creating one set of styles for a page when it's displayed on a desktop computer and a different set of styles when the page is sent to a printer.

You can find detailed instructions for creating multiple style sheets in Chapter 6. You can find additional tips about targeting your designs for different devices in Chapters 7 and 12. In this chapter, we focus on design theory and the specifications of devices that you should consider as you create your designs.

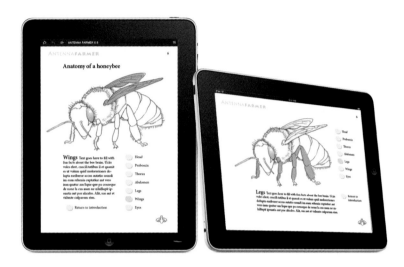

Figure 3-4: You can use CSS to automatically change the position of a sidebar or a second column whenever the iPad is rotated.

Previewing multiple designs in Dreamweaver

If you use Adobe Dreamweaver, be sure to get the Dreamweaver HTML5 Pack. This extension is included in updates to Dreamweaver CS5 and later versions and can be added as an extension to Dreamweaver versions 3 and 4. As you can see in Figure 3-5, the HTML5 extension lets you easily view three different versions of your style sheets at a time by displaying each one in a separate section of the screen. In Figure 3-5, you see how the HTML5 Pack Extension adds a preview that displays the iPhone, iPad, and desktop versions in three separate windows, as viewed from upper left to right and then below.

The Dreamweaver HTML5 Pack for Dreamweaver CS3 and CS4 is a helpful way to quickly check your designs to see how different CSS style sheets affect them, but it doesn't support all the variations of HTML5 and CSS 3 yet. Also be aware that the limited "real estate" in the vertical ratio of these previews makes it hard to ensure that you're using the full space available in portrait mode.

To use Adobe Dreamweaver to view a blog created with WordPress, such as the one shown in Figure 3-5, you need to set up your computer as a web server — a process that's not as difficult as you might imagine. You can find detailed instructions for making Dreamweaver and WordPress work on your desktop computer at www.digitalfamily.com/dreamweaver.

Figure 3-5: Adobe Dreamweaver features an HTML5 extension that displays CSS targeted to the iPhone, iPad, and desktop simultaneously.

Beholding the iPhone and iPad Multimedia Superpowers

Much of the rush into creating mobile multimedia is occurring because Apple's devices are so well-equipped to display images, videos, and other forms of multimedia:

- ✔ **Screen size:** The 3½-inch screen on the iPhone — and especially the 9.7 inch screen on the iPad — make watching video an enjoyable experience.

- ✔ **Screen resolution:** The 480 x 320 resolution of the original iPhone was high enough to allow videos to look good. The 1024 x 768 resolution of the iPad is the same as on a standard XGA computer monitor. Adherence to these standards makes videos display in much the same way as they do on regular desktop displays.

- ✔ **Internal storage:** Like its predecessor, the iPod, the iPhone has gigabytes of memory. The 64 gigabytes (GB) of storage on the iPad rivals the amount on many netbooks. All these devices can store a season's worth of *House* episodes, numerous podcasts or vodcasts (video podcasts), or enough music to fill a weekend at the beach.

↳ **Processor speed:** The proprietary Apple ARM A4 processors in the iPhone and iPad are powerful enough to not only handle decompressing and streaming video but also to multitask and run other applications in the background.

↳ **Content access:** Unlimited data plans allowed iPhone users to watch as many YouTube videos or access as many websites as they wanted, without having to fear the sight of their monthly bills from AT&T. (These plans have been discontinued, but their replacement plans are still decent.) The iTunes Store lets users move audio and videos on and off their devices by using an interface that even preschoolers can master.

Comparing different devices

If you want to design web pages optimized for the iPhone, iPad, and desktop computer, you need to first understand the design differences of these different devices. Table 3-1 gives a quick overview of the resolution, screen, and display differences between the iPhone, iPad, and iPod touch.

If you want to also design a version of a site for desktop computers, consider following the current guidelines on the web and then design for monitors with a resolution of 1024 x 768 pixels. You can find more details in the sections that follow.

Table 3-1	A Comparison of Design Differences in the iPhone, iPad, and iPod touch			
Device Name	**Display**	**Screen Resolution**	**Screen Size in Pixels**	**Icon Size in Pixels**
iPhone 3GS	A 3½-inch (diagonal) widescreen Multi-Touch display	163 pixels per inch (ppi)	Portrait: 320 x 480 Landscape: 480 x 320	57 x 57
iPhone 4.0	A high-resolution retina display and 3½-inch (diagonal) widescreen Multi-Touch display	326 ppi	Portrait: 640 x 960 Landscape: 960 x 640	114 x 114

Device Name	Display	Screen Resolution	Screen Size in Pixels	Icon Size in Pixels
iPad	A 9.7-inch (diagonal) LED-backlit glossy widescreen Multi-Touch display with IPS technology (which is what gives the iPad a wide viewing-angle of up to 178 degrees)	132 ppi	Portrait: 768 x 1024 Landscape: 1024 x 768	72 x 72
iPod touch	A 3½-inch (diagonal) widescreen Multi-Touch display	326 ppi	Portrait: 640 x 960 Landscape: 960 x 640	57 x 57

Understanding screen resolution and color depth

If you're new to creating images, video, and other multimedia for the mobile web, understanding the concepts behind terms like *color depth* and *resolution* can help you as you start creating mobile site designs. *Color depth* refers to the number of colors a screen can display, most commonly referred to by the number of *bits*.

Screen resolution

Hand in hand with color depth, screen resolution affects how crisp and lifelike images appear. As you might expect, the screen resolutions on mobile devices are nowhere near as large as they are on desktop or laptop computers.

Most new LCD monitors or laptop displays have resolutions of at least 1920 x 1080 pixels, and more expensive displays are even higher. The iPhone is tiny by comparison. The original iPhone display (from the iPhone 1 to the 3GS) is 480 x 320 pixels, which allows it to play the vast majority of videos on YouTube in a resolution that makes them look reasonably crisp on the screen, but doesn't come close to what most consumers expect from a television screen. In contrast, the iPad offers a high-resolution display that is 1024 x 768, more than enough to make watching video on the iPad an enjoyable experience. As you prepare your images and videos, consider the different screen resolutions of the iPhone and iPad.

Pixels per inch

Another important factor is the number of pixels per inch (ppi) in an image or a video. Most computer monitors display images at 72 ppi; newer models display 92 ppi. The iPad displays 132 ppi, and the iPhone 4 has a resolution of 326 ppi. Remember that the more pixels per inch, the more detail in the image and the better it appears. The reason that the display on the iPhone 4 has garnered so much attention is that its images are as crisp and sharp as the human eye can detect. A high-resolution image on an iPhone screen probably looks better than most other images you've ever seen on a digital display.

The pixels per inch (ppi) measurement is different from dots per inch (dpi), which is a common way to measure print resolution, because printer quality is measured in dots per inch. Pixels per inch is used as a measure of the resolution of a computer display.

Researchers generally agree that the average human eye can discern, at a distance of one foot, improvements in quality at as much as 300 ppi. That is, if you increase the number of pixels per inch at a normal reading distance higher than 300 ppi (such as with the iPhone 4's retina display), the eye can't detect any increase in quality.

In theory, that means you should optimize your images at 300 ppi, but in practice that creates such large file sizes they would take a prohibitively long time to download, especially over a mobile connection.

We think it may be time to increase the recommended ppi for web graphics — it's always been 72 ppi because that's all anyone would see on a computer monitor anyway. But these days, with increasingly high monitor resolutions, we recommend that you increase your images to at least 92 ppi, and 132 ppi if images are a key part of your web design and you know your visitors use high-speed connections.

Aspect ratios

Aspect ratio is the ratio of the width to the height of an image or video. Aspect ratio is particularly important when you're working with video. A standard TV displays video in 4:3 aspect ratio (or 1:1.33) — the nearly square format that generations of boob tube addicts know and love. Basically, for every 4 pixels across, 3 pixels are down, so the standard-definition TV screen resolution is 640 x 480. Recently, HDTV has caused a move to the 16:9 aspect ratio (or 1:1.85), also referred to as *widescreen,* and a common resolution is 1280 x 720.

The aspect ratio of the iPhone is 3:2 (or 1:1.5), which isn't even standard. The iPad is 4:3, just like a traditional television signal. To display a widescreen or HD image, both the iPhone and the iPad use the *letterboxing* technique, which places thin, black bars above and below the image. In Figure 3-6, you see the effect of letterboxing when a video is played on a screen that does not fit the aspect ratio. On the iPhone, when viewing a standard 4:3 video, you can tap to expand the image to fill the space vertically — but all it does is snip off the edges on either side. If you're working with still images that are dramatically cropped (such as in a panoramic landscape), users either will see a lot of blank space on the screen or have to scroll a lot.

Figure 3-6: Black bars appear at the top and bottom of this training video by author Janine Warner because the video does not fit the aspect ratio of the screen.

Comparing Approaches to Design: Start from the Bottom Up or the Top Down

When you create multiple versions of your site design, at some point you have to step back and think about what the site should look like on each device and how to create a design that works well for all visitors. This list describes two common approaches to site design:

- ✓ **Design for the high end and strip down:** First you create a great-looking design that takes advantage of top-of-the-line features and the large screen size of the iPad. Then you strip the design to a version that works on the smaller screen of an iPhone while maintaining as much of the same look and feel as possible. In our unscientific survey of mobile web designers, we found that people with a design background tend to favor this approach.

- ✓ **Design for the low end and build up:** You determine the minimum amount of text, links, and images you want on your site and then add more design features, multimedia, and interactive content for devices that support it. In our many discussions with developers, we found that programmers and people who specialize in creating wireframes and developing site architecture (covered in Chapter 2) prefer this approach.

Optimizing Designs for the iPhone

The iPhone screen is small, but we encourage you to stop thinking about constraints and start focusing on the amazing new opportunities — such as attracting an audience of people on the move — people who may be standing right outside your restaurant, for example, while they look at the menu on your website and consider whether to eat there.

This section presents a few key points about designing for the iPhone.

- ✐ **Remember that every pixel counts.** You don't have much room to play with, so be sure not to waste a single pixel in your designs.
- ✐ **Create designs with only one column of information for the iPhone.** Multicolumn layouts just don't fit well on small screens. (Refer to Figure 3-1 at the beginning of this chapter for a quick comparison of a design that's optimized for the iPhone versus the iPad.)

When you create a special design for the iPhone, be sure to include a link back to the desktop version of your site. Visitors to your mobile site may already be familiar with the desktop version and may prefer to visit the version that's already familiar to them, even if they're using an iPhone. The mobile version of the Safari web browser aims to display any desktop site as well as a desktop computer does, and, with the exception of the smaller screen size, it comes darned close.

Creating Designs for the iPad

The iPad, with its big beautiful screen, may lead you to believe you don't need to do anything special, but the best design techniques for the iPad are not the same techniques that many of us have used to design for the desktop.

Although the iPad provides far more screen real estate than the iPhone, it still creates new challenges for web designers. Here are a few things to keep in mind when designing websites for the iPad:

Understanding the mobile iPhone & iPad audience

No matter which device you target in your designs, the first element to consider is your audience. When an audience is using an iPhone, you can safely assume that they're mobile and quite likely on the move — they may even be lost on their way to find your location.

Although the iPad is more commonly used at home or in an office, the iPad is a mobile device, and iPad users, especially those with the 3G models, are increasingly carrying their devices around with them.

Keep in mind the following key issues as you design for an audience on the go:

✓ **The need for information is often urgent:** Many people resort to the mobile web because they have to, because they're lost or late, or because they can win a bar bet if they know who won the 1987 Super Bowl.

✓ **Screen real estate is limited:** iPhone sites should be designed to fit on small screens, and designs for both devices should make it easy to find important information, like your address and a map to your location, quickly.

✓ **Users are often distracted:** Having to navigate road or foot traffic while reading content on a screen is just one distraction that may compete for your users' attention.

✓ **3G connections may be affected by low bandwidth:** Limit the size of images and text so that pages load quickly, even at slow connection speeds. Remember, even 3G devices often connect at much slower speeds, especially when people are on the move.

✓ **The interface has limitations:** Links and other navigational options should be big and easy to click with a (fat) finger.

✓ **Processing power and memory are limited:** Large files and scripts that require fast processors don't execute efficiently over 3G or slower connections.

✓ **Factors like time and place affect user actions:** Don't forget that users' actions are likely to be affected by their locations, the time of day, and even the weather (whether it's raining, for example). Be sure to include location-specific information, such as maps and directions.

✓ **Design for both orientations:** The ability to turn the iPad from landscape to portrait mode dramatically alters the screen space for your web designs. Figure 3-3 earlier in this chapter demonstrates how much design space is wasted when a site designed only for landscape mode is viewed in portrait mode.

✓ **Make the most of HTML5 and CSS 3:** When you're designing for the iPad, you don't have to worry about all the web browsers still used on desktop computers, so you can take full advantage of the latest in these web design technologies (covered in Chapters 4-7).

✓ **Test iPad designs on an iPad:** When you create content for the iPad, remember that you're probably using a machine that's quite different from the one your visitors will use when they view your work. Don't test your work in the same place where you develop it. You may still have to do most of the design and coding of your iPad sites while sitting at a desktop or laptop computer, but when you're done, get up, stretch out, and go sit in a comfy chair to see how it feels to use your site and evaluate how it works when you're viewing it on an iPad.

Test your web page designs in different lighting situations. Take the iPad outside to see how your pages look in bright sunlight, and bring the device to bed with you to see how it looks when you hide in the dark under the covers. (We love not needing a flashlight to read on the iPad, the way we did when we wanted to stay up late to read books as children.) You can learn more about testing websites in Chapter 11.

Designing for the Desktop

Throughout this book, we focus on the cutting edge (or, as some would say, bleeding edge) of web design today. When you focus on creating designs for Safari on the Apple iOS, you can take advantage of the latest in HTML5 and CSS 3 and all that this new, multimedia, interactive environment has to offer. But we don't want you to forget that some people who view your web pages may still be using older web browsers on more antiquated devices, such as computers running Internet Explorer 7 on Windows XP.

If you employ the best practices we cover in Part II, you can create great-looking designs for the iPhone and iPad without compromising the experience of your less advanced users. Here are a few things to keep in mind if you want to make sure that your pages look good to the broadest possible audience:

- **Use multiple styles targeted to each device:** Design styles that are specific to the iPad and iPhone, and be sure to include a set of styles that work well on a desktop computer. (You can find tips in Chapters 5 and 6 for targeting your CSS rules.)

- **Create one version of your site that works well on a computer monitor set to a resolution of 1024 x 768.** You should create a page design that's about 960 to 980 pixels wide.

- **Make sure your design works well even if the cool new CSS 3 design features, such as drop shadows and rounded corners, don't display.** Test your pages in an older browser to make sure they look "good enough" and that they're still at least readable and navigable on older web browsers.

Choosing the best design tools

We've seen people mock up web page designs in many different programs, including InDesign, Fireworks, Corel Draw, and even PowerPoint, but our favorites are Photoshop and Illustrator.

We recommend that you create vector shapes in Illustrator so that they scale and then save them as smart objects that work in Photoshop, where you can pull together all your design elements. If you're working with simple vector images, you can save them as a shape layer so that you don't have to return to Illustrator to edit them.

For more on Photoshop and Illustrator, read the edition of *Photoshop For Dummies* by Peter Bauer and *Illustrator For Dummies* by Ted Alspach that matches your setup.

Navigating in a Touch Screen World

The way that your site visitors interact with your pages and navigate your links is dramatically different on an iPhone or iPad than a desktop or laptop computer. Site visitors using an iPhone or iPad are using their fingers — not a mouse, keyboard, or stylus. That means links should be easy to identify and big enough that users don't accidentally click on too many at a time with a fingertip.

Also keep in mind that rollover effects don't work the same way on an iPhone or iPad as they do on a desktop browser. Rollover effects, and similar hover effects, which cause something to happen as a user rolls a cursor over an image or other element on a web page, are automatically converted to "on click" events in an iPhone or iPad.

In Figure 3-7, you see a common design technique on the web – a row of thumbnail images that are linked to larger versions. On your computer, you'd roll your cursor over each image to view the larger version; on an iPad those rollover events would be converted to links, triggered by the touch of a finger.

Design your links to work on the touch screen, and make sure to test whether rollover effects and drop-down menus can be activated with the touch of a finger, as well as a mouse.

To make navigation easy for iPhone and iPad visitors, you need to

 ✔ **Make links easy to click:** Separate links with enough space between them to make it easier to tap them using only a fingertip. (As a guideline, Apple recommends that links be set to occupy at least 44 pixels by 44 pixels of space.) This recommendation is the same for both the iPhone and iPad because it's based on the size of a finger, not on the resolution of the device or the size of the screen. (Even though some fingers are fatter than others, 44 pixels is a good guideline.)

Figure 3-7: The rollover effects in this image gallery are converted to links on the iPad.

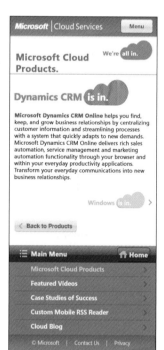

✔ **Make links easy to see:** Style links so that they're easy to distinguish from other text and elements on a page. Remember that your visitors may be distracted or in a hurry and may be in low light or, worse, bright light when using either of these highly portable devices. Distinguish links by using text and images that contrast sharply with the background.

✔ **Organize links:** Group links to related elements together, and if you have a sub-navigation menu within a site, organize those links into their own, easily recognized sections.

✔ **On the smaller iPhone screen, place navigation menus at the bottom of the screen, not at the top:** Navigational links can occupy a lot of room on a mobile screen. Rather than clutter the top of your design with links, include a single Menu button at the top of each page, as shown in Figure 3-8, and create a link that jumps down to the bottom of the page, where you can include more links without burying the content.

Figure 3-8: A Menu link at the top of the page.

The design shown in Figure 3-8 was created for Microsoft by the talented designer Sia Ea, who works at Ansible Mobile.

Simplifying navigation with breadcrumbs

Create a clear hierarchy of links and consider adding *breadcrumbs* to help users find their way back through different levels of your site — this list of links, usually added in small text toward the top of a page, can help visitors identify where they are in the structure of a site. Breadcrumbs generally include links to specific sections and subsections in a site's structure.

The BBC uses breadcrumbs effectively on its mobile site. In Figure 3-9, you can see them just below the BBC Sport logo. The links represent each section of the site that the user has navigated to reach the page. In this example, you can see BBC Home (a link to the home page), BBC Sport (a link to the main page of the sports section), and Football (it's *soccer* in this example, all you Super Bowl fans).

Learning from apps: Don't clutter the screen with navigation options

In the navigation options at most traditional websites, links to all the main pages are always visible. A typical website includes a row of links across the top or the upper left or right side of the screen with common links to the main sections, including the home page, the About Us page, and other important sections.

Breadcrumb navigation

Figure 3-9: The BBC mobile site design adds breadcrumb navigation as you follow links through the site.

Keeping navigation links at the top of every page makes them easy find but clutters the design space. Add your logo and other branding elements, sub-navigation links, and possibly advertising and — yuck — what a mess. No wonder newspaper sites are always described as "busy" and most blog designs are considered boring. Cramming too much information on every page before you even start adding the content makes it difficult to keep things interesting.

Now consider the approach that most designers have taken to creating iPad apps. Yes, this book is about designing websites for the iPad and iPhone, but that doesn't mean you can't benefit from the new breed of app designers that are out there.

After studying a wide variety of iPad apps, including popular magazines *Wired* and *Sports Illustrated,* we've discovered two consistent areas where app designers are placing navigational elements:

- **In the upper left or right corner of the page:** Unlike web pages, the navigational links in most apps are visible only when you tap an icon, such as the Home icon in the upper left, as shown in the Honeybee magazine in Figure 3-10.

- **At the bottom of the page:** Again, an optional set of navigation links appears only when you tap the bottom of the screen, as shown in Figure 3-11.

Figure 3-10: This list of navigation links is visible only when you tap it.

We think that this new design practice could be a useful new way to design web pages as well as apps. The design shown in Figures 3-10 and 3-11 was originally created as an app for the iPad. It was designed using Adobe's new digital publishing tools, which are ideal for creating interactive magazines and enhanced e-books. But after we'd finished creating this design with Adobe's digital publishing tools, which automatically create the navigation links shown in Figure 3-10 and 3-11, we saw no reason not to do the same thing in a web page version.

So we re-created the same design in HTML and CSS and tested it in the Safari web browser. *Voilà!* This approach to navigation works beautifully on the mobile web as well, and it leaves much more room for creating great-looking designs that fill the screen on the iPad.

Even in the web page version of this site, the drop-down menu shown in Figure 3-10 appears only when you tap the Home icon. The menu disappears as soon as you tap a link from the list.

Figure 3-11: Creating navigation links that appear at both the top and bottom of the page design is an emerging best practice for apps as well as for mobile websites.

Using the Best Image Formats and Sizes

If you've been doing web design for a while, you probably have realized that the PNG and GIF formats are generally best for line art, such as logos or cartoons, and that the JPEG format is best for photographs and other images that have millions of colors.

The same format guidelines hold true on the latest versions of the iPhone and iPad, but if you want your images to display well on *all* devices in the iOS family, stick to the PNG format for all your images. It's also a good choice for iPhone and iPad apps because the iOS Software Development Kit (SDK) automatically optimizes PNG images.

The PNG format is the most confusing of the three image formats used on the web, in part because it's the newest. In the early days of the web, designers used the GIF format because all the early web browsers could display it. The PNG format offers superior quality with smaller file sizes, and because web browsers have supported PNG for more than a decade, most designers have upgraded to using PNG instead of GIF. Still, the legacy message that the GIF format is better supported than PNG means that some people have the misconception that GIF is a better option.

Adding to the confusion is the multiple kinds of PNG files that exist. Photoshop supports both PNG 8 (which supports 256 colors) and PNG-24, which supports a far superior 8 bits per channel and is especially well suited to working with transparency. You can still use the JPEG format for photographs and other images, but transparency isn't possible in JPEGs, so the PNG-24 format offers an advantage.

The question that remains is whether the superior color depth of PNG-24 is worth the additional time it takes to load PNG-24 images because of the larger file size that comes with all that color depth.

Ultimately, you have to decide what's more important to you for your designs — the best color and image quality, or fast download speeds.

Either way, you can save any image in the PNG format by using Adobe Photoshop, shown in Figure 3-12, by choosing File⇨Save for Web and then selecting the PNG-8 or PNG-24 from the image format drop-down list, which is open in Figure 3-12.

You find more detailed instructions for optimizing images in Chapter 8.

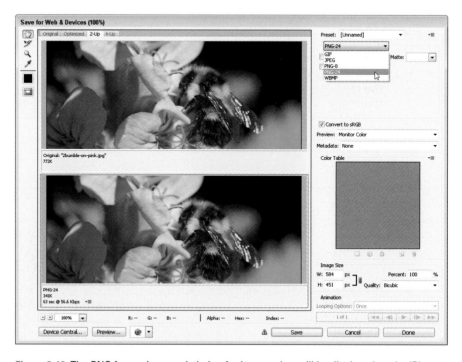

Figure 3-12: The PNG format is a good choice for images that will be displayed on the iPhone or iPad.

Changing the Opacity of Colors for Effect

For years, web designers have been using transparency in websites by saving images in either the PNG or GIF format and making one color transparent. Although this method isn't ideal, it has worked as a way to make images seemingly "float" on a page and to layer one image over another by placing an image in a page over a background image.

Thanks to CSS 3, you can now create transparent backgrounds and even specify different levels of opacity to create more subtle design effects. In Chapter 6, you can find instructions for using the opacity property with RGBa colors to create sophisticated transparency features in your designs, such as the transparent drop-down navigation list shown in Figure 3-13. Changing the opacity of the background behind the drop-down list lets the image behind it show through and creates a more subtle design effect.

Figure 3-13: Changing opacity creates a subtle design effect.

In the example shown in Figure 3-13, we made the background of the menu a transparent gray rather than the solid gray used in the same design shown in Figure 3-10. The opacity settings in CSS 3 provide a great deal of flexibility with the option to use an RGBa color and to specify the amount of transparency.

Creating One Design for All Devices

If the idea of designing an iPhone portrait and landscape design *and* an iPad portrait and landscape design — just for one web page — has you feeling overwhelmed, this section may offer relief.

The Safari web browser does a good job of displaying most websites on the Internet, even if those sites aren't specifically designed for these two devices. If you want the simplest option for any or all of your websites, you can create one design that's "good enough" on the desktop as well as on the iPhone, iPad, and iPod touch.

Designing for the future

Throughout this book, we share the best tips and techniques we know about, but the design situation changes fast and we understand that not everyone has the time to create special designs for both landscape and portrait views in the iPhone and iPad.

If you're feeling limited by the design choices you have available on the iPhone and iPad, don't give up too soon. Both devices continue to evolve, and you can logically expect faster connection speeds, higher-resolution screens, and more interactive functionality. Yep, you might even be able to use Flash on the iPad/iPhone someday. (Though we make no promises on that front, we recognize the high demand for it.)

We worked hard to include all our best tips and the latest techniques in this book, and we also created a special website where you can find our latest design tips and techniques — as well as updates to the content of this book. Visit www.digitalfamily.com/mobile for the latest tricks, errata, insights and advances related to these devices.

If you decide to create just one design, make sure to follow these guidelines:

- **Don't use Adobe Flash.** Sorry — we realize that this is a bummer for Flash developers, but unless Apple changes its stance, anything designed in Flash *doesn't even work* on an iOS device. As a result, we don't use Flash in any of our sites.

- **Create a design that's no more than 980 pixels wide.** Although the iPad displays designs as wide as 1024 pixels in landscape mode and only 768 in portrait mode, Safari automatically resizes your web page design if you create a page and don't make it too wide. We find that keeping the number of pixels to between 960 and 980 is ideal if you want your site to automatically size effectively. Keep in mind, however, that automatically resizing images can lead to blurry text and changes to your designs that may leave them less than pixel-perfect.

- **Create designs that extend more than 600 pixels down the page.** If your sites fit perfectly on a monitor with a resolution of 800 x 600 pixels, they're probably too short to look good on an iPad. In Figure 3-3, earlier in this chapter, you can see an example of the space left over in a web page that was designed to fit in fewer than 600 pixels from top to bottom.

If you're looking for the "Goldilocks" design option (not too long and not too short), design your pages to look like the one shown in Figure 3-14. In this site for actor Yuval David, you see how the iPad displays a page that's 970 pixels wide and nearly 2000 pixels from top to bottom. Notice that the entire design is automatically enlarged in landscape mode to fill the 1024-pixel width and is reduced to only 768 pixels wide to fit in portrait mode.

Figure 3-14: This page on the website of an actor fits well in both landscape mode and portrait mode.

For the best results, test your web page designs on an iPad or iPhone to make sure that your front page fills the entire screen in portrait mode. Also ensure that text and images don't become too blurry to read or look too distorted when they're automatically enlarged or reduced.

Part II
Using Markup and Programming Languages

The 5th Wave By Rich Tennant

iPad

"In fact it does come with a compass."

*T*his part introduces you to the power and advantages of the latest in markup languages and styles. In Chapter 4, you find an introduction to HTML5 and CSS 3. In Chapter 5, we move on to creating a framework with HTML5, and in Chapter 6, you discover how to use CSS 3 to style your designs. Then, in Chapter 7, we explore more sophisticated design options using JavaScript and advanced CSS 3.

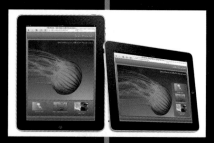

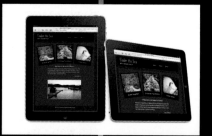

Introducing HTML5 and CSS 3

In This Chapter

▶ Designing for different web browsers

▶ Understanding the history of HTML and CSS

▶ Getting started with HTML5 and CSS 3

▶ Choosing an HTML editor

*S*ince the early days of the World Wide Web, one huge challenge of designing web pages is making them look good in all the different web browsers in use on the Internet. The creators of web browsers and the companies that create software for designing web pages don't always agree on the same standards. A page that looks great in Firefox on your desktop, for example, may be unreadable in Safari on an iPhone.

The challenge of designing for the iPhone or iPad now is that you need a solid foundation in using HTML and CSS and the latest information about HTML5 and CSS 3 to take advantage of the coolest new things you can do.

In Part II of this book, we focus on how to use HTML5 and CSS 3 to design sites for the iPhone and iPad. In Chapter 5, we jump directly into the topic of using HTML5 to create the Framework of a web page. In Chapter 6, we show you how to design pages with CSS 3, and in Chapter 7 we create more advanced features by combining HTML5, CSS 3, and JavaScript.

But those chapters go into all the details and steps. For now, you should understand the basic principles of HTML and CSS and the differences in HTML5 from previous versions of the web's markup language, and why the differences among web browsers are now more challenging than ever.

If you're completely new to working with HTML and CSS, we recommend you find more detailed references on the basics of web design. We assume, if you're reading this book that you're already familiar with HTML and want to focus on what's new in HTML5 and CSS 3.

We're excited to introduce you in Part II to some of the cool new things you can create by using these new web technologies. If you design and test your pages carefully, you can create advanced designs for the latest web browsers on the iPhone and iPad without compromising the audience of people who surf the web on computer screens.

Most professional designers agree that the best way to create web pages is to follow the latest web standards and create the most forward-looking web pages while still supporting some of the previous versions of popular web browsers. This task was difficult enough before mobile devices such as the iPhone and iPad became popular.

Designing for Different Web Browsers

If you want to make an amazing-looking website with lots of useful functionality and tons of "wow factor," design your web pages with the code to make them look good in the web browsers that visit your website.

Though your audience may differ, our goal in this book is to help you create websites that look good in Safari on the iPhone and iPad without compromising the design of the page when viewed in any of the most popular web browsers on the Internet.

In the code examples in this book, we targeted (and tested) our designs using the two most recent versions of each of the most popular web browsers on desktop and laptop computers.

At the time of this writing, the browsers in the following list were the most popular — and the ones we used to test and target our design:

- **Chrome:** Versions 7, 8, 9
- **Firefox:** Versions 3.5, 3.6, 4.0
- **Internet Explorer:** Versions 8, 9
- **Opera:** Versions 10, 11
- **Safari:** Versions 4, 5

Designing for WebKit browsers

Safari and Chrome are WebKit browsers, based on the same WebKit *rendering engine,* which controls how the browser interprets HTML, CSS, and other code. All WebKit browsers follow the same rules (at least most of the time).

The iPhone, iPad, and iPod are all supplied with the Safari web browser, which is slightly different from the version that's available for computer screens, as shown in Figure 4-1. Apple created the WebKit rendering engine and then released it to the open source community, where it has been further developed by Google, KDE, Nokia, Palm, ProFUSION, RIM, Samsung, and others.

Because WebKit works on many different types of phones, websites that work on Safari on the iPhone are likely to work well also on the latest Android phone models, BlackBerry phones by RIM, some Nokia phones, and a growing list of others. Your mileage may vary, and you should always test your designs on the devices that you want your pages to work on; if you target WebKit browsers, however, you should be able to reach most of the smartphone market.

Figure 4-1: The Apple Safari web browser uses the same WebKit rendering engine on the iPhone and iPad as it does on Windows and Mac computers.

You can learn more about WebKit browsers, such as Safari, at the WebKit Open Source Project site at `www.webkit.org`.

Discovering your audience's browser preferences

If you're not sure which browsers your visitors are using, you can probably find out by viewing the traffic logs from your website. Most sites have a way to track traffic, and by searching your web logs, you can see which types of browsers and devices are visiting your site.

Our favorite way to track traffic is Google Analytics, which you can add for free to any site to track traffic sources, measure which browsers visit your site, as well as do many other things. In Figure 4-2, you see how Google Analytics lists all the types of browsers and devices visiting one of our websites. Traffic patterns and browser usage changes over time, so be sure to review your own reports regularly and test your code with each new browser release. Understanding your own visitors can help you choose the path that works best for your site.

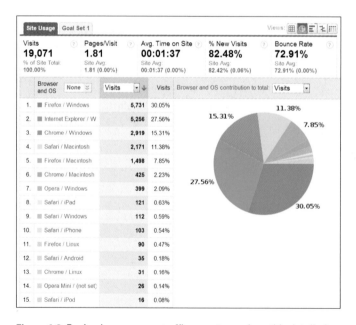

Figure 4-2: Reviewing your own traffic reports, such as this detailed chart from Google Analytics, can help you identify how many visitors to your website use mobile devices.

Comparing HTML and CSS support among web browsers

When you create websites for the iPhone and iPad and visitors to your web-site have one of these devices, you can trust that they have the latest version of Safari, which is one of the best browsers for supporting the latest features of HTML5 and CSS 3.

If you're going to design pages with the right code for the right browsers, you need to identify which browsers support which tags. Fortunately, a number of resources online can help you, including www.caniuse.com and its visu-ally appealing companion site, www.html5readiness.com, shown in Figure 4-3. Another useful site for comparing and understanding browser support for CSS 3 is www.css3please.com.

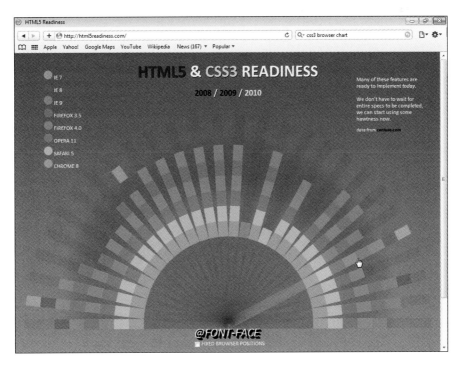

Figure 4-3: You can compare browser support for new tags and styles at the HTML & CSS Readiness site.

Moving to HTML5 and CSS 3

Many different versions of HTML are now in use on the web. All the most recent versions work in the iOS (Apple's operating system on the iPhone and iPad), so you have to decide which one to use. We're diving into HTML5 because we think that the upside of all the new features is too good to wait for and we believe that the W3C is right in making HTML5 the next standard.

If you're concerned about anyone who visits your site using an older web browser, such as Internet Explorer 7 or 8, keep this point in mind: Older browsers don't display the new features of HTML5 or the new styles in CSS 3. As a general rule, if a browser doesn't understand a new tag, it ignores it, so if you design your pages well, you can create designs that *degrade* gracefully. For example, if you use the new text drop shadow features in CSS 3, you see drop shadows around your text in the Safari browser on an iPad but no drop shadows in IE7 on a Windows computer. As long as the text is still readable in IE7, we think it's worth adding the enhancements, such as text drop shadows, that CSS 3 brings to newer browsers.

Similarly, most designs that work well on the Apple iOS on an iPhone or iPad also look good on phones and tablets that run the Google Android operating system, because the browsers on most Android devices also support many HTML5 and CSS 3 features.

Reviewing the evolution of HTML

To help you keep all the options in markup languages in perspective, we begin with a quick review of how we got to where we are now. The World Wide Web was built on good old HTML, the Hypertext Markup Language, which was born out of SGML, the Standard Generalized Markup Language, which dates all the way back to 1986 — the same year that the song "That's What Friends Are For," sung by Dionne Warwick, Elton John, and Gladys Knight, topped the pop charts. (Yeah, it's nice to have friends to lean on when you're reading about all this techy stuff.)

XML, the eXtensible Markup Language, was also born out of SGML. And, if you're starting to think that all these acronyms would make a good skit on *SNL* (the *Saturday Night Live* comedy show), we'd love to consult with you about script ideas. XML caught on so well that it became a standard for sharing data across all kinds of documents and systems.

The popularity of XML led to the evolution of HTML to XHTML. Essentially, XHTML is a more restrictive subset of SGML, one that can be read better by XML parsers because it follows the rules strictly. If you can picture the typical "odd couple," HTML is the sloppy roommate and XHTML keeps the contents of the medicine cabinet in alphabetical order.

You can think of HTML5 as what happens when HMTL grows up, gets a job, and has to start wearing socks, at least most of the time. HTML5 isn't as strict as XHTML (slobs never clean up completely), but it has some grown-up features, such as better ways to present multimedia. At the risk of our beating this metaphor too hard, you can imagine that HTML5 benefits from two new characters on this sitcom — CSS 3 and JavaScript. Combine the power of all three of these current web standards and you can add a lot more interactivity, animation, and even location awareness — features that are especially exciting in the mobile world.

This five-minute version of the history of HTML is only part of the story of how we got to where we are now. In what many of us now consider a misguided effort, the makers of the first mobile web browsers created another markup language, the Wireless Markup Language (WML). Perhaps an understandable reaction to the limited options of early feature phones, WML is now quickly being discarded.

And, while we're introducing acronyms, we should note that the term Wireless Application Protocol (WAP) is used to describe everything related to the mobile web. WAP 1.0 represents the earliest attempts at mobile web design, including sites created with WML.

When the mobile web evolved to WAP 2.0 in 2002, most mobile devices could display pages designed in XHTML Basic (a subset of XHTML that has no support for CSS). Since 2004, most phones can handle XHTML MP, which (mostly) supports CSS 2.

C-HTML, another mobile markup language you may run into on the web, was designed to be used on NTT DOCOMO phones in Japan, but most mobile designers in Japan now predict that the iPhone's growing popularity in Japan means that C-HTML will eventually be replaced by XHTML MP.

If your head is spinning from all these acronyms, don't worry. What follows are more detailed descriptions of the markup languages you're most likely to need for your mobile designs. You'll also find a few tips to help you manage the transition from WML to XHMTL MP to HTML5.

The good news is that all the code designed for the mobile world is based on good old HTML. So if you have a background in HTML, you're off to a great start.

If you want to create a site that will work for any of the more than 6,000 devices in the market, you need a design strategy that includes all these languages and pages created and delivered to match each device. In *Mobile Web Design For Dummies,* which Janine co-authored with David LaFontaine, we cover how to support the lowest common denominator and ensure that your site works on every device across the board.

In this book, however, we focus on creating sites for the *crème de la crème* of mobile browsers.

Creating a Semantic Structure

Creating semantically relevant pages has been good practice on the web since long before the iPad appeared, but HTML5 builds in special tags to make it easier to be consistent in how you use semantics as you design web pages.

The idea of creating semantically relevant pages comes from the inventor of the World Wide Web, Tim Berners-Lee, who envisioned a "web of data" that had *meaning*, or *semantics*.

Creating a web page with semantic structure has long been considered a best practice because it gives the web page more meaning. In HTML4 and XHTML, web designers can create a semantic structure by following well-established rules with HTML tags. For example, the most important headline on a page should be formatted with the Heading 1, or <h1> tag. Similarly, most web designers now define class or ID styles for the main sections of a site with names like header and footer to identify their role and importance on a page.

HTML5 takes this concept a step further by adding a series of new semantic elements. Rather than create a class or ID style and apply it to a <div> tag, in HTML5 you can simply use tags with names like <header> and <footer>. Thus, rather than use ID styles such as <div id="nav">, you can simply use <nav>. Much like <div> tags, however, none of the new tags *does* anything unless you define a set of style rules that correspond to the name. (We cover these and other HTML5 tags in more detail in Chapter 5.)

Building these semantic elements into HTML5 gives designers a more consistent way of structuring HTML pages and is recommended because it makes web pages more accessible for anyone who uses a screen reader to read web pages aloud, as well as for search bots and other programs that need to interpret the content of a web page irrespective of its design. Think of it this way: When you see a web page, you can generally tell by the design which part of the page is the header (it has the navigation area with links) and which is the footer (with the copyright and other details). But none of the bots, readers, and other programs that need to interpret web pages can "see" the design, and that's part of the reason that using semantics is important.

The semantic structure of a page can be independent from the styling and positioning of the content, so you can create a page that has meaning because recognizable sections make up a logical structure. For your visitors who can see the page, you can style sections, such as the header or footer, to display any way you want them to in a browser.

As we create the Framework for an HTML page in Chapter 5, we use semantic tags and organize the content from most important to least important. Later, in Chapter 6, we use CSS 3 to style the page and make it look good to humans (as well as to machines).

Creating an adaptable Framework with the HTML5 semantic tags

Before you create a Framework for a website in Chapter 5, it's helpful to think ahead about how you want your pages to look when you add the styles in Chapter 6. This is where wireframes can really help. (You can find out more about planning and wireframes in Chapter 2.)

In Figures 4-4 through 4-6, you see three different wireframe designs for the front page of a simple blog website — the first one is for the iPhone, and the following two are for the iPad (one for landscape mode and the other for portrait mode).

In Chapter 5, we create a more complex page design for our Jelly Rancher website. In this section, we explore three relatively simple wireframe designs that would be ideal for a basic blog. Wireframe designs, such as the ones shown in Figures 4-4 through 4-6, can help guide you as you create a Framework for your site in HTML.

As you decide how to develop your site, keep in mind that you could create three completely different HTML pages, each with its own style sheet to achieve these three different displays. If you took that route, you'd need to use a device detection script, a complicated program that can detect the type of device used by visitors to your site and then direct them to the best version of each page for that device. If you're designing a mobile website that needs to reach the broadest audience, that's the best way to go, and you can find out more about how to set up device detection in Chapter 12.

The advantage of focusing on the iPhone and iPad is that you don't have to go to all the trouble of creating a device-detection script. That's because the Safari web browser on the iPhone

Figure 4-4: A wireframe showing how the new HTML semantic tags would be displayed in a page designed for the iPhone.

and iPad can read multiple CSS files, something many other cellphone browsers aren't capable of. That means we can use CSS to create designs that work well on the latest browsers on desktop and laptop computers, as well as the iPhone and iPad. (You find more about the design differences between the iPhone and iPad in Chapter 3.)

Although you can create completely different pages for display in each device, we think the most efficient option is to create one page in HTML and then use three different sets of style sheets to adjust the design. With that goal in mind, we show you how to create one page Framework in Chapter 5, and then in Chapter 6, we show you how to use CSS to create different designs from that one HTML page.

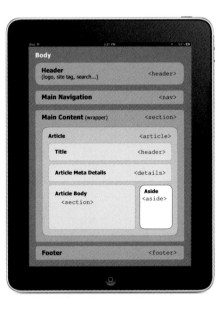

Figure 4-5: Wireframe for iPad in portrait mode.

Figure 4-6: Wireframe for the iPad in landscape mode.

Now here's the part that can seem a little crazy if you're not already familiar with all the things you can do with CSS. The same HTML code can be used to create all three of the designs shown in Figures 4-4 through 4-6. The positioning of the elements, such as the aside, is done with CSS.

Figure 4-3 shows the wireframe for the design we want when the blog page is displayed on an iPhone. Because of the small size of the iPhone screen and the simplicity of this blog design, we created one design that spans the full width of the browser window for both the portrait and landscape views. For the larger iPad screen, we created two designs: the one shown in Figure 4-5 for portrait mode, and a second that better uses the wider space on an iPad when it is in landscape mode, as shown in Figure 4-6.

Looking at what's new in HTML5

There's more than just new semantic elements in HTML5. HTML5 merges HTML 4 and XHTML. HTML5 has two main versions: HTML5 and XHTML5. XHTML5, as you might expect, follows the rules of XML.

HTML5 adds many new tags to the web designer's toolkit, including the new video and audio tags. These new multimedia tags make it possible to add a video stream or an audio stream directly to a web page without requiring that your users have a plug-in. We look deeper into these and other new HTML5 tags in Chapter 5. We cover multimedia formats and options in Chapters 8 and 9.

Writing HTML Code

Before you start creating your site structure in HTML5, knowing which web design tools support this emerging standard is helpful:

- **Text editors:** You can write HTML code manually in any text editor, including NotePad, SimpleText, or WordPad. Though this method isn't the easiest, it enables you to create the code exactly as you like.

- **HTML editors:** If you use an HTML editor, such as BBEdit or Adobe Dreamweaver, as shown in Figure 4-7, you find many features that make it faster and easier to write and test your code. Most HTML editors haven't quite caught up with HTML5 yet, though, so your HTML editor of choice may not offer all the tags covered in this chapter and you may see error messages if the HTML editor you're using doesn't support these tags yet.

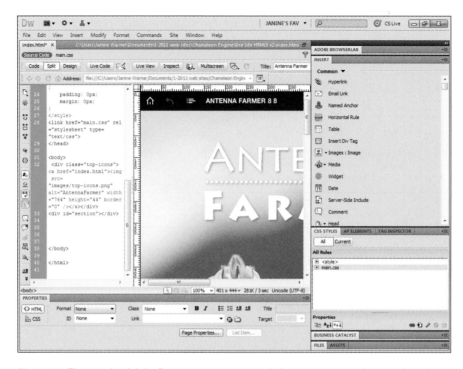

Figure 4-7: The popular Adobe Dreamweaver program helps you create web pages by using HTML and CSS.

Dreamweaver version CS5.5 and later includes special features for designing and previewing HTML5. If you use Dreamweaver version CS3, CS4, or CS5, download extensions that add HTML5 functionality from the Adobe exchange server at www.adobe.com/exchange.

Creating Sites with HTML5

In This Chapter

▸ Creating an HTML5 Framework

▸ Starting with the `<head>` section

▸ Building the `<body>` of a page

▸ Moving scripts to the end of the page

▸ Using the HTML5 video and audio tags

▸ Creating the ultimate contact page

▸ Choosing the best keyboard for form entry

▸ Creating valid HTML code

*W*eb designers often use terms like *architecting, building,* and *constructing* when they talk about creating web pages because there are a lot of similarities between building a house and designing a website — even a site for a mobile device like the iPhone, iPad, or iPod touch.

If you start with a wireframe for your website (as we cover in Chapter 2), you can think of the wireframe like using blueprints to build a house. You can build on that metaphor in this chapter, where we use HTML5 to create a Framework for a web page in much the way you frame a house with two-by-fours.

In Chapter 6, we use CSS to style the HTML Framework, much like you might add drywall, paint, and wallpaper to finish the walls of a home. If you want to complete the metaphor, you could compare the final step — adding the text, images, and other content to your site — to furnishing your house and hanging art on the walls.

To illustrate the process of creating an HTML Framework in this chapter and then styling it with CSS in Chapter 6, we're using a website designed for Mark Loos and his custom jellyfish aquariums. We'd like to give special thanks to

Mark for letting us use his site at `www.jellyrancher.com` as a guinea pig to test the latest in HTML5 and CSS 3.

We designed the original version of the Jelly Rancher site with XHTML and an early version of CSS — long before we were concerned about how the pages might fit on an iPhone screen. Like many sites these days, it was due for a mobile makeover.

In this chapter, we create a simple HTML Framework that can serve as the basic structure of nearly any web page. As you can see in the finished site in Figure 5-1, we created two very different designs for the horizontal and vertical versions of the site, but we did all that with the CSS that we add in Chapter 6. In this chapter, you discover how to create one set of underlying HTML code that you can use to generate both the landscape and portrait versions of a web page.

Not all web browsers on the Internet today support HTML5. In this chapter, we focus on what's possible in the Safari web browser on the iPhone, iPad, and iPod. If you're creating web pages for the broad audience of the World Wide Web, you should test your work in all the most popular browsers. We're having fun exploring the new tags in HTML5, but they're still new and not fully approved as we write this book. When we design web pages for clients today, we still use many of the tried and true HTML tags from the still popular XHTML. (You can find out more about the evolution of HTML in Chapter 4.)

Figure 5-1: The Jelly Rancher jellyfish site features different designs for the horizontal and vertical views on the iPhone and iPad.

Creating a Site Framework in HTML5

In a valid HTML5 page, the only required tags are the doctype (more on doc-type in a moment), title, and a block element, such as the paragraph tag with a little content.

Many of the tags in an HTML5 page will be familiar to you if you've worked with previous versions of HTML. You still surround the entire contents of the page with opening and closing `<html>` tags, the `<head>` tags contain the `<title>` tags, and the contents of the page that will display in a web browser are contained within the `<body>` tags.

Here's the essential structure of a simple HTML5 page. We review the new HTML5 tags, line by line, in the sections that follow.

```html
<!DOCTYPE html>
<html lang="en">
    <head>
        <meta charset="UTF-8">
        <title>This is a simple page title</title>
    </head>
    <body>
        <p>The content for a simple page goes here.</p>
    </body>
</html>
```

We don't think you should ever have to type any of our code samples, so we include all the code you see in this chapter on the website that goes with this book. Just visit `www.digitalfamily.com/mobile` to find all the code in the book, as well as instructions for how to copy and paste the code from our site into your own web pages.

Starting with the doctype

The *doctype,* which tells a browser how to interpret the HTML code in a web page, is one of the most significant changes in HTML5. In HTML4, web authors had to identify the version of HTML by including a link to the Document Type Definition. You may be familiar with the longer doctype used for a page created with XHTML 1.0, which looks like this:

```
<!DOCTYPE html PUBLIC "-//W3C//DTD XHTML 1.0 Transitional//
        EN" "http://www.w3.org/TR/xhtml1/DTD/xhtml1-
        transitional.dtd">
```

No more! In HTML5, the simple `<!DOCTYPE html>` is all you need at the top of your code. When you see this doctype in a web page, it's the first clear indicator that the page was created using the latest version of HTML.

Creating valid <html> tags

The next line of the your site's HTML Framework consists of the <html> tag, which opens the HTML document and specifies what language (spoken language, not computer language) the page uses.

Why identify the language?

- ✔ **The W3C asks you to specify the language.** According to the W3C recommendation, you should declare the primary language for each web page with the lang attribute inside the <html> tag.

- ✔ **Specifying a language makes your page accessible to people who use screen-reader software.** Screen-reader software (such as JAWS) needs to know what language your pages are written in so it can pronounce your words properly.

- ✔ **Search engine optimization is improved.** You reap SEO benefits if you're writing in English — and especially if you're writing in some other language. According to the Google Zeitgeist, 50 percent of Google users search in languages other than English, and many of these users set their Google preferences to search only for pages in specific languages. Google's language autodetection algorithms are better than most, but why make Google's job more difficult?

Adding the <head> section

Your brain is in your head, which should make it easy for you to remember that the <head> section in an HTML page is at the very top and it provides the intelligence that helps the browser interpret the content in the body section that follows it.

The <head> section contains the <title> and <meta> tags, CSS, and other elements that are not displayed in the browser. This is generally called *meta information,* or information about information, because it describes what kind of information is on the page. The following sections explain the types of content you might want to include between the opening and closing <head> tags.

When you're done adding all the code in the <head> of an HTML5 page optimized for the iPhone and iPad (along with the doctype and <html> tags), your HTML Framework looks something like the one shown in Listing 5-1. As you read through the following sections, you find more detailed explanations of these tags.

Listing 5-1: The Doctype and Head in HTML5

```
<!DOCTYPE html>
<html lang="en">
<head>
<meta charset="utf-8" />
<title>Jelly Rancher - Specializing in Jellyfish Aquariums</
         title>
<meta name="viewport" content="width=device-width; initial-
         scale=1.0; maximum-scale=1.0; user-scalable=0;" />
<meta name="apple-mobile-web-app-capable" content="yes" />
<meta name="apple-mobile-web-app-status-bar-style"
         content="black-translucent" />
<meta description="Order custom jellyfish aquariums hand-
         crafted by oceanographer Mark Loos." />
<link rel="apple-touch-icon" href="apple-touch-icon.png" />
<link href="css/main.css" rel="stylesheet" type="text/css" />
<!--iPad portrait -->
<link href="css/ipadP.css" rel="stylesheet" media="only
         screen and (min-device-width:  768px) and
         (max-device-width: 1024px) and (orientation:
         portrait)">

<!--iPad landscape -->
<link href="css/ipadL.css" rel="stylesheet" media="only
         screen and (min-device-width: 768px) and
         (max-device-width: 1024px) and (orientation:
         landscape)">

<!--iPhone portrait -->
<link href="css/iphoneP.css" rel="stylesheet" media="only
         screen and (min-device-width: 320px) and (max-
         device-width: 480px) and (orientation: portrait)">

<!--iPhone landscape -->
<link href="css/iphoneL.css" rel="stylesheet" media="only
         screen and (min-device-width: 320px) and
         (max-device-width: 480px) and (orientation:
         landscape)">

</head>
```

Specifying the character set

The <head> section is also where you can specify the character set, written
as charset. The *character set* enables the browser to know what characters
to display. For instance, the letter *ä* may be displayed as a small rectangle in
the browser if the specified character set doesn't include the special character needed to create the letter *ä*.

Typically, the `charset` is sent to the browser via the web server in the Response Header. You can ask your hosting provider whether your web server does this, but to be safe, most designers add it in manually with this tag:

```
<meta charset="utf-8" />
```

If you're creating a website that supports several languages, make sure you use the correct encoding for each language. See the latest list of character sets at www.iana.org/assignments/character-sets.

Using iOS-specific meta tags

In HTML5, you can include meta tags specific to iOS (Apple's operating system for the iPhone, iPod touch, and iPad). These tags enable you to control how your site appears or how your users interact with it via the touchscreen on an iPhone or iPad. If a visitor arrives at your site using a device that doesn't support these features, the browser simply ignores them. Here's a quick introduction to the iOS-specific tags:

- `viewport` — When you visit most web pages on an iPhone or iPad, you can pan around the page and zoom by using pinch and stretch finger gestures to shrink or enlarge the page and its contents. This feature helps make websites that were designed for desktop computer screens possible to read on the smaller screen on an iPhone. However, if you've optimized your design for these devices in the first place, you may want to prevent users from panning and zooming because it's unnecessary and may confuse them.

  To block the pan and zoom features on a page that you've designed to perfectly fit the iPhone or iPad screen, use the meta `viewport` tag, which sets the window to the width of itself and prevents scaling:

  ```
  <meta name="viewport" content="width=device-width;
          initial-scale=1.0; maximum-scale=1.0; user-
          scalable=0;" />
  ```

  This `viewport` meta tag setting is best used if your site is designed to fit perfectly on the small iPhone screen. If your site isn't optimized for small screens, it's best not to use this meta tag because you'll want to allow visitors to enlarge sections of the page and scroll around as necessary to read your content.

- `apple-mobile-web-app-capable` — This meta tag tells the Safari browser that it doesn't need to have the navigation options at the top and bottom of the screen on the iPhone or iPod touch. It also removes the navigation options at the top of the iPad screen.

This feature doesn't work the first time someone visits a website. It works only if a visitor to your site has bookmarked the page by saving a Web Clip icon (covered in the section, "Creating a Web Clip icon," later in this chapter). When someone uses the link from the Web Clip icon to visit your site, this meta tag hides the navigation.

```
<meta name="apple-mobile-web-app-capable" content="yes"
      />
```

If you choose to use this tag, you must ensure that your site doesn't need the typical navigation options that the browser provides. When you remove the bars at the top and bottom of the iPhone and iPad, you gain some valuable real estate for your designs, but you lose the back and forward arrows and other navigation features built into these devices. If you use this option, make sure your website includes navigation elements to help visitors move through your website.

✔ apple-mobile-web-app-status-bar-style — The default style of the toolbar on an iPhone or iPad is opaque black. If you want to change the style of the status bar to a translucent black, you can use yet another iOS-specific meta tag. This meta tag also works only if the user visits a website via the link from a Web Clip icon.

```
<meta name="apple-mobile-web-app-status-bar-style"
      content="black-translucent" />
```

If you remove both of the interface bars and set the status bar to translucent, you have an extra 124 horizontal pixel lines of screen real estate in Safari on the iPhone and iPod touch. That's over 25 percent more room on the small screen! A translucent black status bar also allows content of the page to flow underneath the status bar.

Including meta tags for SEO

In HTML5, you can continue to use all the meta tags you already know and love, including the meta description, which is important for search engine optimization.

```
<meta description="Order custom jellyfish aquariums hand-
      crafted by oceanographer Mark Loos" />
```

The meta description tag appears in the head area at the very top of your HTML code. Humans never see this text because it's not displayed on a web page, but meta description tags are often used in search engine results and thus can make a big difference in whether someone clicks on your site or not. You can add descriptions to any or all of the pages in your site. Although search engines vary, most display only the first 250 characters.

You can add the meta `keywords` tag, but most search engines are known to ignore keywords in the meta `keywords` tag, so we don't describe it here.

Creating a Web Clip icon

Much like you can bookmark web pages in a desktop browser, you can save a link to any web page on an iPhone or iPad by clicking the Export icon circled in red in Figure 5-2 and then choosing Add to Home Screen, as shown in Figure 5-3.

A Web Clip icon looks just like the icons that come with native iTunes apps. When a visitor to your website adds a Web Clip icon to her Home screen (the desktop of her device), it creates a link to your website, much like a bookmark in a desktop web browser.

Figure 5-2: You can save a Web Clip icon to the Home screen with a link to any web page by clicking the Export icon, circled in this figure.

Figure 5-3: Choose Add to Home Screen to create a link to the web page.

This Web Clip icon gives your visitors a great shortcut back to your website, and it's a powerful way to keep them thinking about you. Unfortunately, many users of the iPhone and iPad don't even realize it's possible to save a link to a website in this way.

Here's how it works: When a user taps the middle button in the button bar at the bottom of the iPhone or iPod touch (see Figure 5-2), Safari offers several options, shown in Figure 5-3.

When you choose Add to Home screen, a small image, called a *Web Clip icon,* is saved to the Home screen of the iPhone or iPad with a link to the web page. This link makes going to a website by clicking an icon just as easy as launching an app. Click a Web Clip icon, and the iPhone and iPad launch Safari and open the page in a browser in one slick action.

As a web designer, you can create an image to serve as your Web Clip icon. If you don't, the iPod touch, iPhone, or iPad saves a screenshot of whatever is displayed on the screen and uses that as the icon. Because a random screenshot is often a less-than-ideal image to represent your website, we recommend you go to just a little extra effort and specify the image that you want to use as the icon on the Home screen.

In Figure 5-4, you can see that we've created a Web Clip icon from the main image used in this design. This image is cropped and simplified to serve as a better icon than a screen capture of the entire page, which would include the text and other images at such a small size that they would be impossible to read.

Here's how you create a Web Clip icon and specify it in the code of your page:

Figure 5-4: You can create a small image, like this jellyfish, to serve as the Web Clip icon for any web page.

1. **Use a graphics program, such as Photoshop, to create the image you want to serve as your icon.**

   The image should measure 114-x-114 pixels and be saved in the PNG format.

   Note: High-resolution devices display the icon at 114 x 114. Older iPhones display it at 57-x-57 pixels, iPads display 72-x-72 pixels. You can create one of each size, or you can let the device scale down the image automatically. Also note that you can use a JPEG image in newer iPhones and the iPad, but if you want to make sure the icon works on all devices, saving it as a PNG image is the safest option.

2. **Name the image** `apple-touch-icon.png` **and upload it to the root directory of your website.**

3. **(Optional) If you want to save the image in a subdirectory or you want to use a different Web Clip icon for the home page than you use for internal pages in your site, you can add this code to the <head> section of any web page to specify the name and location of the image.**

```
<link rel="apple-touch-icon" href="images/apple-touch-
      icon.png" />
```

Sending the right CSS

Since CSS version 2, it's been possible to create styles specifically targeted to different devices by changing the media type. For example, it's common to create a special style sheet for printers that removes background images and other design elements that can make a page difficult to read when it's printed.

CSS 3 takes this idea a step further, making it possible to target the iPad and iPhone in the portrait and landscape orientations. The Jelly Rancher site that we use as an example in this book includes two sets of styles: One set of styles works well in the latest desktop browsers, and the additional style sheets are designed for the iPhone and iPad. In Figure 5-5, you see the result of using two styles sheets to cause the same HTML page to display differently in landscape and portrait modes.

We started by creating one style sheet designed for desktop browsers that we named `main.css`. That style sheet is linked to the page with the following code:

```
<link href="css/main.css" rel="stylesheet" type="text/css" />
```

Next we added links to the style sheets we created for the landscape and portrait modes on the iPad and iPhone. Note that CSS 3 doesn't specifically include a way to target the iPad or iPhone, but you can use CSS 3 to target any screen size. Thus, we've targeted the iPhone and iPad by specifying maximum and minimum widths that equal the size of each device. To further distinguish styles sheets, we added the orientation to identify which style sheet should be applied by the browser when the device is in portrait or landscape mode.

Figure 5-5: Using CSS 3, you can alter the design when a page is viewed in landscape or portrait mode on the iPhone and iPad.

Here are the links to the two style sheets for the iPad:

```
<!--iPad portrait -->
<link href="css/ipadP.css" rel="stylesheet" media="only
         screen and (min-device-width:  768px) and
         (max-device-width: 1024px) and (orientation:
         portrait)">

<!--iPad landscape -->
<link href="css/ipadL.css" rel="stylesheet" media="only
         screen and (min-device-width: 768px) and
         (max-device-width: 1024px) and (orientation:
         landscape)">
```

We include notes in the code between comment tags `<!-- -->` to make it easy on us (and you) to identify the different style sheets in the HTML. For example, the line `<!--iPad portrait -->` in the preceding code is an optional comment. It isn't read by a browser, because it's included in the comment tags.

Here are the links to the two style sheets for the iPhone:

```
<!--iPhone portrait -->
<link href="css/iphoneP.css" rel="stylesheet" media="only
        screen and (min-device-width: 320px) and (max-
        device-width: 480px) and (orientation: portrait)">

<!--iPhone landscape -->
<link href="css/iphoneL.css" rel="stylesheet" media="only
        screen and (min-device-width: 320px) and
        (max-device-width: 480px) and (orientation:
        landscape)">
```

Using multiple style sheets has advantages and disadvantages:

- **Advantage:** Using multiple style sheets to create designs targeted to specific devices is relatively simple when compared with the more advanced programming required if you want to do device detection on the server and send completely different HTML files to different devices. (In Chapter 6, you find out more about creating and linking to style sheets.)

- **Disadvantage:** Targeting devices with multiple style sheets works only in the latest web browsers. If you want to create different designs for all the devices used on the Internet today, this approach won't work. Older phones, such as the Motorola RAZR, can't read multiple style sheets. To reach the broadest audience on the web, you need more advanced programming, and you need to identify each device as it arrives at your site and use a script on the server to deliver the best version of your site to each device. You find out more about device detection in Chapter 12.

- **Advantage:** The user's browser downloads only the CSS that matches the media query. For example, the iPhone doesn't download the CSS sheets you've created specifically for the iPad.

- **Disadvantage:** It takes longer to download multiple items than to download one because the browser on an iPhone has to request each of the files from the server. As a general rule, the fewer items downloaded, the faster the page is displayed. Similarly, if you want to prevent some of your content, such as high-resolution images, from being downloaded to the iPhone, you need to use device detection on the server. You can use CSS to hide elements in your design on any device, but if you use CSS to do so, visitors still have to wait for all the content to download, even if it's not displayed. Using the more advanced techniques, covered in Chapter 12, you can deliver only the necessary content to each device.

Body building (between the <body> tags)

You place all the content that you want your visitors to see, everything that will be displayed in a web browser, in the *body* of your page, between the opening and closing <body> tags.

Within the <body> tags, you can still use all the tags from previous versions of HTML (with a few notable exceptions).

In the sections that follow, you discover the most important new structural HTML5 tags that you can use in the body of your web pages. HTML5 introduces new structural tags, which are also called *semantic tags* because they add more meaning to HTML code by better identifying each type of content they format. Here are the new structural tags introduced in HTML5:

✓ <header> — Defines the header of any section or page. The header tag is the ideal place for the name of the site.

Here's the HTML code that makes up the header of all the internal pages in the Jelly Rancher site. ***Note:*** We altered this code slightly for the front page to accommodate the larger image in the header.

```
<header>
   <h1><a href="index.html">Jelly Rancher</a></h1>
   <h2>Specializing in<br>
     Jellyfish Aquariums</h2>
</header>
```

✓ <nav> — Defines the main navigation links in a page or section. The main navigation links are typically placed just after the header and then repeated at the bottom of the page. Within the <nav> tag, we follow the common convention of formatting our list of links with an unordered list, using the <ul> tag to surround the entire list of links with in the <nav> tags, and then making each navigational element a separate list item with the <li> tag.

```
<nav>
    <ul>
       <li><a href="index.php">Home</a></li>
       <li><a href="aquariums.php">Order Custom
          Aquariums</a></li>
       <li><a href="Mark-Loos.php">About Mark Loos</a></
          li>
       <li><a href="contact.php">Contact</a></li>
    </ul>
 </nav>
```

✓ <article> and <section> — Use these tags to define any article or a distinct section of a page.

In the example Jelly Rancher site, the next element we add is the main content section of the page. For this part of the page, we can use either the <article> tag or the <section> tag. You can use these two tags interchangeably. Thus you can have a section with several articles within it. Or you can have an article that has multiple sections. Either way, make sure that when you use these tags, you're defining areas of the page that go together in a meaningful way. In the code example that follows, we used the <article> tag to define the main content, and we used the <section> tag to separate sections in the article:

```
<article>
  <section>
    <h2>This is a headline for the first section</h2>
    <p>content</p>
    <p>more content...</p>
  </section>
<section>
    <h2>This is a headline for the second section</h2>
    <p>content</p>
    <p>more content...</p>
  </section>
</article>
```

✔ `<footer>` — Defines the footer for any section or page. You can use the `<footer>` tag within a section or article tag, but it's most commonly used at the very bottom of a page. Usually the footer has a lot of legal text in it.

You know how when you get one of those credit card offers in the mail it has all that small legal text? The semantic idea behind the `<small>` tag is the same. In HTML5, you can use the small tag in the footer container to format legalese, such as copyright information, causing it to display in small text without diminishing its importance semantically.

You can use all the tags in the preceding list more than once in a document. For example, you can have a `<header>` inside each `<article>`. Just make sure you never put a `<header>` inside another `<header>`.

In addition to these key structural elements, HTML5 includes other new elements, such as the following:

✔ `<aside>` — This element is ideal for tips, small sidebars, and other, well, asides. Within the main content section of the Jelly Rancher site, we use the `<aside>` tag to create a sidebar with related information.

```
<article>
  <h2>This is a headline</hs>
    <p>content</p>
    <aside>
      <h3>Aside Headline</h3>
      <p>Aside content</p>
    </aside>
    <p>more content...</p>
</article>
```

✔ `<canvas>` — The canvas tag is used to display graphics. It's only a container, but you can use JavaScript to render 2D shapes and images.

✔ `<figure>` — The figure element is best used for an illustration, a diagram, or a photo.

✔ `<figcaption>` — A figure caption element must always be inside the figure element, and it's best used to contain the caption for a figure.

HTML5 adds many great new tags to a web designer's toolkit, but that doesn't mean you can't still use tags from previous versions of HTML. For example, it's still good practice in HTML5 to use the heading tags for headlines on a web page. As you see in the example from the Jelly Rancher site earlier in this section, even though we're using the new <header> tag, we've formatted the most important headline text with the <h1> tag and the second most important text with the <h2> tag. Those good ol' heading tags have been with us since the earliest versions of HTML and are still valuable today.

Making the entire header a link

In the old days of web design, the banner at the top of most web pages was created with a big, long graphic. Designers resorted to using a graphic because it was the only way to use any font they wanted, and most designers included things like logos in the banner. With HTML5 and CSS 3, you can use any font you want in your web pages, and you can even create design features like drop shadows without having to use graphics.

That's great for creating faster-loading pages that are more accessible and easier for search engines to read, but it does cause a common problem. How do you link the entire banner area of your page if it's not a graphic?

We like to link the banner of our sites back to the site's home page to help visitors find their way home easily. This link is especially useful on the smaller screens of an iPhone. A quick solution to making your entire banner a link is wrapping an anchor tag around text, images, or any block-level element. Block-level elements, such as a paragraph tag, <div> tag, or a heading tag, begin a new line in the document by default. In contrast, inline elements, such as the <strong> tag, don't cause a line break.

Here's how the code looks that turns our banner, created with the <h1> tag, into a link:

```
<header>
   <a href="index.html">
      <h1><a href="index.html">Jelly Rancher</a></h1>
      <h2>Specializing in Jellyfish Aquariums</h2>
   </a>
</header>
```

Moving scripts to the end of the page

JavaScript makes it possible to add more advanced interactive features to a web page. In the early days of JavaScript, most developers put their scripts at the top of the document, within the <head> tags.

Understanding the exceptions: When scripts belong on top

In some situations, you can't move scripts to the bottom of your HTML document. If you use JavaScript to build part of your page, you may need it to execute as the page is loaded. In that one exception, the JavaScript needs to be at the top of the page. If you're creating content on your page with JavaScript, make sure you put the code above where you want the content to be shown.

In the Jelly Rancher sample site, a simple JavaScript at the bottom of the HTML file changes the position of the page on an iPhone by sliding it up on the screen just far enough that the address bar disappears. This provides 60 more precious rows of pixels on the iPhone screen. Users can always pull the screen back down if they want to see the URL field.

The problem with that approach is that scripts at the top of the page can block other elements from downloading, which can make your pages take longer to load for visitors. Thus, today the best practice is to place all your scripts at the bottom of the page, usually just before the closing </body> tag. This way, visitors can see most of your page content while one or more scripts download.

Not matter where you place scripts on your pages, JavaScript should always be contained between the opening <script> and closing </script> tags.

Checking out the whole HTML document

Piece by piece, we've been building a well-formed HTML5 document. This code forms the base of all the pages in our sample website. Keep in mind, however, that the actual code on each page does vary. Some elements may not be needed on every page; other pages may include tags for special features, such as video. To help you appreciate how all the pieces fit together, Listing 5-2 presents the entire HTML Framework for the example site, ready for us to add the real content.

Listing 5-2:   HTML5 Framework for the Jelly Rancher Site

```
<!DOCTYPE html>
<html lang="en">
<head>
<meta charset="utf-8" />
<title>Jelly Rancher - Specializing in Jellyfish Aquariums</
          title>
```

```
<meta name="viewport" content="width=device-width; initial-
         scale=1.0; maximum-scale=1.0; user-scalable=0;" />
<meta name="apple-mobile-web-app-capable" content="yes" />
<meta name="apple-mobile-web-app-status-bar-style"
         content="black-translucent" />
<meta description="Order custom jellyfish aquariums hand-
         crafted by oceanographer Mark Loos." />
<link rel="apple-touch-icon" href="apple-touch-icon.png" />
<link href="css/main.css" rel="stylesheet" type="text/css" />
<!--iPad portrait -->
<link href="css/ipadP.css" rel="stylesheet" media="only
         screen and (min-device-width:  768px) and
         (max-device-width: 1024px) and (orientation:
         portrait)">

<!--iPad landscape -->
<link href="css/ipadL.css" rel="stylesheet" media="only
         screen and (min-device-width: 768px) and
         (max-device-width: 1024px) and (orientation:
         landscape)">

<!--iPhone portrait -->
<link href="css/iphoneP.css" rel="stylesheet" media="only
         screen and (min-device-width: 320px) and (max-
         device-width: 480px) and (orientation: portrait)">

<!--iPhone landscape -->
<link href="css/iphoneL.css" rel="stylesheet" media="only
         screen and (min-device-width: 320px) and
         (max-device-width: 480px) and (orientation:
         landscape)">
</head>
<body id="home">
  <header>
    <h1><a href="index.html">Jelly Rancher</a></h1>
    <h2>Specializing in
<br>Jellyfish Aquariums</h2>
  </header>
  <article>
    <header><h2>Main article headline</h2>
    </header>
    <details>A detail</details>
    <section>
      <p>content</p>
      <aside>
        <header>
          <h3>Aside Header</h3>
        </header>
```

(continued)

Listing 5-2 *(continued)*

```
        <p>aside content</p>
      </aside>
      <p>more content…</p>
    </section>
  </article>
  <nav>
    <ul>
      <li><a href="index.html">Home</a></li>
      <li><a href="jelly-tales.html">Jellyfish Tales</a></li>
      <li><a href="aquariums.html">Order Custom Aquariums</
            a></li>
      <li><a href="Mark-Loos.html">About Mark Loos</a>
      <li><a href="contact.html">Contact</a></li>
    </ul>
  </nav>
  <footer> <small> Copyright 2011. All rights reserved.
          Contact Mark Loos.</small> </footer>
</body>
<script language="javascript" type="text/javascript">window.
          onload = function() {
 setTimeout(function(){window.scrollTo(0, 1);}, 100);
}
</script>
</html>
```

We don't think anyone should type more than necessary, and we certainly don't expect you to type all that code from Listing 5-2 into your own web pages. That's why we created the website that goes with this book. Just visit `www.digitalfamily.com/mobile` to find all the code examples.

Adding Audio and Video in HTML5

Although previous versions of HTML made it possible to add audio and video to web pages, those versions all required that your visitors had a plugin to play the audio or video file. This was especially problematic because each audio and video format seemed to require its own player.

HTML5 makes it easier to add audio and video to your pages, but it doesn't solve the problem that several video formats are in use on the web and not all of them work on all devices. For example, Flash video was fast becoming the most popular video format until the iPhone and iPad came along — none of the Apple iOS devices play Flash video and developers are quickly changing to the MP4 video format because it works on more platforms.

In Chapter 9 you find a review of the most popular video formats on the web, as well as instructions for using two of the best video hosting services: YouTube and Vimeo. These video services offer the simplest options for adding video to your page. Among the features they offer: both Vimeo and YouTube convert videos into multiple formats for you and then use sophisticated device detection systems to ensure the best version is delivered to each of your site visitors.

Playing audio and video without a plugin

If you are hosting your own audio or video (meaning you're not using a third-party service like YouTube), the new HTML video tag offers an exciting advantage — the new tags in HTML5 no longer require a plugin player to play audio and video files.

When you use the new HTML5 video tag on an iPad, the video can be displayed in the body of the page. On an iPhone, Safari launches the iPhone's media player to display the video (instead of playing it within the web page you're viewing). Then, when users are finished watching, they have to tap the Done button to return to the page in the web browser.

HTML5 audio and video tags are very similar and can be implemented in two ways. (We include examples of both options in the audio and video code examples that follow.) You can insert audio or video:

- ✏ With a single source reference inside the tag.

- ✏ As part of a list with several source options. This is useful if you want to include audio or video in multiple formats to ensure your visitors find a version that works in their web browsers. When you list multiple video or audio source files, the browser will go through the list until it finds the first version it can play.

If you have multiple source elements, iOS recognizes only the first one. This is important because, if you want your video to play well on desktop computers, you may want to include video saved using more than one codec option. Because iOS devices only support H.264+AAC+MP4, this effectively means you must always list your MP4 first. This bug is fixed in iOS 4.0 and later.

HTML5 adds three new tags for adding multimedia to your pages:

- ✏ `<video>`: Use this tag to insert one or more video files. You can also include any or all of the video attributes listed in Table 5-1.

- ✏ `<audio>`: Use this tag to insert one or more audio files. You can also include any or all of the audio attributes listed in Table 5-1.

✔ `<source>`: You can combine the source tag with the audio and video tags to add multiple file types. Note the source tag is limited to these three attributes:

- `media`: Specifies the type of device the media is optimized to display on. The default value is *all*, but you can also specify screen or print.
- `src`: Identifies the URL to the source file of the source tag.
- `type`: Specifies the mime type of the file.

You find examples of the `<source>` tag used in combination with the `<audio>` and `<video>` tags in the sections on adding audio and video that follow.

In Table 5-1, you see the options you can use when you insert a video or audio file using the new HTML5 tags.

Table 5-1	HTML5 `<video>` and `<audio>` Tag Attributes		
Attribute	**Value Type**	**Description**	**Recommended Use**
audio Works only with video.	Muted	Defining the default state of the audio. Currently, only "muted" is allowed.	If you want to make sure the user doesn't get surprised by the sound in your video, you can set this to muted.
autoplay Works with audio and video.	Autoplay	If present, the video or audio starts playing as soon as it's ready.	Don't use this unless you warn your user in some way.
controls Works with audio and video.	Controls	If present, controls will be displayed, such as a play button.	When this attribute is set to none, you must provide some other means of controlling the media.
height & width Works only with video.	Pixels	Sets the height and width of the video.	*Tip:* Instead of using the height and width attribute, use CSS and you can make the size smaller on an iPhone than in an iPad or desktop browser.

Attribute	Value Type	Description	Recommended Use
`loop` Works with audio and video.	Loop	If present, the video or audio will start over again, every time it is finished.	Use this attribute to loop your video.
`poster` Works only with video.	URL	This will define the thumbnail for the video that's shown before the user taps Play.	Use this attribute to show the user what to expect from the video.
`preload` Works with audio and video.	Preload	If present, the video will be loaded at page load, and ready to run. Ignored if "auto-play" is present.	This attribute helps your video play faster. It is recommended.
`src` Required for both audio and video.	URL	The URL of the video or audio to play.	You must specify a source for your audio or video.

If your visitors are using an iPhone that runs iOS 3.2, they won't be able to see the video if you include a `poster` attribute. The `poster` attribute of the `<video>` tag allows you to display a custom image while the video is loading, or until the user presses Play. This bug is fixed in iOS 4.0.

Adding audio with HTML5

Many people listen to music, podcasts, and other audio files on their iPhones and iPads. Here is an example of the code needed to add an audio file in one format, using a single source:

```
<audio src="favoritesong.mp3" controls="controls"
          preload="auto"></audio>
```

If you have several sources, you can use the source tag to define each in the order the browser should attempt to play them in:

```
<audio controls="controls" preload="auto" >
  <source src="favoritesong.mp3" />
  <source src="favoritesong.ogg" />
  Sorry, your browser does not support the audio tag. We
        recommend you download the latest version of the
        Safari or Chrome web browser to view this page.
</audio>
```

Because (by default) HTML ignores tags it doesn't understand, you can include text between the <audio> or <video> tags and it will be displayed only if the visitor's browser does not support the tag. It's good practice to add a message before the closing tag with a message for visitors who don't use a browser that supports HTML5. You can enter your own text or alter our message, but we like offering a simple instruction about how a visitor can view the content: "Sorry, your browser does not support the video tag. We recommend you download the Safari or Chrome web browser to view this page."

Adding video with HTML5

Adding video can bring your website to life. In Figure 5-6, you see how we used video to enhance the Jelly Rancher site.

The video tag can be used to add one video file, or combined with the <source> tag to include the same video in multiple formats.

In the video code examples that follow, we include the poster attribute to preload a single image in place of the video. Note that the .jpg image included in the poster attribute will display when the page loads, as it does on the video page in our sample Jelly Rancher site shown in Figure 5-6. When a user clicks play on an iPhone, the page disappears and the video player launches to play the video. On an iPad, this code will cause the video to play where it is inserted in the page.

Figure 5-6: We used the HTML5 <video> tag to insert the video into this page on the Jelly Rancher website.

Here's the code to add a single video file to a page using HTML5:

```
<video src="videos/myvideo.mp4" controls="controls"
          preload="auto" poster="images/previewphoto.jpg" >
Sorry, your browser does not support the video tag. We
          recommend you download the Safari or Chrome web
          browser to view this page. </video>
```

Here is the code to add the same video in two formats (you find out more about video formats in Chapter 9):

```
<video controls="controls" preload="auto" poster="images/
          previewphoto.jpg" >

          <source src="videos/myvideo.mp4" type="video/mp4"
          />
          <source src="videos/myvideo.ogg" type="video/ogg"
          />

Sorry, your browser does not support the video tag. We
          recommend you download the Safari or Chrome web
          browser to view this page.
</video>
```

The `<video controls>` tag at the beginning of this code example adds controls when a video is played on an iPad. On an iPhone, the `<video controls>` tag has no effect because the built-in video player on an iPhone is launched when a video is played and it has its own controls. On an iPad, you can embed video in the page and without the `<video controls>` tag, your visitors won't have a way to stop, pause, or restart a video.

Creating the Ultimate Contact Page

Any good website should have a contact page. On a mobile site, such as one for iPhones, design that contact page to make reaching you in a variety of ways as easy as possible. This section explores features you can add to take advantage of the web browser and phone that iPhone users have in a single device (and iPad users, too, if they use Skype or have an iPad 2 with FaceTime). In this section, we show you how to make the ultimate contact page.

A great contact page on a mobile site should fulfill two key goals:

- ✔ Your users should be able to save your contact information easily to the contacts management system on their device.

- ✔ Your users should be able to contact you in any and every way their phones support.

The first goal is relatively easy because this feature is built in to all Apple devices. See the upcoming "Saving contact information" section for details.

To help you accomplish the second goal in your designs, we suggest you enable your site visitors to do the following:

- ✔ Dial a phone number. (It is a phone after all.)
- ✔ Send an e-mail.
- ✔ Send a text message.
- ✔ Place a phone call via Skype.
- ✔ Initiate a FaceTime session with video.
- ✔ Get directions to your location.
- ✔ Scan a 2D barcode to automatically add more information (for the iPad only, as you discover in the section "Adding 2D barcodes," later in this chapter).

In the most current browsers that support HTML5 and other current website features, adding these elements is easy, as you discover in the following sections.

Mobile users are more likely to be on the go, in a hurry, and in need of your information urgently.

Placing a call with the touch of a finger

Touch a telephone number on an iPhone, and a dialog opens automatically, giving you the option to place a call (or to cancel), as you see in Figure 5-7.

The Apple iOS automatically recognizes phone numbers, so when a user taps the link, the dialog box shown in Figure 5-7 opens to initiate a call.

Not all phones are as smart as the iPhone. If you want to create a link that will place a call on any mobile device with phone capabilities, just add the `tel` protocol to the URL like this:

```
<a href="tel://+12121234567">Get in Touch</a>
```

The Internet is international. No matter what country you're in, make sure you enter phone numbers in the international format with your country code in case the user is not in the same country you are. If your phone number is in the United States, including the +1 at the beginning of the number (as we did in this example) ensures callers from outside the U.S. can use the link to initiate a call just as easily as anyone within the U.S.

If the user clicks and holds the linked phone number on an iPhone, a different dialog box appears, giving the user four options:

- ✔ Call the number.
- ✔ Send a text message to the number.
- ✔ Create a new contact to automatically save the number.
- ✔ Add the number to an existing contact.

This is great to know if you own an iPhone, but because many iPhone users don't realize that these options will appear, you may want to include a line of text in your contact page explaining these options.

Sending an e-mail automatically

Since the early days of the web, it's been relatively easy to turn an e-mail address into a link that launches the users e-mail program and initiates an e-mail to any address. If you've created a website before, chances are good that you've used the link tag with the `mailto` attribute. Well, the good news is that the same tag works just as well on an iPhone or iPad.

Here's an example of the code for an e-mail link:

Figure 5-7: When a user touches or clicks a phone number link, a dialog box appears to confirm that the user wants to place the call.

```
<a href="mailto:janine@DigitalFamily.com?subject=Found your
         email in your Dummies book">Email Janine</a>
```

When a visitor to your site clicks a link with this special code, an e-mail is automatically started with the e-mail program your visitors have set up on their mobile phones or other devices.

You can automatically include a subject line with any e-mail link – a great way to save your iPhone users from having to enter it on a small keypad. As you see in the preceding code example, we added a question mark followed by `subject=`, followed by the text we want to use in the subject line of any messages that are sent to us from the site. When you include a subject line in an e-mail like this, the subject automatically appears in the new message as it's created, as shown in Figure 5-8.

Can you see me now? Enabling video calls with FaceTime on the iPhone 4

Users have other ways to call from an iPhone. FaceTime is a new video chat service that shipped with iPhone 4 and iPad 2. With a FaceTime link, your user can start a FaceTime video call to your computer, iPad 2, iPod touch, or iPhone 4 directly from your web page.

You can create a FaceTime link to a phone number or an e-mail address. Use a phone number if you want to initiate a FaceTime call to an iPhone 4. To call an iPad, an iPod touch, or a Mac computer, use an e-mail address. Here's an example of the code for a FaceTime link with a phone number:

```
<a href="facetime:+12121234567"> Video call me with FaceTime
     </a>
```

Here's an example of the code for a FaceTime link with an e-mail address:

```
<a href="facetime:mark@jellyrancher.com">
```

When the user taps a FaceTime link, he's shown a message and given the chance to confirm the FaceTime call or cancel it, as shown in Figure 5-9.

Saving money with Skype calls

You can initiate Skype calls by touch on the iPod touch, iPhone, and iPad. You must have Skype loaded on your device to make it work, and you have to have Wi-Fi coverage, but it's a surprisingly easy way to add phone calling capabilities to an iPod touch or iPad, and to save money on calls on computers and iPhones. We use Skype a lot, especially when we're traveling and working with people in other countries.

If you've never used Skype before, all you need to do is set up an account. Their basic service is free (and works great on all iOS devices). Although you can make calls to and from phone numbers using Skype, most accounts are activated by a Skype name, which you set up when you set up your account.

Because Skype is such a popular application, many people already have it loaded on their systems. And we've been in places where we couldn't connect to the cellular network to make phone calls, but we did have a Wi-Fi connection. In that case, Skype was the only way to make a call. For all these reasons, including a Skype link is a great idea.

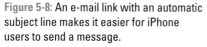

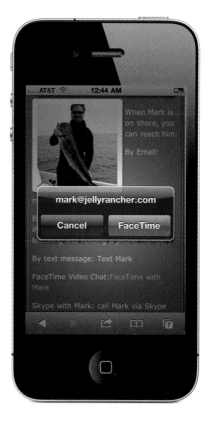

Figure 5-8: An e-mail link with an automatic subject line makes it easier for iPhone users to send a message.

Figure 5-9: When a user taps a FaceTime link, a dialog box appears to confirm that the user wants to place the call.

When you have your Skype name, you can use the following code to add a link that will automatically trigger a call via Skype:

```
<a href="skype:YourSkypeName?call">Call me on Skype</a>
```

Note: In place of the text `YourSkypeName`, in the code example, make sure to include your exact Skype name with no spaces. The question mark (?) followed by the word `call` indicates that the link will initiate a call via Skype.

If you want to get even more advanced with your Skype links, you can include a Skype button (a graphic that represents your Skype link, as shown in Figure 5-10). You can even set up a connection to automatically update your Skype status on your contact page. Thus if you're available via Skype, the I'm Available link displays, but if you're away or busy, the Skype button changes to let your visitors know you're not available. You can create the code you need to copy into your pages for these advanced Skype features by visiting `www.skype.com/intl/en-gb/tell-a-friend/get-a-skype-button`.

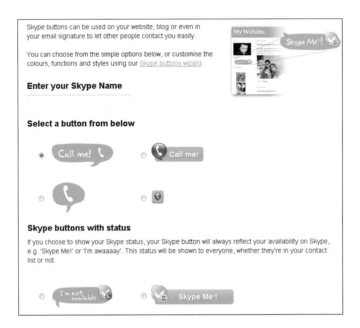

Figure 5-10: You can include a button on your site that can trigger a Skype call and update your current availability on Skype automatically.

Mapping your location

When you're designing for the mobile web, keep in mind that visitors to your site may be on the road. (We can all hope they're not driving while they surf your site!) If they're trying to find you, save them some trouble and include a link to a map on your contact page.

To create a link to a map to your restaurant, office, paint ball shop, or anywhere else you want your visitors to be able to find, follow these steps:

1. **Point your browser to** `http://maps.google.com`.

2. **Enter the address you want the map to lead to and click the Search Maps button.**

3. **Copy the link to the page and include it in a link tag, as shown in the following example:**

```
<a href="http://maps.google.com/maps?q=1800+Cabrillo+M
    emorial+Drive+San+Diego,+CA+92106-3601"> Show
    this location on a Google Map</a>
```

For best results, don't use the iFrame link provided by Google; just copy the URL and paste it into a link tag.

The key here is to set the query (?q=) to the address you want the map to show. In place of spaces, use the plus (+) sign. In this case, we're showing a map to the Cabrillo State Park. For even better accuracy (or to include a map to a location that doesn't have a traditional street address) you can also include the latitude and longitude of the location. If you want to add a little information on the map itself, you can add a label by adding text inside of parentheses. In Figure 5-11, you see the acronym LAX is included in the map. Here's an example of a map link that would take you to the Los Angeles airport, also known by the airport code LAX:

```
<a href="http://maps.google.com/maps?q=33.93-
      118.40(LAX)">Open a map to LAX</a>
```

Saving contact information

When you touch and hold a phone number or an e-mail address on an iPhone, iPad, or iPod touch, built-in features trigger a message, as shown in Figure 5-12, that includes an easy way to create a new contact or add the information to an existing contact.

If you want to make sure your visitors know that saving your contact information is an option (a surprising number of iPhone users polled haven't discovered this feature), you can include a message in your contact page that explains the feature. For example: "Touch and hold the phone number to add to your iPhone or iPad contacts."

If you don't want visitors to your site to be able to touch and hold a telephone number to open the options list shown in Figure 5-12, you can add a meta tag that prevents Safari from automatically detecting this type of contact information. We can't think of too many reasons you'd want to do this, but here it is, just in case. Just add this code to the header of any web page:

```
<meta name="format-detection" content="telephone=no">
```

Sending an SMS

Short Message Service (SMS) is the technical name for what most people simply call a *text message*. The Text Message option is automatically included in the list of options available on the iPhone and iPod when you touch and hold a phone number. As shown in Figure 5-12, the iPhone makes it easy to call, text message, and even save contact information.

Figure 5-11: Including a link to a location, such as the Los Angeles airport, on a Google Map makes it easier to find you in the real world.

Figure 5-12: Touch and hold a phone number on an iPhone and you get a menu of options, including the ability to send an SMS text message.

Fitting Text Onscreen with Soft Hyphens

To design a site that looks good in both the landscape and portrait view of the iPad and iPhone, you have to either alter your designs considerably or cram them together to fit everything into portrait view.

In our Jelly Rancher website design, we ran into a common mobile problem. The text we used under the three small images at the bottom of the page didn't quite fit when the page was displayed in portrait view. That's because our friend Mark uses ten-dollar words like *Oceanographer* that take up too much room in the tiny portrait view on the iPhone.

To solve the problem, we added a soft hyphen. A *soft hyphen* doesn't display unless a line of text must be broken because of the way the text flows in a way that requires the hyphen. The soft hyphen appears only when the page is in portrait view on an iPhone, as shown in Figure 5-13. The code to create a soft hyphen is

```
&shy;
```

Here's an example of the entire line of code we used to add a soft hyphen in the middle of the word *Oceanographer:*

```
<a href="Mark-Loos.html">Oceano&shy;grapher <br>Mark Loos</
     a></li>
```

Because we want the word *Oceanographer* to automatically hyphenate only when the page appears in portrait view on an iPhone — and nowhere else — we were pretty psyched to find the soft hyphen solution.

Handling Forms on the iPhone and iPad

Forms are an important part of many websites, enabling you to collect data from site visitors, search features, and other interactive options. For the most part, when you create HTML forms for the iPhone or iPad, you use the same form tags included in earlier versions of HTML. When you're designing forms for the iPhone and iPad, pay special attention to how the user will input data.

Here are a few things to keep in mind when creating forms for mobile devices:

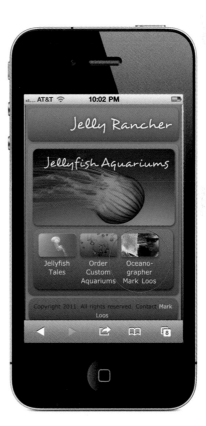

Figure 5-13: You can hyphenate a long word only when necessary by using the soft hyphen option in HTML5.

  ✔ **Keep it short.** Limit the questions or fields your users must fill out to only the essential ones. Remember, the iPhone's keyboard has made it easier to enter data than the simple 0–9 telephone keypads of the old-fashioned feature phones, but it's still not a device any sane person would choose to type the entire contents of a novel. This tip is more for the iPhone and iPod touch than the iPad.

✔ **Choose the best input option.** You find tips for specifying the input keyboard on the iPhone and iPad in the sections that follow.

✔ **Respect their privacy.** The iPhone and iPad are highly personal devices. If you're going to ask for personal information, such as phone numbers or e-mail addresses, make sure you have a clear and respectful privacy policy that's easy to find on your site.

Choosing the Input Keyboard on the iPhone

Don't make the mistake of thinking that a "keyboard is a keyboard" when it comes to mobile web design — or even worse, thinking that there's nothing you can do to control what kind of keyboard shows up when you ask your users to input some data into the forms on your website.

In fact, you can choose from five very different software keyboards, each with its particular strengths and use cases. In the following section, we demonstrate what each one looks like, explain under what circumstances it should be chosen, and provide the necessary HTML code.

Using the standard keyboard

As the name would indicate, the standard keyboard (shown in Figure 5-14) appears by default whenever users are called upon to enter information into an iPhone. Note that there is a spacebar, but no special characters appear, and to add punctuation, the user must tap the .?123 key in the lower left corner.

This keyboard should be used whenever you want your users to write a message using standard spelling and grammar, such as in a comment section, or when asking them what they thought of your service.

Figure 5-14: The standard keyboard is best when your users need to type regular words and sentences.

Following is the input type for the standard keyboard type="text":

```
<form name="myform" action="handler.cgi" method="POST">
<input type="text" value="Enter your name" />
<input type="submit" value="Send me your name!" />
</form>
```

Using the telephone number keyboard

The telephone keypad, as shown in Figure 5-15, works great when you want your users to be able to type phone numbers quickly without having to tap the button to switch from a standard keyboard to one that looks just like a telephone.

This keyboard is best used whenever you are trying to get your users to enter a phone number (theirs or someone else's). Note that the number keys also contain the standard `ABC` letters, just like a push-button telephone keypad, as well as the +*# key in the lower left corner.

Figure 5-15: The telephone keypad is best for typing phone numbers quickly.

The input type for the telephone keypad is `type="tel"`:

```
<form name="myform" action="handler.cgi" method="POST">
<input type="tel" value="Enter your phone number" />
<input type="submit" value="Send me your number!" />
</form>
```

Using the web URL keyboard

The web URL keyboard, as shown in Figure 5-16, works great when your users might want to enter the URL for a website more easily. Note the differences between this keyboard and the standard keyboard in Figure 5-14: The URL keyboard has buttons to allow users to quickly enter the type of information necessary for a web address, such as .com or @123.

Figure 5-16: The web URL keyboard makes it faster to type web addresses that use the special characters and syntax of the Internet.

If you've ever struggled with the standard keyboard on an iPhone, where you have to switch back and forth between the alphabetical keyboard, the number keyboard, and the special character keyboard, you can appreciate what a time-saver this particular format can be. The default settings for this keyboard are for the letters to be lowercase.

The most recent updates to Apple's iOS operating system have a special Easter egg in them — if you keep pressing the .com key, a shortcut menu pops up, allowing you to choose from other common URL suffixes, such as .org or .net. You should use this keyboard as the default in a field where you're asking your users to submit the URL of their (or someone else's) website.

The input type for the web URL keyboard is type="url":

```
<form name="myform" action="handler.cgi" method="POST">
<input type="url" value="What's your favorite site?" />
<input type="submit" value="Tell me your favorite!" />
</form>
```

Using the e-mail keyboard

The e-mail keyboard, shown in Figure 5-17, differs from the web URL keyboard above in one crucial way: It includes an @ (the at sign) that makes it easy to enter an e-mail address.

You should use this keyboard when you're asking your users to enter their e-mail addresses (or the address of someone they want to e-mail your content to), so you can send additional information, or a registration code.

Figure 5-17: The e-mail keyboard allows your users to easily enter their e-mail addresses.

The input type for the e-mail keyboard is type="email":

```
<form name="myform" action="handler.cgi" method="POST">
<input type="email" value="Enter your email address" />
<input type="submit" value="Send me your address!" />
</form>
```

Using the numeric keyboard

The numeric keyboard, shown in Figure 5-18, is for when you want your users to just type in a string of numbers, such as in the field for a street number, or the number of items they want to order. Note the difference between this keyboard and that of the dedicated telephone keyboard — there's no button here for them to push to insert special characters.

Figure 5-18: The numeric keyboard is for when you want your users to enter just numbers (and no special characters) into a form field.

The HTML code for this keyboard is `<input type="text" pattern="[0-9]*" />`.

The input type for the numeric keyboard is `type="text"`, but it's shown only when the pattern specifies a number only:

```
<form name="myform" action="handler.cgi" method="POST">
<input type="text" pattern="[0-9]*" />
<input type="submit" value="Your favorite number?" />
</form>
```

Reining in autocorrect

You can also control the automatic capitalization and automatic correction in form fields. This can be helpful if the user is entering something that should not be changed from what they enter. We all hate it when autocorrect changes something that we didn't want changed.

If you're asking your users to enter text that's typically outside the dictionary (such as names, URLs, or unusual spellings), turning off autocorrect is recommended. Similarly, if you want to stop the iPhone from automatically capitalizing the next word after a period, such as when they are entering a complicated web address that contains periods (such as `www.go.espn.com`), turning off the autocapitalize function can save your users a lot of backspacing and correcting. You can set these functions to the Off position either separately or together in the same HTML tag.

When you use them together, the HTML code looks like this:

```
<textarea type="text" autocorrect="off" autocapitalize="off">
```

Creating Valid HTML5 Code

One of the challenges of creating HTML5 code today is following standards and making sure you are creating *valid* code. What do we mean by standards and who decides what is valid? We think the W3C does, but we have taken the liberty to include a few browser-specific tags when we think they're warranted. Although not all browsers or web design programs follow the rules set out by the W3C, we still consider it the ultimate authority.

The W3C provides tools to help you ensure that your code is valid. You can use the W3 validator to check your pages by typing any URL into `http://validator.w3.org`. Take it from us: Checking your code early and often can save you a lot of time later. You can find out more about testing and validating the code in your web pages in Chapter 11.

6

Designing with the Advantages of CSS 3

Many designers are excited about the new features in CSS 3, including the ability to use almost any font on your web pages, to add drop shadows to text and other elements, and to create gradients — without resorting to using images. These long-awaited design improvements offer a compelling reason to start using CSS 3 right away.

In addition to new design options, CSS 3 offers the ability to target specific devices with styles — you can create style sheets targeting the iPhone and iPad, the desktop, and other devices. CSS 3 also adds styles that create animation, interactivity effects, and transitions that were previously possible only by using a program such as Adobe Flash.

In this chapter, we introduce the most popular CSS 3 features, including the ability to add drop shadows to text and to create rounded corners, so that you can immediately start designing pages with CSS 3. In the next chapter, we get into more advanced CSS 3 features and show you how to combine JavaScript with CSS to create more complex design features.

In Figure 6-1, you can see how we've used media queries to alter the design of the page about oceanographer Mark Loos based on the orientation of the iPad. The layout is wider when the iPad is in Landscape mode than when it's in Portrait mode.

Figure 6-1: Using CSS 3, you can create style sheets that display pages differently in Landscape and Portrait modes on the iPhone and iPad.

In Chapter 5, you discover how to create a web page framework by designing a document using the latest HTML5 tags. In this chapter, you add the style that makes the page look good on each device.

Displaying New Code in Many Browsers

Apple created the operating system, *iOS,* which runs on the iPhone, iPad, and iPod touch and in a special version in Apple TV 2. Safari, the default iOS browser, supports nearly the entire CSS specification as described by the World Wide Web Consortium (W3C), the open international organization that develops web standards. Led by the inventor of the web, Tim Berners-Lee, it brings together browser creators, leaders, and users to create the specifications for the protocols that define the World Wide Web.

Similar to HTML5, CSS 3 is still under development as we write this book. The specification won't reach its final Proposed Recommendation stage until 2022, according to the W3C's timeline. Even if the specification may not be final for many years, browser developers typically implement parts of the working drafts of new versions of HTML and CSS as they update their browsers. Developers implementing parts of a working draft refer to it as *experimental* CSS and usually insert the browser name in the rule. That's why you see multiple versions of the same style rules, as you can see in the example we show you in the next section for creating rounded corners.

Many designers shy away from using experimental CSS, preferring to wait until the standards are approved, or at least until most web browsers support them consistently. Implementing experimental CSS is easier when every browser plays by the same rules, and it can lead to problems if the specification is changed again later. However, CSS 3 offers so many exciting new features and so few negative side effects — if you design your pages carefully — that you have little reason to hold back. CSS naturally degrades in browsers. (If the browser doesn't support a CSS style, it's ignored.)

When you focus a design on the iPhone, iPod touch, or iPad, you have the advantage of knowing that your visitors will be using the Safari web browser. It's based on the WebKit layout engine, which can render CSS 3 as well as any desktop browser can. WebKit is also used in Google Chrome. Thus, most sites that look good in Safari for the desktop also look good in Chrome. (As with most elements of web design, though, you might see exceptions.)

In this book, we focus on designing for the iPhone, iPod touch, and iPad, by showing you how to create pages that display well in the desktop Safari browser versions 3 and 4. However, we assume that most of you still have to work in the real world and that not all visitors to your sites may be using Safari. To create CSS 3 styles that work in Firefox or Internet Explorer or another browser, you may need to add special code for those browsers. For tips on how to make your designs display well on more than just WebKit browsers such as Safari, read on.

Making your CSS 3 work across browsers

If you're designing for the desktop as well as for the iPhone and iPad, you can still use the experimental CSS 3! Eventually, the CSS 3 in your site will likely be supported. The example in this section shows you how to hedge your bets for the future. For any of the `-webkit-` code examples in this book (that cover our beloved Safari versions 3 and 4), create another identical CSS rule with `-moz-` to cover Firefox and one CSS rule with just the root name to cover the newest browsers: Opera 10.5, Internet Explorer 9, Safari 5, Chrome, and future browsers.

Here's an example of a set of rules to round the corners of a box:

```
-webkit-border-radius: 12px; /* Saf3-4 */
-moz-border-radius: 12px; /* FF1+ */
border-radius: 12px; /* Opera 10.5, IE 9, Saf5, Chrome */
```

Resetting HTML Elements with CSS

The new semantic tags in HTML5 work well in Safari on the iPhone and iPad, but not in most of the older web browsers still common on the web. To make these new elements work in older browsers, all you have to do is set the style rules for display to block to define the semantic tags as block-level elements. This action makes them act like <div> tags in older browsers.

Because not all browsers interpret HTML and CSS in the same way, many web developers begin designing pages by creating styles that remove any border, padding, or margins included in an HTML tag by defining a style that sets those values to 0 (as you see in the following example).

The process of resetting elements helps ensure that any styles you create will display more consistently across different web browsers because all your tags start with the same blank slate. It's good practice for Safari on the iPad and iPhone, and for other browsers.

In this example, we set the display to block and simultaneously set the border, padding, and margin to 0, to ensure a more consistent display across different web browsers:

```
article, aside, footer, header, menu, nav, section, details,
        table, body, h1, h2, h3, p, ul, li, {
                            border:0; margin:0; padding:0;
                            display: block;

}
```

Styling Text with CSS 3

When you create CSS 3 for an iPhone or iPad site, you not only enjoy the benefits of custom fonts and drop shadows but also gain the challenge of sizing text on screens with different dimensions. Worry no more: In this section, you find out how to best manage the sizing of text and then discover the joys of styling text by using CSS 3.

Understanding CSS size options

As in previous versions of CSS, you can specify sizes for fonts and other elements in so many ways that confusion can set in. If you're familiar with print, you probably recognize point sizes and pixel sizes, but these aren't necessarily the best options when you're designing for the Internet. On the web, where display windows can vary from giant monitors to tiny cellphone screens, using relative sizes can help you create more flexible and adaptable designs — something you can't do as well with fixed pixel or point sizes. As you work in Dreamweaver to create web pages, be sure to become familiar with the sizing options described in this list:

✔ **Percentage-based relative sizes:** You can use percentages to make text larger or smaller, relative to the base size. For example, you can define the text in a caption style as 90 percent so that your caption text appears at 90 percent of the size of the rest of the text on the page. You can then make headlines 150 percent (for example) and subheads 125 percent.

✔ **Em and ex:** Another size option is *em,* which refers to the space taken up by a capital letter *M* in the font face specified in a style. The *ex* option is similar, but it's based on the size of a lowercase *x* in the specified font face. Although these two options may seem complex (especially when you're new to web design), these two sizes are highly recommended, especially when you're creating designs where the text may be resized because the size is adjusted relative to the displayed text size. Although this concept can get confusing, em and ex work much like percentages — and adapt even better to different user settings and monitor sizes.

Many web designers prefer the em and ex size options, especially when they specify text size, because these size options adjust well when the text size is altered by users or by device differences.

Adjusting text size

To help make it easier to read text on the iPhone, the default setting for the `text-size-adjust` rule is `auto`: The text is automatically scaled to the screen. On the iPad, the default is `none` because the larger screen doesn't require text to be resized automatically. On many websites, this adjustment makes the page easier to read, but if you've carefully designed your pages and targeted your styles specifically to the iPhone or iPad, you may want to prevent automatic resizing.

Here are three examples of how you can use this option:

```
-webkit-text-size-adjust: auto;
-webkit-text-size-adjust: none;
-webkit-text-size-adjust: 80%;
```

Here's the code we build on in the preceding two sections, with the addition of the `webkit-text-size-adjust` rule set to `none`; including this bit of code in the style for all these tags at one time makes none of the text in the tags automatically resize:

```
/* This style helps older browsers understand HTML5 and
         resets common tags to 0 */
article, aside, footer, header, menu, nav, section,
         details,body, h1, h2, h3, p, ul, li, {
                              border:0;
                              margin:0;
                              padding:0;
                              display: block;
                              /* stops WebKit resizing text */
                              -webkit-text-size-adjust: none;


}
```

Adding text shadows

Using CSS 3, you can add drop shadows to text and to any block-level element, such as a `<div>` tag. We explain in this section how to add shadows to text, and we cover block-level elements later in this chapter.

A helpful way to increase the contrast between text and the background is to add a text shadow. Text shadows not only make your page designs more interesting but also make text much more readable, especially if your design has a complex background or the foreground and background colors don't have much contrast.

Here's the syntax for text shadows for WebKit browsers:

```
text-shadow: horizontal vertical blur radius color;
```

Here's how filling in these placeholders affects the text shadow:

- `horizontal` and `vertical` — The first two values, which specify the horizontal and vertical offsets, are required. They specify the distance the drop shadow extends below and to the right of the text.

- `blur radius` — The third setting, which specifies the amount of blur in the shadow, is optional. If you don't include a blur radius, the default is 0, which makes the specified color appear as a solid color.

- `color` — Specify a color using its hexadecimal color code (the traditional 6-character color codes) or its RGBa color code, which enables you to specify among red, green, and blue, as well as opacity. (More on RGBa in a moment.)

The following line of code adds a text shadow to the <h1> tag. The numbers specify that the text shadow extends two pixels to the right and below the text with a 3-pixel blur. This example uses a gray color specified with the hexadecimal color code #999.

```
h1 {text-shadow: 2px 2px 3px #999;}
```

If you specify the color as an RGBa color, you can define a partially transparent color. RGBa colors are defined by a series of numbers that specify how much red, blue, or green you want. The range of numbers is 0 to 255. The fourth number defines the amount of opacity or transparency. (The range is 1 for full opacity to 0 for full transparency.) For example the .6 in the following example indicates an opacity level of 60 percent; 40 percent of the underlying color shines through.

The style defined for the preceding <h1> tag applies to any text formatted with the Heading 1 tag. The style below is a class style (indicated by the dot before the name). Class styles are more versatile and can be applied to any text on a page.

```
.shadow {text-shadow: .2em .2em .3em rgba(153,153,153,.6);}
```

In CSS, sizes can be specified in many different measurements, including pixels, percentages, and the em option used in the preceding example. For more on sizes, see the earlier sidebar "Understanding CSS size options."

Enhancing your site with custom fonts

To most web designers, the font of fonts does *not* runneth over. The 11 fonts built in to the Apple iOS, shown in Figure 6-2, are woefully inadequate. Serious designers spend hours searching for just the right font to convey the feeling they want to elicit in a design. That's why many designers are excited that CSS 3 offers a new solution.

The @font-face option, new in CSS 3, enables you to link to any font that's available from a web server. Add a little drop shadow and other

Figure 6-2: By default, Apple iOS limits designers to these 11 fonts.

styling elements with CSS, and you can create fantastic font effects without resorting to the old workaround for limited fonts: saving images of styled text created in Photoshop.

Finding fonts online

Although you can upload any font you have to your own server and link to it, an online font repository offers many advantages, the font is stored on the repository's servers and it provides the CSS to include the font in your site. Online font repositories also take care of any licensing issues. Fonts, much like images, are generally protected by copyright law; be sure that you have permission before uploading a font and making it available on the web.

We recommend that you start by using the fonts available from the Google Font Directory or from Font Squirrel, as described in this list:

- **Google Font Directory:** The Google Font Directory, shown in Figure 6-7, lets you easily use any font in the directory on your web pages. In the sections that follow, you find detailed instructions for using a font from the Google Font Directory in your page designs.

- **Font Squirrel:** FontSquirrel.com makes it easy to use any number of free fonts on your web pages. Essentially, the folks at Font Squirrel have collected all the best free fonts (again, no worries about licensing issues). To include one of these free fonts, just download a font-face kit. It includes sample code and the four types of fonts needed to support browsers that now implement the @font-face part of CSS 3.

  Font Squirrel also has one of the best font generators online. If you have a custom font, use the font generator to generate the four font types and the code you need in order to use any font on your web pages.

  For instance, when we created a site for Intel, we put its font through the generator on Font Squirrel and then were able to use the custom-created "Intel font" rather than an image of its logo. *Note:* Font Squirrel requires that you have permission to use a font before you upload it and run it through its generator.

The Apple iOS supports True Type Fonts (TTF) and Scalable Vector Graphics (SVG) versions of a font. Because TTF and SVG are *vector based,* they can be scaled up or down with no loss of quality, making them an ideal choice when designing for the iPhone and iPad. TTF files are generally smaller, so we prioritize TTF higher than SVG. If a user has an iOS older than 4.2, the device downloads and uses the SVG automatically rather than use the TTF.

Using fonts in your page designs

After you generate the code you need on Font Squirrel, you can start using the font on your web pages in a few simple steps. The following example shows the code you see if you run a custom font through the Font Squirrel generator.

First, you add the font to the head area of your page by using this syntax:

```
@font-face {
    font-family: 'GoodDogRegular';
    src: url('GoodDog-webfont.eot');
    src: url('GoodDog-webfont.eot?iefix') format('eot'),
        url('GoodDog-webfont.woff') format('woff'),
        url('GoodDog-webfont.ttf') format('truetype'),
        url('GoodDog-webfont.svg#webfontx1QlgLst')
            format('svg');
    font-weight: normal;
    font-style: normal;
}
```

Then you include the font in a style rule, and you can apply it to any text on your page.

```
.stylename {
  font-family: 'GoodDogRegular';
}
```

Follow these steps to add any of the fonts in the Google Font Directory to your pages:

1. **Open any web browser (we recommend Safari: the desktop version is closest to the version in iOS) and visit** `http://code.google.com/ webfonts`.

2. **Click the name of any font to select the font you want to use in your design.**

3. **Click the Use This Font tab at the top of the page to generate the code you need, as shown in Figure 6-3.**

4. **Copy the link in the first field and paste it into the head area of your web page.**

5. **Copy the code for the font family from the second field on the Google Font Directory font page (also shown in Figure 6-3) and paste it into the CSS style sheet for your web page.**

   In the example shown in Figure 6-3, you see that Google has generated the rule in a style for the <h1> tag. You can use this code to create a style for the <h1> tag with the font you selected, but you also have the option of adding the font rule to any other CSS style.

6. **Apply the rule to text in your web page.**

   If you use the entire h1 rule provided by Google, any text formatted with the <h1> tag displays in that font. If you create a new class or ID style with the font as part of the rule, you apply the style to your text for the font to appear, just as you would have to apply any other style.

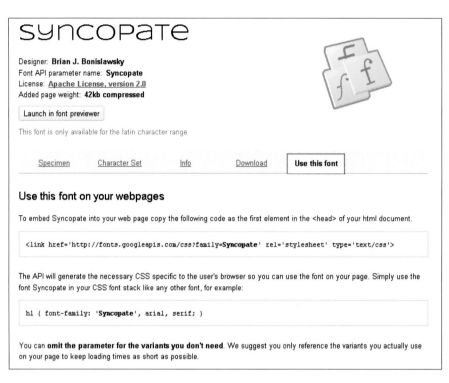

Figure 6-3: The Google Font Directory helps you easily generate the code you need in order to use a growing collection of fonts in your web pages.

Combining style rules

There are many ways to define rules using embedded fonts in your web pages and many ways to combine style rules to create more efficient CSS. In the Jelly Rancher site, we created a style that defined the font, color, padding, and text shadow for all our headlines at once, like this:

```
h1, h2, h3, h4 {
                             text-shadow: .01em .01em .3em
          #333;
                             font-family: 'GoodDogRegular',
          sans-serif;
                             padding: .3em;
                             color: #F6FFFC;
                             font-size: 1.5em;
}
```

We then created additional styles to specify the size of the headlines differently, like this:

```
h1 { font-size: 3em; }
h2 { font-size: 2.5em; }
h3 { font-size: 2em; }
```

Polishing Design Elements with CSS 3

Until the advent of CSS 3, many common design elements — including gradients, rounded corners, and drop shadows — could be created on a web page only by using image files. Now you can create popular design elements, such as rounded corners, with just a touch of code, as you see in the sections that follow.

Softening the edges of a box with rounded corners

If you created a box with rounded corners using previous versions of CSS, images, and HTML tables, we probably don't have to tell you what a pain it was, or how you had to create four images (one for each corner), and how you had to carefully adjust everything so that the corners lined up *just so.*

Whether or not you tried the old technique, you're sure to appreciate how much easier creating rounded corners is when you use the CSS 3 property `border-radius`.

When you use `border-radius`, you specify the length of the radius as the value to create the rounded corners. You can then make your rounded corners as rounded as you like, and you can apply the style to any or all of the corners of a box. In Figure 6-4 you see a diagram designed to help you see how changing the radius changes the curved corner.

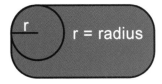

Figure 6-4: The radius of the rounded corner.

You can apply `border-radius` to any box object, such as a `<div>` tag or an `<h1>` tag. Here's the syntax for creating rounded corners in CSS 3 for WebKit browsers (note that `r` represents *radius,* the distance from the center of a circle to the curved corner):

```
-webkit-border-radius: r length;
```

If you want to specify a different radius for each corner, your style might look more like the following bit of code. In Figure 6-5, you see how

Rounded Corners

Figure 6-5: Change the radius of any or all corners.

the values change if the rounded corner is only applied to the upper right and lower left corners:

```
-webkit-border-top-left-radius: 0;
-webkit-border-top-right-radius: 25px;
-webkit-border-bottom-right-radius: 0;
-webkit-border-bottom-left-radius: 25px;
```

You can have even more control over the radius if you specify two values for the radius, like this:

```
-webkit-border-radius: 50px 100px;
```

When we designed the Jelly Rancher site, we added one font height of rounding to the box so that it remains in scale with our text, as shown in Figure 6-6. By using the em unit as our unit of measure, we can keep the design in scale on both the iPhone and iPad. This is a helpful practice when you want to add rounded corners around a text element, such as a headline:

```
-webkit-border-radius: 1em;
```

In the example shown in Figure 6-6, we've also used a drop shadow and a gradient. We show you how to create gradients in the section that follows. Later in this chapter, we describe how to add drop shadows using CSS 3.

Figure 6-6: Use the em measurement to design rounded corners that scale with the text size.

Creating gradients

Gradients are a favorite effect of graphic designers everywhere because gradients create a smooth transition of color. Adding gradients to the background of a web page or to sections within a page adds richness and depth to a design. In Figure 6-7, you can see the difference between a radial and a linear gradient.

In previous versions of CSS, if you wanted to use a gradient in the background of an element, such as a `<div>` tag, you had to use an image. If you were clever, you created a 1-pixel-wide graphic that was as tall as you wanted the gradient and then inserted it as a background so that it repeated to fill the space. If you designed a background image well, the image file size could be small but the limitations many. For example, you had to make the gradient as tall or taller than the space you wanted to fill, which limited your ability to create flexible page designs. Similarly, matching a second background image behind the gradient, if a design had this type of image, was no simple task. In short, adding gradients to page designs was possible, but also a true hassle.

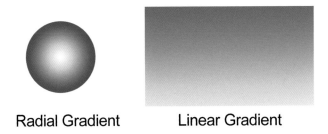

Radial Gradient   Linear Gradient

Figure 6-7: You can create both radial and linear gradients with CSS 3.

Enter CSS 3 and designers everywhere can celebrate the new gradient options to solve all those old problems at once. Gradients generated with CSS 3 download faster and automatically adjust to fill the space perfectly. CSS 3 gradients can be designed as linear, or radial, and you can apply different bands of color at different spacing along the continuum. All in all, CSS 3 gradients can be used in most situations where a designer would want to use one and are a significant improvement to CSS.

When you add a gradient to a background — whether it's the background of the entire page or an element within a page, such as a <div> tag — the gradient automatically adjusts to fill the entire space unless you specify a size. Gradients can also be used in the border of elements and to fill the center of a bullet in an unordered list.

Here's the simplest syntax for creating a linear gradient in CSS 3 for WebKit browsers:

```
-webkit-gradient( linear, <point1>, <point2>, from(<color>),
        to(<color>) );
```

Radial gradients are created this way:

```
-webkit-gradient( radial, <point>, <radius>, <point>,
        <radius>[, <stop>]* ) <color>;
```

Here are two examples of gradients used as a background image:

✔ The following code creates a linear gradient with two colors:

```
background-image: -webkit-gradient(
    linear,
    left bottom,
    left top,
    color-stop(0.32, #FFFFFF),
    color-stop(0.66, #245FAB)
);
```

✔ This code example creates a radial gradient with multiple colors:

```
background: -webkit-radial-gradient( radial, center
        center, 0, center center, 70.5, from(green),
        to(yellow));
```

Here's the code we used to create the gradient in the background areas of the body, headings, and asides in the Jelly Rancher website, as shown earlier in this chapter, in Figure 6-1.

```
body { background-image: -webkit-gradient(linear,left
        top,left bottom,color-stop(0, blue),color-
        stop(.25, #98fc45),color-stop(1, transparent)); }
```

In our example, you can see that we create a linear gradient that starts at the top and moves to the bottom. You can vary the gradient by starting it at the upper left corner and ending at the lower right corner, which would form the gradient along a diagonal path. We also show several color stops in the example, each of which represents a color along the gradient. The gradient example progresses as follows:

✔ Start with the color blue: `color-stop(0, blue)`.

✔ Change into the hexadecimal color #98fc45 at 25 percent: `color-stop(.25, #98fc45)`.

✔ Then #98fc45 becomes transparent through the rest of the gradient until the background is completely transparent: `color-stop(1, transparent)`.

Designing with transparency

In addition to the keyword `transparent`, CSS 3 has another way to produce transparent or translucent elements, as shown in the following chunk of code. CSS 3 introduces the new color selector RGBa, which we introduce you to in the section "Adding drop shadows to box elements," earlier in this chapter. RGBa is the same as the original RGB color selector, except that it takes a value that describes the alpha, or transparency, of the styled element.

```
<div style="background: rgba(0, 0, 255, 0.2);"></div>
<div style="background: rgba(0, 0, 255, 0.4);"></div>
<div style="background: rgba(0, 0, 255, 0.6);"></div>
<div style="background: rgba(0, 0, 255, 0.8);"></div>
<div style="background: rgba(0, 0, 255, 1)  ;"></div>
```

These elements are all blue, but they have a different amount of transparency, as illustrated in Figure 6-8. Note how the solid red block shows through. In the Jelly Rancher site, we used gradients with transparency to let the background show through. In Figure 6-9, you can see that we used it to create a layered effect. If we change the bottommost color of the page, all the layered colors let the change filter through a tint. The result is that the entire site can change with a single change of the background.

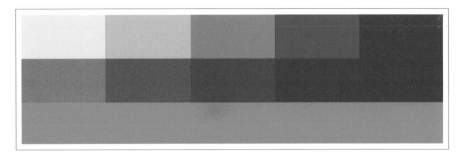

Figure 6-8: You can use CSS 3 to create effects using RGBa color transparency.

Adding drop shadows to box elements

In addition to text shadows, CSS 3 gives you the power to add shadows to box elements, such as <div> tags. In Figure 6-9, you see how we used drop shadows to set off sections, such as the aside, in this page of the Jelly Rancher site

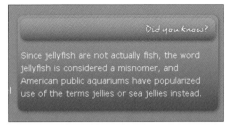

Figure 6-9: You can add drop shadows to text, <div> tags, and other elements by using CSS 3.

Much like the text shadow covered earlier in this chapter (see the earlier section "Adding text shadows"), the first value tells the Safari browser the horizontal offset, the second represents the vertical offset, and the third value describes how blurred the shadow should be. Again, the default is 0, and if you don't specify the blur, the shadow's color is completely solid.

Here's the syntax for box drop shadows for WebKit browsers:

```
-webkit-box-shadow: horizontal vertical blur color;
```

An RGBa color gives you greater control over the shadow's appearance because you can add transparency. Similarly, using the em measurement creates a shadow that adjusts better if the size of the text changes.

The following style adds a drop shadow to all <div> box elements on a page:

```
div {  -webkit-box-shadow: .15em .25em .5em rgba(27, 27, 27,
        .6);}
```

Using Media Queries to Target Devices

When you design web pages with CSS, you can create one style sheet that's used no matter which device a page is displayed on, or you can create multiple style collections designed specifically for each device. CSS 3 adds the ability to use a media query to target your style sheets based on the screen resolution, aspect ratio, and other distinguishing factors of a device. These additional options are especially useful when you're designing for the iPhone and iPad.

In Chapter 5, we introduce this concept as we cover the HTML Framework. In this section, we get more specific about the many ways you can create, target, and associate styles with your content. Refer to Figure 6-1 to see how we used media queries to alter the design of the page about oceanographer Mark Loos, based on the orientation of the iPad, to display a wider design when the iPad is in Landscape mode than when it's in Portrait mode.

The ability to target devices in CSS makes it possible to use different style sheets for different types of displays: desktop and laptop monitors, iPad-size screens, or iPhone-size screens. If you don't use media queries to target your CSS, the iPhone and iPad automatically adjust your designs for you, shrinking or enlarging the page to best fit the screen.

If you truly care about designing for optimum display on the iPhone and iPad, finding out how to use media queries to target your style sheets to each device is a helpful strategy.

Media queries build on capabilities that CSS 2 offers: the ability to target style sheets based on media type. Media types enable you to use one style sheet to control how a page appears on a computer monitor, for example, and a second one to change the appearance of the same page when it's sent to a printer. For example, in a print-specific style sheet, you might remove a busy background image or change the text color to give it more contrast on a white sheet of paper.

When you use a media query in CSS 3, you can factor in more values than you can with just media type. These additional values include screen resolution and aspect ratio and determine whether a device displays color — values that are especially useful when you're designing for the iPhone and iPad, which both have Portrait and Landscape modes.

Specifying media types and features

A *media query* is made up of a media type, such as screen or print (the two most common), and an optional expression that checks for particular features, such as the height or width.

These media types are supported in the iOS:

- ✔ `all`: Suitable for *all* devices
- ✔ `print`: Designed for print preview and for display when a page is printed
- ✔ `screen`: For content displayed on any screen

Don't be confused by the `handheld` media type, which is best for feature phones and other devices with small screens, limited bandwidth, and monochrome displays that support only bitmapped graphics. iOS devices are categorized as `screen` media types.

You can combine media types with the media features described in Table 6-1. *Note:* If the media type doesn't support the feature, it has no effect.

Table 6-1	Media Features in CSS 3
Media Feature	**Options**
Width	`min-width, max-width`
Height	`min-height, max-height`
device-width	`min-device-width, max-device-width`
device-height	`min-device-height, max-device-height`

(continued)

Table 6-1 *(continued)*

Media Feature	Options
aspect-ratio	min-aspect-ratio, max-aspect-ratio
device-aspect-ratio	min-device-aspect-ratio, max-device-aspect-ratio
Color	min-color, max-color
color-index	min-color-index, max-color-index
Monochrome	min-monochrome, max-monochrome
Resolution	min-resolution, max-resolution
Scan	Grid

Applying styles to your page designs

You can apply style sheets by linking them, importing them, or embedding them as internal styles into the head region of your page's HTML. You can even target devices using inline styles — a handy option if you want to apply a specific rule only to certain devices (see the example in the "Creating inline style rules" section that follows).

You can use a combination of these options, and you can import, or link, multiple external style sheets to the same web page. After you define the media type with the media features you want to target, you specify how the styles should be applied to the page by using one of the options explained in the following sections.

Targeting devices when linking external style sheets

The most common (and generally most recommended) option is to link external CSS style sheets to every HTML page. The code for the CSS and HTML are saved in separate files, and the <link> tag connects the two.

You can link multiple style sheets to one HTML page. For example, you can create one style sheet for styles that format text and another style sheet for layout styles. You can also create external style sheets for different purposes, such as one for print and one for screen display. One huge advantage of using external style sheets is that they make creating new pages faster and easier, and they make it possible to update styles across many pages at a time. ***Note:*** You can attach more than one external style sheet to the same web page.

Include the `<link>` tag within the `<head>` and close `</head>` tags at the top of the HTML code of a web page. The following example includes two style sheets — one designed for a computer screen and the other designed for print:

```
<link rel="stylesheet" type="text/css" media="screen"
        href="screenstyles.css">
<link rel="stylesheet" type="text/css" media="print"
        href="printer.css">
```

You can use a similar technique to target iPhone and iPad devices. Thus, in addition to (or instead of) the two previous style sheets for print and screen, you can link to style sheets that target the iPhone and iPad. This example links four separate style sheets to a web page, each designed for optimal display in the iPhone or iPad in landscape and portrait modes.

The comment tags are optional. When you comment code in HTML, you use these tags:

```
<!-- comment here --!>
```

We include comment tags only to make the code easier for humans to read.

```
<!--iPad portrait -->
<link href="css/ipadportrait.css" rel="stylesheet"
        media="only screen and (min-device-width:  768px)
        and (max-device-width: 1024px) and (orientation:
        portrait)">

<!--iPad landscape -->
<link href="css/ipadlandscape.css" rel="stylesheet"
        media="only screen and (min-device-width: 768px)
        and (max-device-width: 1024px) and (orientation:
        landscape)">

<!--iPhone portrait -->
<link href="css/iphoneportrait.css" rel="stylesheet"
        media="only screen and (min-device-width: 320px)
        and (max-device-width: 480px) and (orientation:
        portrait)">

<!--iPhone landscape -->
<link href="css/iphonelandscape.css" rel="stylesheet"
        media="only screen and (min-device-width: 320px)
        and (max-device-width: 480px) and (orientation:
        landscape)">
```

Using imported style sheets

The ability to import style sheets, using the CSS rule @import, is similar to the HTML tag used to link style sheets to a document. You can use either of these options to apply the styles in an external style sheet to a web page, but the @import option is best used to organize multiple style sheets into one file.

The web browsers available on older mobile devices, such as low-end cellphones, don't support the @import rule with multiple style sheets.

When you're working with many style sheets in a single website, you can combine them into one by importing them into a single file. To do so, you first create a new style sheet file (using the .css extension), and then you can import other external style sheets into that style sheet by using the @import rule.

With multiple styles imported into one style sheet file, you can then link to just that one style sheet from every HTML file. If you're working with multiple style sheets that need to be linked to multiple HTML files, this technique can be more efficient. Combining style sheets can help keep things better organized, and if you add or remove a style sheet later, you need to change the reference only once to update all HTML documents that rely on the styles.

Here's an example of how to use the @import rule to link multiple style sheets to one document:

```
<style type="text/css" MEDIA="screen, projection">
@import url(/stylesheets/main.css);
@import url(/stylesheets/iPhone.css);
@import url(/stylesheets/iPad.css);
</style>
```

The @import option is a CSS construct. When you link a style sheet to an HTML file, you use the HTML <link> tag (shown in the previous section). If you use this option, the @import rule must be listed first in the document.

Using internal styles

The difference between internal and external style sheets is that, using internal styles, the CSS code is stored in the <head> area at the top of the HTML page, not in a separate file that's linked or imported into the document. The styles in an internal style sheet can apply only to contents of that page.

External style sheets generally offer the greatest efficiency because they can be applied to any or all pages in a website, but if you're creating styles to be used *only* on one page, an internal style can make it easier to keep track of styles applied to specific pages. This technique can also save a little download time because the browser doesn't need to download more than one file in order to apply a style to an HTML file.

Creating inline style rules

Inline styles can apply to only one element, and they're applied to an HTML document at the place where the style is used. Of all the CSS options, inline styles are the least common on the web because they offer none of the new efficiencies of CSS, such as the ability to make global updates and reuse style rules throughout a site.

Inline styles offer one advantage that can come in handy on occasion, especially if you want to override other styles that are used throughout a site. For example, if you want to create a special style that makes your featured content red, you might create an inline style that changes the text color because you want to apply that style only where the featured text appears on the page.

Inline style rules can be assigned using the @media element. Here's an example of two styles that change the display of the <h1> tag only on the iPhone causing text in the <h1> tag to display in a larger size with more line spacing when the iPhone is in landscape mode and in a smaller size when the iPhone is in portrait mode.

We include /* Portrait */ and /* Landscape */ as comments in the following code to help make it easier to read. Note that in HTML code, the comment tags are created using <!-- -->. In CSS, you use the /* */ commenting tags like this:

```
/* Comments inside these tags won't display or affect the
        styles. */

<style type="text/css">
/* Portrait */
@media screen and (max-width: 320px)
{
                        h1 { font-size: 1.2em; line-
        height: 1.2em; }
}

/* Landscape */
@media screen and (min-width: 321px)
{
                        h1 { font-size: 1.4em; line-
        height: 1.4em; }
}
</style>
```

Positioning elements for optimal display

In the Jelly Rancher site, we used the ability to target CSS to specific devices to change the design in a number of ways. The Jellyfish Tales page is a good example. In this design, shown in Figure 6-10, we alter the positioning of the three thumbnail images based on the orientation of the device.

In Portrait mode, the images should appear at the top of the page so that they don't get lost on smaller screens. In Landscape mode, display them on the right side of the page, to better take advantage of the horizontal display area. In Figure 6-10, you can see how these two style sheets cause the same HTML page to display differently based on the orientation of the iPhone.

The following bit of code makes these different displays possible.

```
@media screen and (min-device-width: 320px) and (max-device-
        width: 480px) and (orientation: portrait) {
/* iPhone portrait targeted */
aside {
                        display: table-row;
                        float: left;
                        width: 90%;
}
@media screen and (min-device-width: 320px) and (max-device-
        width: 480px) and (orientation: landscape) {
/* iPhone landscape targeted */
aside {
                        float: right;
                        display: table-column;
                        width: 100px;
}
```

Figure 6-10: The position of the three thumbnail images in this page changes based on the orientation of the iPhone.

Note that the three thumbnail images are contained in the HTML5 semantic element aside and that we used the display attribute table-row. The table-row and table-column attributes orient the block element so that it acts like part of a table. The float rule moves the element to the top of the screen, somewhat counterintuitively, by setting the float to the left, which aligns the row to the top of the page. In Landscape mode, floating the display to the right causes the row of images to change position to the right side of the screen.

To create a framework in HTML that can be altered to create two designs such as these by using CSS, you can use an attribute of the CSS rule display, which makes the three images line up in the page as though they're in a table.

Hiding Elements You Don't Want to Display

With more space on the iPad than on the iPhone, you may find it best to hide certain elements in your designs when you display a page on the smaller screen.

Hiding the contents of a <div> tag or another element is relatively easy with CSS 3, but it doesn't prevent the content from being downloaded to the device: Your content fits the space better, but you're still making your site visitors download everything. This solution works well for hiding a few small items, but if you want to take this strategy a step further, in Chapter 7 you can find instructions for using PHP to remove the content from the page on the server before it's downloaded.

The simpler, less technical solution is to use CSS to hide the element: You do that by simply creating a style with the rule display: none.

We used this trick to shorten the subhead of the Jelly Rancher site. On the iPad, we used the longer version: *Specializing in Jellyfish Aquariums.* On the smaller iPhone screen, we shortened it to simply *Jellyfish Aquariums.* In Figure 6-11, you can see the difference and how this change makes the design fit better on each device.

To make it easy to isolate and hide the subhead on the iPhone, we wrapped a <span> tag around the part we don't want to display. We used the <span> tag because it's an inline element, not a block element, and doesn't force a line break in the middle of the subhead when it displays in its full version on the iPad.

Figure 6-11: You can use CSS to hide elements, a great trick for doing tasks such as shortening the subhead of this jellyfish site on the iPhone.

Here's the HTML code we used:

```
<header> <a href="index.html">
    <h1>Jelly Rancher</h1>
    <h2><span>Specializing in<br>
        </span> Jellyfish Aquariums</h2>
</a> </header>
```

And, here's the style that hides only the contents of the <span> tag:

```
body div h2 span, details {
      display: none;
}
```

Conquering the Cascade

One of the most frustrating aspects of working with CSS is that sometimes styles conflict. You can define a new style and apply it to an element, for example, and then find that the style has no effect or that it changes the element in ways you didn't expect. You can overcome this challenge in web design by understanding how the *cascade* effect works in Cascading Style Sheets. The cascade refers to the way that one style's rules spill down the page like water, building one on top of another.

In the early days of HTML, web designers placed style information close to the elements they styled using attributes such as `font color`. If you wanted to turn your text yellow, for example, you simply surrounded it with a font tag with the color attribute set to yellow, like this: `<font color="yellow">`. With the style inline with the text, the cause and effect were easy to see, and conflicts were rare.

Separating content from style with CSS has made tracking the hierarchy of styles harder to do because each element on a page may be affected by multiple style rules. The way the cascade works in CSS makes this process even more complex. Following the cascade of rules through several rule definitions is hard, especially when all the new CSS 3 options are added.

Figure 6-12 provides a quick reference for resolving style conflicts. It ignores many of the more complex cascading rules, but simply understanding these basics will help you resolve most conflicts by helping you quickly determine which of your style rules has priority. A style rule with higher priority wins over an identical style rule with a lower priority.

	Lowest priority		Highest Priority
Rule Origin	Browser Default Rule	Reader's Style Sheet	Author's Style Sheet
Reference Method	Linked Stylesheet	Embedded Stylesheet	Inline Stylesheet
Selection Method	DOM Element Selector Depth	CLASS	ID

Figure 6-12: The general cascading order rules in CSS.

The hierarchy of styles works as described in this list:

✓ **Origin of the rule:** To determine which CSS value is applied, the first distinction is the origin of the rule. As authors, our CSS has a higher priority than the default values of the browser or any user stylesheet. (Remember that your users, as well as your users' browsers, may have styles that affect your pages). *Note:* The keyword `!important` can override all the others and be challenged only by another instance of `!important`.

✔ **Specificity of the selector:** Rules are next evaluated by the specificity of the selector, defined by giving each contradicting rule a 3-digit number specifying the value according to these rules:

- The number of ID attributes in the selector

- The number of attributes and pseudo-classes in the selector

- The number of element names in the selector

Whichever rule has a higher value wins. Here's an example:

```
body#home div:first-of-type { color:red; }
body#home { color:green; }
body div:first-of-type { color:blue; }
```

The first rule receives a score of 1-1-2 (1 ID, 1 pseudo-class, 2 elements). The second rule gets a score of 1-0-1 (1 ID, 0 pseudo-classes, 1 element). The final rule receives a score of 0-1-2 (0 IDs, 1 pseudo-class, 2 elements).

Based on these rules, you might deduce that the text of the first <div> tag in the body of the page identified as home will be red (and you'd be right). Any other text on the page would be green. And, the text of the first <div> tag on a page that doesn't have a body ID of home would be blue.

✔ **Order on the page:** Finally, the rules are sorted by the order in which they're presented in the page. Consider it the tiebreaker. After all other rules are considered, the first rule to appear in a style sheet wins.

Many browsers now have built-in testing tools, or add-ons you can install, that show you which CSS rules apply to each element in a web page. These tools (we recommend the popular Firebug add-on), make testing CSS much easier. You can download Firebug (for free) from www.getfirebug.com.

For a detailed list of CSS selectors and other resources, visit www.Digital Family.com/mobile.

7

Animating and Interactivity

In This Chapter

▶ Creating interactive features with CSS 3

▶ Using transitions, transformations, and animations

▶ Using scripts to enhance the user experience

Much like the first layer in a birthday cake, you build the foundation for a well-structured site using HTML5 in Chapter 5. You style the site with CSS 3 in Chapter 6, adding the second layer to the cake. Now you're ready to add the icing and decorations — the best part — adding more advanced CSS 3 features, and extending the capabilities with JavaScript.

The relatively simple programming language JavaScript runs within a web browser. Using JavaScript, you can enhance CSS 3 features, add interactive messages, and even create complex games and web applications.

In this chapter, we explore how to create transformations, transitions, and animations with CSS 3. Using these exciting features, you can change the positioning of elements on a web page, and even create animated effects previously only possible using a program such as Adobe Flash or by using programming that's far more complex than CSS 3.

We can't cover all the cool, new CSS 3 features in this book, and we certainly can't tell you everything there is to know about JavaScript, but you can find an introduction to the most exciting new features, and tips and resources for adding scripts more easily, by using frameworks, such as jQuery.

Creating Interactive Features with CSS 3

If your goal is to convey information creatively, one of the best options for adding animation and other interactive features to a website today is to use CSS 3.

We love Adobe Flash, and we understand why it has been a popular tool for creating animations for the web. Now, however, we recommend that you avoid it, especially if you're designing for the iPhone or iPad, which don't even support Flash. In Figure 7-1, you see the Groonies iPad game, which looks like many of the game apps you might download from the iTunes App Store. In the Groonies game, you can roll the dice, move players along the virtual board, and flip cards, such as the one shown open in Figure 7-1. All this was created at `http://themanyfacesof.com/the-goonies`, using CSS 3 (and a little JavaScript). (See the later sidebar "Replacing Flash with HTML5, CSS, and JavaScript," for more on why we no longer recommend using Flash.)

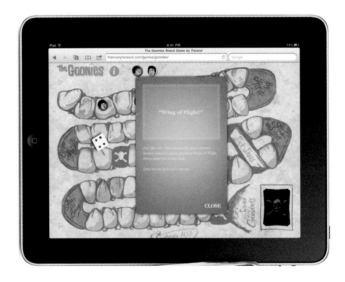

Figure 7-1: The rich, interactive game *The Groonies* was created using CSS 3 and JavaScript.

In this book, we focus on creating the best designs for the iPhone, iPad, and iPod touch. The features we create in this chapter with CSS 3 are designed for WebKit browsers. These features aren't designed to work in other browsers, including Firefox and Internet Explorer. See the sidebar "Making CSS 3 work in more web browsers," later in this chapter, to find out more about creating CSS 3 features that work in other browsers.

Replacing Flash with HTML5, CSS, and JavaScript

Adobe Flash has been a popular video and animation tool for more than a decade. Flash makes it easy to animate images and text. The interface in the Flash development tool is set up for designers to quickly create and animate ideas that convey a deeper meaning than static images. Flash is also a great way to add fun little effects, create games, and play video. Many new forms of entertainment have been created and distributed through Flash.

Unfortunately, none of the iOS devices (including the iPhone, iPad, and iPod touch) support Flash. If your site uses Flash and someone visits your pages with one of these devices, the visitor sees nothing. Nada. Zip.

Our best advice is to re-create your Flash animations and other interactive features by using HTML5, CSS 3, and JavaScript, as we describe

in this chapter. Here are a few additional advantages of replacing Flash content on your sites:

✔ **You experience better search engine optimization.** Although Google has gotten better over the years, it still doesn't search through Flash files for information as effectively as it does through content formatted with HTML and CSS.

✔ **Download speeds are faster.** Animations designed in Flash are generally larger than the equivalent animations designed in HTML5, CSS, and JavaScript.

✔ **Interactive features don't require plug-ins.** Animations and other interactive features created with CSS and JavaScript run in the Apple iOS without requiring a plug-in, which means that they run faster and smoother.

The animations and other features in this chapter work in most popular browsers that use WebKit, including Safari (on Mac, Windows, and iOS for iPad/iPhone/iPad) and Chrome (on Mac, Windows, and devices that run Google's Android operating system). We introduce the topic of how to design for WebKit browsers in Chapter 4. To read more about the latest features supported by WebKit browsers, visit `http://webkit.org`.

Making text spin around, change color, or resize itself just because you can do so is never a good idea. As with the infamous `<blink>` tag (which was overused in the early days of the web), we recommend that you use animations sparingly in your web pages.

Introducing the CSS 3 Transitions, Transformations, and Animations

CSS 3 adds many new designs features, but animation is the most exciting. Using CSS 3, you can make characters walk across the screen, boxes flip over, and images fade away. To demonstrate how animation works with CSS 3, we start by creating a simple ball that bounces in a black box, as you see in the two figures shown side by side in Figure 7-2.

We didn't use any images to create the bouncing ball animation (refer to Figure 7-2). The ball itself — and the action that makes it appear to bounce from the top of the screen to the bottom and back again — was all achieved with just a few lines of CSS 3 code.

Before we get into the details of how we created the bouncing ball in our example, you should understand that CSS 3 introduces three main ways to create interactive effects and animations: transformations, transitions, and animations.

You can create many great design effects with these features, but the most interactive sites you see on the web today, such as *The Groonies* (refer to Figure 7-1), require JavaScript in addition to HTML and CSS.

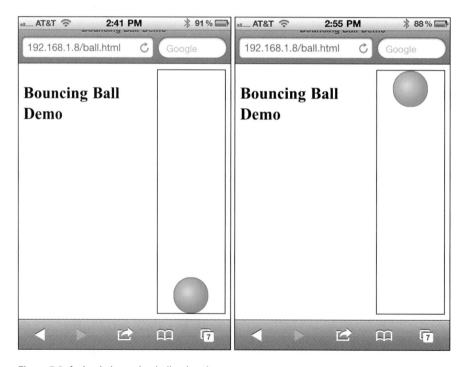

Figure 7-2: A simple bouncing ball animation.

Creating transformations with CSS 3

The CSS 3 transform properties enable you to *transform* an element to create effects in 2D and 3D. You can specify a list of transformations to change multiple aspects of an element. If multiple options are specified, each is applied in the order listed. Transformation options include the ones described in this list:

- scale — Changes the height and width of an element. You can specify two numbers to define a different scale for width and height. However, this element is generally used with only one number to scale an element proportionately. The first of the following examples transforms the element to scale to half its size, and the second transforms the element to half as wide and twice as tall:

  ```
  -webkit-transform: scale(0.5);
  -webkit-transform: scale(2, 0.5);
  ```

- translate — Use this property to *translate,* or move, an element from position A to position B equally along the x and y axes. You can also use translateX and translateY to move elements along only one axis at a time. For example, this code causes an element to move 150 pixels from the left and 150 from the top:

  ```
  -webkit-transform: translate(150px, -150px);
  ```

- skew — Use this property to *skew,* or change the position of an element based on a specified value that skews an element on the x and y axes. For example, this could skew an element 20 degrees on the x axis:

  ```
  -webkit-transform: skew(15deg,  4deg);
  ```

- rotate — Use this property to *rotate,* or change the position of an element based on a specified value that controls the angle of rotation. For example, the first example in this code rotates an element 5 degrees to the right, the second one rotates the element –5 (negative 5) degrees. As you can see in Figure 7-3, it causes the photos on the right and left in this design to angle away from the center image:

  ```
  -webkit-transform: rotate (5deg);
  -webkit-transform: rotate (-5deg);
  ```

In the SCUBA site example shown in Figure 7-3, notice that the two outside images rotate to the left and right, respectively, using the CSS Rotate feature — but only on Safari, Firefox, and Chrome. Visit this page with IE and the boxes are all in a straight line, but they don't look bad that way, so there's no harm done.

Figure 7-3: The right and left images in this design are angled away from the center image by using the rotate property.

Also notice how we've tucked an image into the bottom of the design so that when you turn the iPad/iPhone from landscape to portrait view, content fills the entire screen.

Next, suppose that you want to add a cool CSS 3 technique that happens when you tap one of the three photos. Can you tell we like ocean dwellers and SCUBA diving?

Creating transitions with CSS 3

The CSS 3 transition properties make it possible to change the state of an element. Using transitions, you can do things like change an element's color or make text fade away when someone taps it.

Using transitions, you can cause an element to enlarge when it's touched (or clicked), as shown in Figure 7-4, but CSS 3 has its limitations. After the larger image is enlarged, as shown in Figure 7-4, you have no way to close it unless you combine CSS 3 with JavaScript. Although a discussion about writing JavaScript is beyond the scope of this book, you can find, at the end of this chapter, some useful frameworks to make it easier to add JavaScript features.

Making CSS 3 work in more web browsers

Both HTML5 and CSS 3 are still under development as we write this book. The CSS specification has not yet been approved by the W3C, but many browser developers have already implemented parts of the working drafts of CSS 3, including the features covered in this chapter. When browser companies implement parts of a working draft they call it *experimental* CSS and they usually include the browser name in the rule. That's why there are multiple versions of the same style rules featured in this chapter.

The features covered in this chapter are designed to work in the Safari web browser. Most of them also work in Chrome, because both browsers are based on the WebKit. For Safari and Chrome, you need to add the `-webkit` prefix to each style. For Firefox, you add the `-moz` to the beginning of each style rule. For the Opera web browser, ad `-o`. If you want to follow the W3C recommendations (even though they aren't yet approved), don't add anything to the beginning. Here's an example of a transition and a transformation for each of these four options:

The code for the Safari web browser looks like this:

```
-webkit-transition-timing-function: linear;
-webkit-transform: scale(1.5, 2);
```

For Firefox, here's what you would use to create the same transformation:

```
-moz-transition-timing-function: linear;
-moz-transform: scale(1.5, 2);
```

In the Opera web browser:

```
-o-transition-timing-function: linear;
-o-transform: scale(1.5, 2);
```

The current W3C recommendation is simply this:

```
transition-timing-function: linear;
transform: scale(1.5, 2);
```

Warning: Not all browsers implement experimental rules in exactly the same way. For instance, here are two rules for a linear gradient:

```
-webkit-gradient(linear, left top, left bottom, from(#444444),
    to(#999999));
background-image: linear-gradient(top, #444444, #999999);
```

See `http://developer.apple.com/devcenter/safari/` for the full list of CSS 3 rules for iOS devices and see `http://www.w3.org/TR/#tr_CSS` for the complete list of recommended CSS 3 rules from the W3C.

See our introduction to CSS 3 and a more detailed explanation of the browser differences in Chapter 6.

The `webkit-transition` includes several properties (*Note:* If multiple options are specified, each one is applied in the order listed.):

Figure 7-4: You can use CSS 3 to enlarge an element, such as the image on the left.

- `-webkit-transition-property` — Specifies which property, such as text color, the transition affects.

- `-webkit-transition-duration` — Specifies the number of seconds until a transition occurs. The duration can be expressed in seconds as 1s, 2s, and so on, or in milliseconds, such as 500ms, 250ms, and so on.

- `-webkit-transition-delay` — Specifies any delay before a transition begins. For example, you add a three-second delay by including `webkit-transition-delay: 3s`.

- `-webkit-transition-timing-function` — Specifies the speed curve of a transition and enables you to change the speed over the duration of a transition by specifying as many as five predefined values:

    - `ease` — The default value; creates a transition effect that starts slowly, grows fast, and then slows again

    - `linear` — Creates a transition with the same speed from beginning to end

    - `ease-in` — Creates a transition that starts slowly

    - `ease-out` — Creates a transition that ends slowly

    - `ease-in-out` — Creates a transition that starts and ends slowly

    - `cubic-bezier` — An advanced option that makes it possible to define your own values; a function, based on the Bezier curve that has been used in computer graphics since the 1960s, uses a sequence of numeric values from 0 to 1.

Creating animations with keyframes

Much like Adobe Flash, more complex CSS 3 animations rely on keyframes. *Keyframes* are the points within an animation where something changes. Whenever you want to change an animated object, you need to create a new keyframe.

For instance, if we want to animate a ball bouncing, as shown in Figure 7-5, we would have a keyframe at the top of the bounce and another one at the bottom of the bounce. In this example, the ball is 50 pixels in diameter, and the container for the ball is 350 pixels tall. The first keyframe, therefore, places the ball at the bottom of the container, and the last one places it at the top of the container.

Here's the code that makes this work:

```
@-webkit-keyframes bounce {
        from { margin: 300px auto 0;}
        to { margin: 0 auto 0;}
}
```

An `@-webkit-keyframes` block contains rules that define each keyframe. A keyframe defines the style for that moment within the animation. You can have a start and an end as in the example shown here, or you can define any number of points in-between. Some web browsers apply this style more smoothly than others, but Safari on the iPhone and iPad make this work quite well.

In this simple bouncing ball example, we define an animation called `bounce` to have two keyframes: one for the start of the animation (the `from` block) and one for the end (the `to` block). These two keyframes move the ball *from* the bottom *to* the top.

When you define an animation with a set of keyframes, you can use the following `webkit-animation` properties:

- ✔ `animation-name` — defines the animation used. We point it to *bounce,* the keyframe set we defined earlier. If the name isn't found (it's missing or misspelled), the browser assumes the default value of `none` and no animation is produced:

  ```
  -webkit-animation-name: bounce;
  ```

- ✔ `animation-duration` — defines the length of the animation. The time value format is a number followed by a time unit identifier. The time unit identifiers are `ms` for milliseconds and `s` for seconds (`1000 ms`, `1s`). The animation of the bouncing ball lasts one second. Figure 7-5 illustrates how the browser automatically creates the *tweened* frames — the frames between the top and bottom. You define the start and end and the browser fills in what's "in-be*tween*."

```
webkit-animation-
        duration: 1s;
```

✔ animation-iteration-count — defines the number of times an animation cycle is played. The default value is 1, and that value makes the animation play from start to end once. A value of infinite causes the animation to repeat forever. As you might guess based on that information, in the following example, the animation plays ten times:

```
-webkit-animation-
        iteration-
        count: 10;
```

✔ animation-direction — defines whether the animation should play in reverse every other cycle. If alternate is specified, every other animation cycle is played in the reverse direction. When an animation is played in reverse, the timing func-

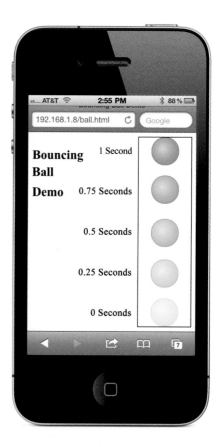

Figure 7-5: The bouncing ball with portions of seconds demarked.

tions are also reversed. This is why we need to define the ball as only bouncing up. The alternate animation is played in reverse, bringing the ball back down to the bottom of the box (not unlike gravity).

```
-webkit-animation-direction: alternate;
```

Put it all together and the style rule that makes the bouncing ball animation work looks like this:

```
#animationDemo #ball {
-webkit-animation-name: bounce;
-webkit-animation-duration: 1s;
-webkit-animation-iteration-count: 10;
-webkit-animation-direction: alternate;
}
```

When you enter one or more properties, be sure to follow this order:

1. transition-property
2. transition-duration
3. transition-timing-function
4. transition-delay

We used the following statement for the bouncing ball demonstration:

```
#animationDemo #ball { bounce 1s 10 alternate;}
```

For a complete list of CSS properties you can animate by using transitions, visit www.w3.org/TR/css3-transitions.

Improving the User Experience with Scripts

HTML5 and CSS 3 make it possible to add many types of animations and design elements to your pages, but for the most advanced interactive features on the web, you need to use a little JavaScript or PHP or another type of programming.

In this chapter, we try to give you all the information you need in order to complete the tasks we cover, but if you're completely new to programming or want to find out more than we can cover in this book, we recommend the JavaScript introduction at www.w3schools.com/js/js_intro.asp. You don't have to know much JavaScript to use what we cover in this book, but the introduction provided at the W3Schools.com link may help you apply and extend our examples for your own projects.

Saving space on the tiny iPhone screen

On the relatively small iPhone screen, every pixel is precious. That's why one of our favorite scripts — and one we use in nearly every page we design for the iPhone — is designed to scroll the page down automatically, hiding the address bar and giving us more space for our designs.

The JavaScript that follows slides the window 60 pixel rows up. That gives us back the nearly 15 percent of screen real estate that the URL field takes up at the top of the browser window. When you add this JavaScript to a web page, it will automatically hide the address bar in Safari on the iPhone and the iPod touch without affecting any other browsers. This script is ignored by Firefox, Internet Explorer, and even Safari when it's used on an iPad or a computer.

Here's the code that makes this work. Simply add this code to bottom of any web page, just before the `</body>` tag:

```
<script>
window.onload = function() {
setTimeout(function(){window.scrollTo(0, 1);}, 100);
}</script>
```

This script was published by Apple in 2007 when the first iPhone was released. The script tags tell HTML that JavaScript is coming: In HTML5, JavaScript is the default scripting language, so you don't need to have anything in that tag but script. Here's how it works:

1. The first line, `window.onload = function()  {`, tells the browser to run this script when the page first loads.

2. The second line, `setTimeout`, waits one-tenth of a second (defined by the numeral 100 at the end of that line).

3. After one-tenth of a second, `function(){window.scrollTo(0, 1);}` executes and scrolls the window to the x coordinate 0 and the y coordinate y, better known as the top of the page.

Using frameworks to add advanced features with scripts

If HTML5 and CSS 3 aren't enough of a challenge for you and you want to add more advanced features with scripts, you can save time and trouble by starting with one of the popular JavaScript frameworks, such as jQuery.

The following sections describe some of our favorite frameworks and tell you how they can help you add rich features to your iPhone and iPad web designs.

jQuery Mobile

```
http://jquerymobile.com
```

This is the mobile version of the very powerful jQuery JavaScript library. The mobile version works across most smart phones and offers user interface components that go far beyond a JavaScript library. User interface elements include enhanced styled forms (as shown in Figure 7-6), a large variety of list types, searching, page transitions, themes, and more.

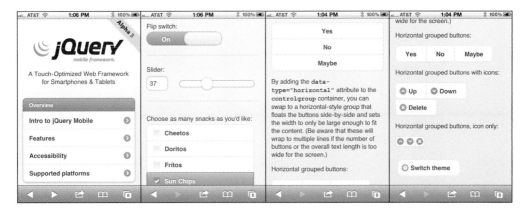

Figure 7-6: jQuery Mobile makes it easier to create web app elements, such as forms.

With the support of device manufacturers and the .mobi group, this project has the most sponsors of any of the mobile frameworks. This typically indicates the lasting power and quality of an open source project, making jQuery Mobile a good bet now and into the future. Similar to most mobile frameworks, as we write this book, this framework is still in development.

Sencha

```
www.sencha.com
```

Because Sencha is a commercial framework development company, after its tools are out of the beta development phase, they will probably cost money to use. These tools will likely serve you better if you need a commercial-level product that comes with customer support.

Reviewing the features and demos on the Sencha website, this company clearly is developing tools that can be used to create rich-media advertising, as well as complicated interactive features, such as the *Solitaire* game, as shown in Figure 7-7.

IUI

```
http://code.google.com/p/iui/wiki/Introduction
```

IUI is the oldest iPhone web app framework. Created by developer Joe Hewitt, its user interface looks much like an iPhone application. One great feature is that this tool builds in Offline Storage (you find more information about Offline Storage at the end of this chapter). Offline Storage is what enables a web app to work even when a user is not connected to the Internet.

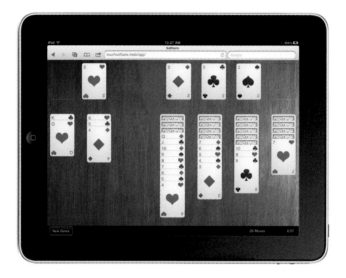

Figure 7-7: Sencha creates commercial development tools and frameworks that can be used to create games.

iWebKit

```
http://snippetspace.com
```

One of the first web app frameworks, iWebKit (see Figure 7-8), focuses on achieving a user interface that is as close to the iOS native user interface possible using HTML5, CSS 3, and JavaScript. This framework includes helpful widgets, forms, and the ability to display RSS feeds, making it a great place to start if you want to focus only on creating web apps for iOS devices.

Impact

```
http://impactjs.com
```

The Impact Engine is a framework that focuses on enabling developers to create games that feel like installed native apps. It's a great choice if you are interested in making games using HTML5, CSS 3, and JavaScript. The current price is $99.

Cubiq.org
http://cubiq.org

Sometimes you just want to keep things simple. Cubiq, created by Matteo Spinelli, a web designer and developer in Florence, Italy, is a great way to add interactive features without delving into all the complexities of the framework tools listed earlier in this section. Spinelli has created several projects that make it super easy to add specific features to your site, including:

- ✔ **iScroll:** Created because of the difficulty of using position:absolute within the virtual iPhone window, iScroll makes it easier to have a fixed bar at the top or bottom of the page.

- ✔ **Hardware Accelerated Accordion:** An *accordion* shows the header or first line of a section. When the user touches it, it expands so the user can see the rest of the text in that section. Accordions are useful when screen real estate is scarce, like it is on the iPhone or iPod touch. Accordion effects on mobile are difficult and usually choppy and jerky, not smooth. Matteo uses the CSS 3 translate property to

Figure 7-8: The iWebKit tool is designed to help you create designs that look a lot like native apps on the iPhone.

better control opening and closing. It's a smart technique because the iPhone uses hardware acceleration with this property to ensure that the transform is smooth.

- ✔ **Slide-in menu:** If you would like to tuck your navigation up past the top of your page and enable users to pull it down when they need it (as shown in Figure 7-9), this one's for you. After you add the slide-in menu to your site, it can be styled and set up to hold your navigation using any icons or design you prefer.

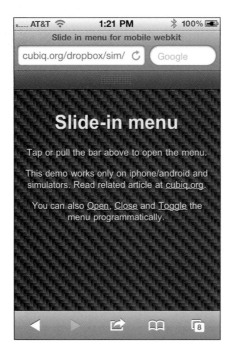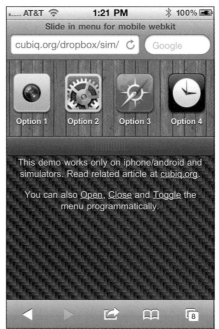

Figure 7-9: Visit Cubiq.org to find everything you need in order to create your own slide-in menu, like this one.

✔ **Add to Home Screen:** Spinelli's Add to Homescreen script adds a float-ing balloon at the bottom of your web page on an iPhone and at the top of the page on an iPad, to call attention to the Add to Home Screen feature on the iPhone. The message, shown in Figure 7-10, dynamically stays in place at the bottom of the page when the user scrolls. Matteo included the ability to customize the length of time before the message appears and disappears. It's also available in 13 languages.

Users can choose the Add Bookmark, Add to Home Screen, Mail Link to This Page, or Print option. When a user selects Add to Home Screen, a small icon is saved on the iPhone's Home screen. You can find instruc-tions for creating a custom icon for your site in Chapter 5.

Figure 7-10: Adding a callout message to the iPhone and iPad makes it more likely that visitors will bookmark your site with a Web Clip icon on the Home screen.

Part III
Adding Multimedia and Web 2.0 Features

The 5th Wave   By Rich Tennant

"You ever notice how much more streaming media there is than there used to be?"

*L*est you think that making your website iPhone and iPad friendly means stripping out all the cool stuff, this part is dedicated to helping you add multimedia and other advanced features to your sites. In Chapter 8, you discover how to optimize images. In Chapter 9, you find tips for working with audio and video, and in Chapter 10, you discover the best shopping carts and transaction services for mobile e-commerce.

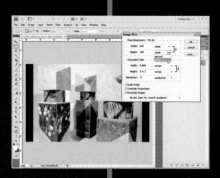

8

Optimizing Images

In This Chapter

▶ Designing images for the iPhone and iPad

▶ Optimizing images in Photoshop

▶ Inserting images into mobile page designs

▶ Creating mobile-friendly galleries

*P*hotographers, graphic designers, and other artists are discovering the iPad is the ultimate portable portfolio. Even if you aren't an artist, having eye-catching images on your website is one of the best ways to attract image-conscious iPhone and iPad enthusiasts.

The "wow factor" of the iPhone and iPad is that they're well suited to displaying beautiful, lifelike images. For the web designer, displaying images correctly on the iPad and iPhone is an undertaking that requires at least a working knowledge of graphics standards, careful planning, and an appreciation of the limitations of mobile displays.

The introduction of a new web platform dictates having to adjust images to have the best quality while occupying the smallest possible file size. These qualifications ensure that images download as efficiently as possible. In this chapter, we guide you through the process of changing the size and resolution of images so that they download quickly but still offer the quality graphics that iPhone/iPad users expect.

We also describe image formats and the best resolution to use, and we tell you how to optimize photos and other graphics when you're designing for the iPhone, iPad, or iPod touch.

Desiging Images for the iPhone and iPad

Cramming a high-resolution image that can be blown up to poster size onto an iPhone screen makes no sense. Not only would the photos not display correctly, but downloading a file that large would also take an inordinately long time and your visitors would likely abandon your site. Rather than force visitors to download large images on the home page of your mobile site, which iPhone users would access, you should ensure that your designs honor the constraints under which your users labor.

Sizing up image-sizing strategies

If you plan to put images on your mobile website, the design process goes more smoothly if you have a strategy to handle the different screen sizes, resolutions, and aspect ratios.

- ✔ **Sizing one image to fit both screens:** A practical and timesaving way to create images optimized to work on both the iPhone and iPad is to create one web-optimized image that looks good on both devices. It isn't a perfect science, but both the iPad and iPhone 4 have such great-looking displays that you can scale an image up or down quite a bit and it can still look quite good. Although this method isn't foolproof, creating one optimized image is the simplest option, and it will work for many sites.

- ✔ **Using multiple image sizes:** If you have the resources and the time, the best solution is to tailor a site to each device's capabilities and screen size. Using this approach, you create multiple versions of each image in different sizes, from 320 pixels wide to 1024 pixels (if you want the image to stretch across the iPad's screen in Landscape mode). Then you deliver the size that best fits the device with some kind of device detection script (such as those covered in Chapter 12).

Because setting up a device detection script is complex and creating multiple versions of every image adds a lot of work to the average web site, many people use services, such as Galleria (covered later in this chapter), to quickly create slide shows with many images that are optimized for each device as they're delivered.

- ✔ **Displaying image portfolios or galleries:** If you design portfolio sites — where the whole point is to empower clients to show off their work anywhere, at any time (and to look their absolute best) — you may have a legitimate need to include higher-resolution images with larger file sizes. The best way to handle this situation is to create one page with low-resolution thumbnails or short text descriptions and then link to the larger images. You can see an example of this approach at the www.inplainsightart.com site. As shown in Figure 8-1, the thumbnails at the top of the page link to larger versions, shown in the page below it. This way, your most important pages load quickly with small versions of your images that all your visitors can view, and those who are interested in high-resolution images can choose to download the larger versions one at a time.

You have many ways to create galleries that work on both the iPhone and iPad. The main concept to remember is not to use Flash. See the section "Creating Mobile-Friendly Galleries and Slide Shows," later in this chapter, for details.

Images by artists Amy Baur and Brian Boldon, www.inplainsightart.com

Figure 8-1: The small thumbnails shown in the top page from this website link to the larger images, as shown in the bottom page.

As you design galleries like these, remember that one of the differences between a web browser on a desktop computer and a touchscreen is that you can't roll over an image with a mouse on an iPhone or iPad. Instead, rollover events, such as those commonly used with an image gallery like the one shown in Figure 8-1, are converted into links on an iPad or iPhone.

Choosing an image format

If you work with photos or other images that have millions of colors, the JPEG format is the best choice for the mobile web, just as it is for the desktop web. Using JPEGs, you can shrink the file size by applying compression. The more compression that's applied, the smaller the image, but if you compress the image too much, the image can look like it was sandblasted and left out in the sun.

For images with limited colors, such as line art, logos, and cartoons, the best format for mobile devices and web pages is PNG. Some designers will tell you that the GIF format is the safer choice — and maybe it was, for older mobile devices and low-end feature phones. But the iPhone and iPad support the PNG format, and it does a better job of maintaining image quality and small file sizes than GIF does. With both GIF and PNG files, you optimize (or reduce) the file size by decreasing the number of colors.

Don't be confused by the two types of PNG files. Photoshop supports both PNG-8, which supports 256 colors, and PNG-24, which supports a far superior 8 bits per channel and is especially well suited to working with transparency. You can still use the JPEG format for photographs and other types of images, but because transparency isn't possible in JPEGs, the PNG-24 format offers an advantage. Just remember that all that color depth also creates larger file sizes that take longer to download.

You can find out more about how to optimize the PNG and JPEG formats in the section "Optimizing Images in Adobe Photoshop," later in this chapter.

Keeping file sizes small

After you know how to optimize PNG and JPEG images and can appreciate the goal of making them as small as possible, you may ask, "How small is small enough?"

Mobile web designers obsess over ways to make their page sizes smaller, without crossing the invisible line between "It loads too slowly" and "It looks junky." Although it's a mostly subjective judgment call, the following points are good to remember:

- **The larger the graphics files, the longer people have to wait for them to download before they can see them.** You may have the most beautiful picture of Mount Fuji on the front page of your website, but if it takes forever to download, most people aren't patient enough to wait to see it.

- **When you build pages with multiple graphics, consider the cumulative download time of all graphics on the page.** Even if each image has a small file size, their total size can add up. Smaller is definitely better on the mobile web.

- **Most web pros consider 75K (kilobytes) to 150K to be a good maximum *cumulative* size for all elements on a desktop web page.** If your page is viewed over a 3G network, and you've limited the total size to no more than 150K most visitors will find the download time acceptable. If you expect many visitors on slower connection speeds, however, consider reducing the size.

  In the past, because the 2.5G data connections on the original iPhone delivered data from about 80 to 100 Kbps, a 150K desktop page in this size range took as much as 20 seconds to transmit. Most mobile users get frustrated and abandon a page that takes that long. The 3G and 4G networks promise data speeds that range from 500 Kbps to 1 Gbps, although the actual speed delivered to customers is the subject of rather fierce debate. Even so, if you keep your home page relatively small, your users are much more likely to stick around — and to click through to your interior pages, where you can experiment with bigger, more eye-catching designs and multimedia features.

If your page is meant to be used by people at home or in offices where they have access to Wi-Fi connections, you can assume that the page will load on an iPad or iPhone almost as fast as it would on a desktop or laptop. Always remember to experiment when you're pushing the limits in this way. Refer to Chapter 11 for more on testing web page load times before you publish your pages.

Optimizing Images in Adobe Photoshop

If you're familiar with using a graphics-editing program, such as Adobe Photoshop or Fireworks, to create graphics for the web, consider this section a good review as you start designing for the iPhone and iPad. If you aren't familiar with the Save for Web dialog in Adobe Photoshop, this section shows you step-by-step how to optimize images for faster download times.

We use Adobe Photoshop CS5 in the examples in this section, but because the features we use are nearly identical in Photoshop Elements, you can use these same instructions to complete these tasks in either program. Similarly, the Save for Web dialog hasn't changed in the last few versions of Photoshop, so if you're using version CS2, CS3, or CS4, these instructions should work just fine. (See the nearby sidebar "Comparing Adobe web graphics programs" to learn more about the differences.)

Making images download faster

The most important thing to keep in mind when creating images for the web is that you want to *optimize* your images to make your file sizes as small as possible so that they download as quickly as possible.

How you optimize an image depends on how the image was created and whether you want to save it as a JPEG, PNG, or GIF. You find instructions for optimizing images with Photoshop in the sections that follow, but the bottom line is this: No matter what program, format, or optimization technique you choose, your biggest challenge is finding the best balance between small file size and good image quality. Essentially, the more you optimize, the faster the image will download, but the compression and color reduction techniques used to optimize images can make them look terrible if you go too far.

As a general rule, do any editing, such as adjusting contrast, retouching, or combining images before you reduce their size or optimize them because you want to work with the highest resolution possible when you're editing. Also, resize an image before you optimize it. You find instructions for resizing an image in the next exercise and instructions for optimizing in the sections that follow.

Comparing Adobe web graphics programs

Most professional designers strongly prefer Adobe Photoshop, although we have to say that we've been impressed with Photoshop Elements, which is a "light" version but offers many of the same features for a fraction of the cost. The following is a list of some of the most popular image-editing programs on the market today. All these image programs are available for both Mac and Windows:

✓ **Adobe Photoshop** (www.adobe.com/photoshop): By far the most popular image-editing program on the market, Photoshop is a widely used standard among graphics professionals. With Photoshop, you can create original artwork, edit and enhance photographs, and so much more. Photoshop has a wealth of powerful painting and selection tools, special effects, and filters that enable you to create images far beyond what you can capture on film or create with many other illustration programs. In previous versions, Photoshop came bundled with a program called *Image Ready,* a companion program designed for web graphics. In CS3, those web features were included in Photoshop; and in CS4, they've been enhanced. Switching between Photoshop and Dreamweaver is easier than ever.

✓ **Adobe Photoshop Elements** (www.adobe.com/elements): If you don't need all the bells and whistles offered in the full-blown version of Photoshop, Photoshop Elements

is a remarkably powerful program — for about a sixth of the price. If you're a professional designer, you're best served by Photoshop. But if you're a hobbyist or small business owner and want to create good-looking images without the high cost and learning curve of a professional graphics program, Elements is a great deal and well-suited to creating web graphics.

✓ **Adobe Fireworks** (www.adobe.com/fireworks): Fireworks was one of the first image-editing programs designed to create and edit web graphics. Originally created by Macromedia, the program is now part of the Adobe Web Suite and is fully integrated with Dreamweaver. Fireworks gives you everything you need to create, edit, and output web graphics, all in one well-designed product. Although Fireworks lacks many of the advanced image-editing capabilities of Photoshop, Fireworks shines when creating web graphics and is especially popular among web designers who rave about the ability to create a design in Fireworks that can easily be sliced and converted into a web page in Dreamweaver.

If you have an Internet connection and want to do basic image editing for free, visit http://www.gimp.org or www.photoshop.com/express. Both sites make it possible to edit and optimize images online without purchasing a software program.

Resizing graphics and photos

Resizing is important for two reasons: The images must be small enough to display well on a computer monitor, and you want them to download quickly to a user's computer. The smaller the image is, the faster it will download.

Although you can change the display size of an image in a web page by altering the height and width settings in Dreamweaver or any other web editor, you get much better results if you change instead the physical size of the image in an editor program such as Photoshop.

When you alter an image's height and width in the HTML code, you simply instruct a web browser to display the image in a different size. Unfortunately, browsers don't do a good job of resizing images because browsers don't change the image itself, but just force it to fit in the assigned space when the browser loads the page. If you set the image to display larger than its actual size, the image is likely to look fuzzy or distorted because the image doesn't contain enough pixels for all the details to look good in a larger size. If you set the code to display the image smaller than it is, the image is likely to look squished, and you're requiring that your users download an image that's larger than necessary.

Reducing an image's size for use on the web requires two steps. First, you reduce the resolution of an image, which changes the number of pixels in the image. When you're working with images for the web, you want to reduce the resolution to 72 pixels per inch (ppi). We stick with 72 ppi in our examples, but if you're wondering why we chose that number or you're starting to think that a higher resolution may be warranted for the iPhone and iPad, see the sidebar that's appropriately named "Why only 72 ppi?" Second, you reduce the image's physical size by reducing its dimensions. You want to size your images to fit well in a browser window and to work within the design of your site.

Follow these steps to lower the resolution and reduce the size of an image in Photoshop (in Photoshop Elements or Fireworks, you follow a similar process although the specific steps may vary):

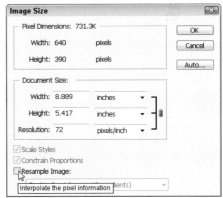

Figure 8-2: To best prepare images for the web, change the resolution to 72 ppi so that they download faster.

1. **With an image open in Photoshop, choose Image⇨Resize.**

   The Image Size dialog box opens, as shown in Figures 8-2 and 8-3.

   If you don't want your original image to lose quality (or you just want to play it safe), make a copy of your image and resize the *copy* for your website.

2. **To change the resolution of your image, first deselect the Resample Image check box at the bottom of the Image Size dialog box, as shown in Figure 8-2.**

   For best results, always deselect the Resample Image check box when you change the resolution.

3. **Click and drag to highlight the number in the Resolution field and replace it by typing in the number** 72.

4. **Click to select the Resample Image check box.**

   With the Resample Image check box deselected, you can't change the Pixel dimensions so it must be checked when you change the image size.

5. **Enter a height and width for the image in the Height and Width fields.**

   As shown in Figure 8-3, we're reducing the width of this image to 500 pixels. If the Constrain Proportions check box at the bottom of the dialog box is selected (as it is in this example), any changes you make to the height automatically affect the width (and vice versa) to ensure that the image proportions remain constant. We prefer to work this way, but if you want to change the image and not maintain the proportions, you can deselect this box.

6. **Click OK to resize the image.**

   If you want to return the image to its previous size, choose Edit⇨Undo. Beware that when you save the image, the changes become permanent.

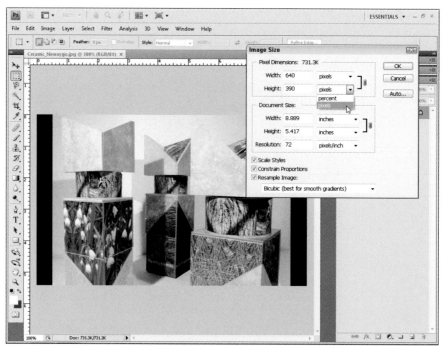

Images by artists Amy Baur and Brian Boldon, www.inplainsightart.com

Figure 8-3: When you resize an image in Photoshop in the Pixel Dimensions area, you can specify the new size in pixels or as a percentage of the original size.

Why only 72 ppi?

When you save images for the web, most web designers recommend that you save them at a resolution of 72 pixels per inch (better known as ppi). Most computer monitors display no more than 72 ppi, so any resolution higher than that is wasted on the web because you'd be making your visitors download more pixels than they can see. However, if you want to print an image, you want all the pixels you can get, usually at least 200 ppi or higher, which is why most images you see on the web look terrible if you try to print them in a large size. When you're designing for the high-resolution iPhone and iPad screens, you may want to increase the number of pixels per inch to better match the resolution of these devices. Remember that the iPad displays 132 ppi; the iPhone 4 displays 326 ppi. We certainly don't recommend that you create images with a 326 ppi resolution for use on the Internet, but if you want your images to look their best and you don't mind sacrificing a little download time, you may be happier with the results if you set the resolution of your images to 92 ppi, or even 132 ppi. (You can see how to change the image resolution and optimize images in Photoshop in the earlier section "Resizing graphics and photos."

Choosing the best image format

One of the most common questions about images for the web concerns when to use GIF or PNG and when to use JPEG. Table 8 -1 provides the simple answer.

Table 8-1	Image Formats for the Web
Format	**Best Use**
GIF (Extension is `.gif`)	For line art (such as one- or two-color logos), simple drawings, animations, and basically any image that has no gradients or blends. The GIF format is no longer recommended because the PNG format offers superior image quality.
PNG 8 and 24 (Extension is `.png`)	PNG generally produces better-looking images with smaller file sizes than GIF and supports transparency. Choose PNG 8 for the smallest file sizes, choose PNG 24 to optimize multicolored images when you want to use transparency.
JPEG (Extension may be `.jpg` or `.jpeg`)	JPEG is the best format for colorful, complex images (such as photographs); images containing gradients or color blends; and any other images with millions of colors.

Optimizing JPEG images for the web

The JPEG format is the best choice for optimizing continuous-tone images, such as photographs and images with many colors or gradients. When you optimize a JPEG, you can make the file size smaller by applying compression. The more compression, the smaller the image, but if you compress the image too much, the image can look terrible. The trick is finding the right balance, as you discover in this section.

If you have a digital photograph or another image that you want to prepare for the web, follow these steps to optimize and save it in Photoshop (in Photoshop Elements or Fireworks, the process is similar although the specific steps may vary):

1. **With the image open in Photoshop, choose File⇨Save for Web & Devices (or File⇨Save for Web).**

   The Save for Web & Devices dialog box appears.

2. **In the top-left corner of the dialog box, choose either 2-Up or 4-Up to display multiple versions of the same image for easy side-by-side comparison.**

   In the example shown in Figure 8-4, we chose 2-Up, which makes it possible to view the original image on the top and a preview of the same image as it will appear with the specified settings on the bottom (if you're working with a vertical image, the previews appear side by side). The 4-Up option, as the name implies, displays four different versions for comparison.

3. **On the right side of the window, just under Preset, click the small arrow to open the Optimized File Format drop-down list and choose JPEG. (This drop-down list is open in Figure 8-4.)**

4. **Set the compression quality.**

   Use the preset options Low, Medium, High, Very High, or Maximum from the drop-down list. Or use the slider just under the Quality field to make more precise adjustments. Lowering the quality reduces the file size and makes the image download more quickly, but if you lower this number too much, the image will look blurry and blotchy.

   Photoshop uses a compression scale of 0 to 100 for JPEGs in this dialog window, with 0 the lowest possible quality (the highest amount of compression and the smallest file size) and 100 the highest possible quality (the least amount of compression and the biggest file size). Low, Medium, and High represent compression values of 10, 30, and 60, respectively.

5. **Specify other settings as desired (the compression quality and file format are the most important settings).**

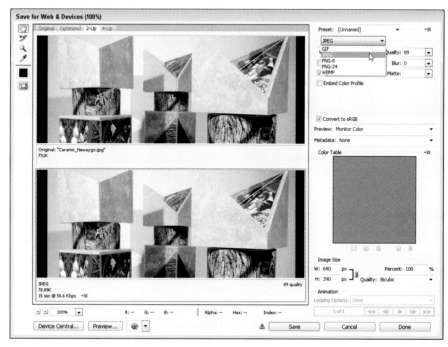

Figure 8-4: The JPEG format is best for photographs and other images with millions of colors.

6. **Click Save.**

   The Save Optimized As dialog box opens.

7. **Enter a name for the image and save it into the images folder in your website folder.**

   Photoshop saves the optimized image as a copy of the original and leaves the original open in the main Photoshop work area.

Repeat these steps for each image you want to optimize as a JPEG.

At the bottom of the image preview in the Save for Web & Devices dialog box, Photoshop includes an estimate of the time required for the image to download at the specified connection speed. In the example shown in Figure 8-4, the estimate is 15 seconds at 56.6 Kbps. As you adjust the compression settings, the size of the image changes and the download estimate will automatically adjust. You can change the connection speed used to make this calculation by clicking the small arrow just to the right of the connection speed and using the drop-down list to select another option, such as 256 Kbps for Cable Modem speed. Use this estimate as a guide to help you decide how much you should optimize each image.

Optimizing images in PNG formats

If you're working with a graphic, such as a logo, cartoon character, or drawing that can be displayed in 256 colors or fewer, your best bet is to use the PNG 8 format and reduce the total number of colors used in the image as much as possible to reduce the file size. If you want to make a color in the image transparent, and you're working with a photograph or another type of image with millions of colors, your best options is PNG 24.

To help make up for the degradation in image quality that can happen when colors are removed, PNG uses a dithering trick. *Dithering* involves alternating pixels in a checkerboard-like pattern to create subtle color variations, even with a limited color palette. The effect can smooth the image's edges and make it appear to have more colors than it actually does.

To convert an image to the PNG 8 or 24 format in Photoshop, follow these steps (in Photoshop Elements or Fireworks, the process is similar although the specific steps may vary):

1. **With the image open in Photoshop, choose File⇨Save for Web & Devices (or File⇨Save for Web).**

   The Save for Web & Devices dialog box appears. In this example, shown in Figure 8-5, you see the black-and-white logo for the website at www. inplainsightart.com. An image with limited colors is best saved in the PNG 8 format.

2. **In the top-left corner of the dialog box, choose 2-Up or 4-Up to display multiple versions of the same image for easy side-by-side comparison.**

   In the example shown in Figure 8-5, we chose 2-Up, which makes it possible to view the original image of the logo (in the top), as well as a preview of the optimized version different same image displayed in the window in the bottom.

3. **Select a preview image to begin changing its settings.**

   Click any image to make it active in the dialog window.

4. **On the right side of the dialog window, just under Preset, click the small arrow to open the Optimized File Format drop-down list and choose either PNG 8 or 24.**

   If you choose PNG 8, you'll get the smallest file sizes. Choose PNG 24 only if you want to optimize an image with many colors and still be able to set one color to transparent.

5. **In the Colors box, select the number of colors, as shown in Figure 8-5.**

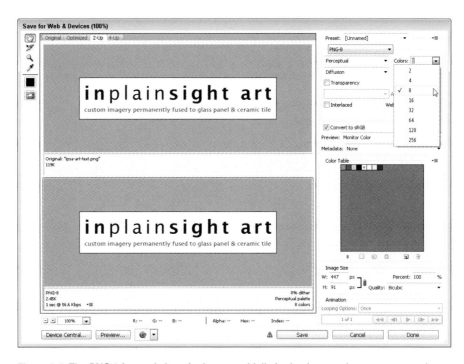

Figure 8-5: The PNG 8 format is best for images with limited colors, such as cartoons and line art.

The fewer colors you use, the smaller the file size and the faster the image will download. But be careful; if you reduce the colors too much, you lose details. The ideal number of colors depends on your image; if you go too far, your image will look terrible.

6. **If you want to maintain a transparent area in your image, select the Transparency check box.**

   Any area of the image that was transparent when you created the image in the editor appears transparent in the preview window. If you don't have a transparent area in your image, this setting has no effect.

   Transparency is a good trick for making text or an image appear to float on a web page. That's because a transparent background doesn't appear on the web page. You can select transparency as a background option in the New File dialog box when you create a new image in Photoshop or Photoshop Elements.

7. **If you choose Transparency, also specify a Matte color.**

   You want the matte color to match the background of your web page so that the dithering along the transparent edge will blend in with the background. If you don't specify a matte color, the transparency is set for a white background, which can cause a *halo* effect when the image is displayed on a colored background.

8. **Specify other settings as desired.**

   The remainder of the settings in this dialog box can be left at their defaults in Photoshop.

9. **Click Save.**

   The Save Optimized As dialog box opens.

10. **Enter a name for the image and save it into the images folder (or any other folder) in your local site folder.**

Repeat these steps for each image you want to optimize as a GIF or PNG for your site.

Trial and error is a great technique in the Save for Web & Devices dialog box. In the preview window displaying the optimized version of the logo in Figure 8-5, we used fewer and fewer colors, which reduced the file size with increasingly degrading effect.

Inserting Images into Page Designs

You can insert images into pages designed for the iPhone and iPad just as you would insert them into any other web page, using the HTML image tag. The following well-crafted image tag inserts a photograph that's 320 pixels x 110 pixels and is saved as a JPEG:

```
<img src="Glass-Artwork.jpg" alt="Glass Trestle" height="110"
        width="320" />
```

This list describes a few best practices for inserting images into any web page. These practices are especially important when you're designing for the mobile web:

✔ **Use Alt text.** Be sure to include alternative (Alt) text to describe the image. If your users are in areas where connections to the mobile web or Wi-Fi hotspots are iffy, they may have chosen to turn off the display of images. In this case, the Alt text may be all your visitors see. If you insert a logo or another image with text, be sure to include the text in the Alt field of the image tag (as shown in the earlier image tag code example).

- **Limit the size of images.** Use a relatively narrow width (320 pixels or smaller) to fit within the limited space of the basic iPhone screen. Another workaround is to specify the width using a percentage so that the image automatically adjusts to the screen size. For example, if you set the `size` attribute in the image tag to `width=95%`, the image fills 95 percent of the width of the display area. If you use a percentage for width, you don't need to specify a height.

- **Specify a height and width for each image.** Using the height and width attributes, as shown in the earlier image tag code example, helps the mobile Safari browser load pages more efficiently because the browser doesn't have to download each image before it can determine its height and width.

- **Use supported image formats.** Apple devices can display JPEG, PNG, and GIF images — even animated GIF images.

Creating Mobile-Friendly Galleries and Slide Shows

Many desktop websites feature galleries and slide shows. Unfortunately, many of these implementations rely on Flash to work, and as you're no doubt abundantly aware by now, Apple's mobile devices don't support Flash. Here's what you need to know about slide shows versus galleries:

- **Slide shows:** After you click the Play button in a slide show, the images cycle through in the order that the creator of the slide show set up, and as rapidly (or as slowly) as that person thought optimal. Good slide shows have buttons you can press to advance to the next picture, pause, or skip backward. Bad slide show buttons replicate the experience of being trapped in a boring relative's basement, forced to watch hours of bland vacation photos.

  Slide shows often incorporate a sound to accompany photos, such as a voiceover describing them or a musical track. Adding sound to photos requires them to be synced to appear and disappear to the cues in the soundtrack, which can be tricky.

- **Galleries:** Galleries tend to be more passive. Usually, they have an array of thumbnail shots of the photos, and when users click or tap one, the selected photo expands to fill most of the page. Some galleries use Flash or Microsoft Silverlight technology (neither of which work on Apple's devices) to animate transitions from one image to the next; the developer community is working hard to update these galleries so that they work on all platforms.

The best option for the iPhone/iPad is to create slide shows or galleries with CSS or JavaScript, or both. If you know enough about JavaScript, you can create your own scripts, but many programs and extensions can help. The following sections introduce a few options for galleries and slide shows.

Make sure the photos you add to any gallery you create are optimized for the mobile web, as we explain earlier, in the section "Optimizing Images in Adobe Photoshop."

Finding a gallery plug-in or service

You can use an expanding array of programs, plug-ins, and online photo services to spruce up your mobile site with slide shows and galleries. We can't possibly list them all, but we've chosen some favorites, described in the following list, and provided step-by-step instructions on how to add a gallery to a website by using the Galleria service:

- **Jaipho:** (www.jaipho.com) This free JavaScript gallery is designed for the iPhone/iPad and lets you easily create a gallery that mimics the look and feel of the original iPhone Photos application. You can quickly scroll through photos, both vertically and horizontally. Just tap a photo to enlarge it and then tap again to return to browsing. Jaipho includes a companion application — *Pipho* (www.jaipho.com/content/pipho-php-image-gallery-iphone) — which is installed on the server to help users easily add images to galleries by uploading them.

- **MobileMe:** (www.me.com) The Apple online service MobileMe includes mobile-optimized photo galleries that let you easily share photos on an iPhone or iPad. You pay an annual fee for the service, which includes video and photo hosting. As you can see in Figure 8-6, the actor Yuval David uses his MobileMe account to make it easy to create a portfolio of photos.

- **Dreamweaver extensions:** (www.adobe.com/exchange) *Extensions* are little plug-ins or widgets that you can add to Dreamweaver to empower it to do things that weren't possible in the original program. Free and paid extensions are available on the Dreamweaver Exchange page, and they're continually being added to or updated. Search for "slideshow" or "gallery" and read the descriptions of the features of the plug-in to find the one that best suits your needs and creative vision.

- **Shadowbox:** (www.shadowbox-js.com) Shadowbox is one of the most popular and flexible plug-ins for users of WordPress blogs, but you can use Shadowbox on any web page. Using Shadowbox, you can easily scroll through a gallery of images. Chapter 13 covers image sizing options in WordPress in more detail.

- **Visual LightBox:** (http://visuallightbox.com) This free plug-in is similar to Shadowbox, but it works on sites that don't have WordPress installed. You can also set Visual LightBox to import images from Flickr or other photo-sharing sites.

Figure 8-6: The actor Yuval David made his photos easy to view on an iPhone by creating a MobileMe Gallery.

Using Galleria to build a photo portfolio

You can create many different kinds of galleries and slide shows using JavaScript, but why start from scratch when many online resources can give you a head start? One of our favorites is Galleria (galleria.aino.se), shown in Figure 8-7. It's one of the handiest JavaScript galleries we've found that works well on sites designed for the desktop or the iPhone and iPad. Galleria is also free (always a good price), and can be customized using fairly simple CSS to match the general look and feel of your site. (Galleria charges for its custom themes, but the fully functional script and theme we used in the example in this section was free.)

Figure 8-7: Visit Galleria to get everything you need to create a gallery that displays well on the iPhone/iPad and on desktop computers.

Galleria is in a constant state of refinement, so new features may have been added by the time you read this chapter. The already existing features are quite nice, though.

After you set up your page for Galleria, you can choose to have your photos display in a limited space or choose full-screen mode. You can also add captions, make thumbnails display in a swirling carousel, and even set up a Flickr feed so that your site pulls in photos that have attributes (such as *roadside diners*) that you specify. Galleria is free to download and try out, but if you enjoy using it, you should make a contribution (we did).

When you create a gallery with Galleria (or any jQuery-based plug-in), you should include a link to the jQuery library on your web page. Alternatively, you can download and install jQuery on your server, but it's simpler to link to one of the popular hosts, such as Google, that make it easy to access the jQuery library on the Internet.

jQuery is the most popular open source JavaScript library. It's designed to make it easier to add interactive features to web pages without spending years learning about functions, classes, prototypes, closures, and other heavy-duty computer programming features. Many online services and plug-ins use jQuery. Using a service like Galleria, you can copy-and-paste code snippets that perform common tasks for you. If you want to find out more about what you can do with jQuery, consult *jQuery For Dummies,* by Lynn Beighley.

In the next section, we walk you through the process of creating a gallery on Galleria, but first, you find instructions for linking to the jQuery library on Google's content delivery network (CDN). The easiest method to make jQuery work on your web pages is to use the `<script>` tag to link to the jQuery library, like this:

1. **Open the web page where you want to add the gallery in your favorite web design program.**

   You can use any web editing tool that makes it possible to view and edit the HTML code, and you can add a gallery to an existing page or create a new page.

2. **Scroll to the bottom of your web page and click to insert the cursor just above the** `</body>` **tag.**

   You can add the jQuery link in the `<head>` tags at the top of the page, but the best practice is to add jQuery code at the end of a web page, to help reduce the amount of time visitors spend staring at a blank screen, waiting for the page to load.

3. **Insert the following code to link to the jQuery libraries on the Google server:**

   ```
   <script type="text/javascript" src=https://ajax.googleapis.com/ajax/libs/
           jquery/1.5.2/jquery.min.js></script>
   ```

4. **Save your web page.**

   For more documentation on including jQuery libraries, visit `http://code.google.com/apis/libraries/devguide.html`.

See the helpful *Beginner's Guide* in the Documentation section on the Galleria site at `http://galleria.aino.se`.

After you have the jQuery library installed, follow these instructions to download everything you need from the Galleria website:

1. **Launch a browser and navigate to** `http://galleria.aino.se` **(refer to Figure 8-7).**

   This page contains information on the latest builds of Galleria and examples of galleries created with their themes and script. Feel free to click around a little and look at the pretty pictures. That's the point, after all!

2. **Click the Download button at the top of the page.**

   The browser takes you to the GitHub download page for Galleria. GitHub encourages you to sign up to receive updates or share your own code. You don't have to do this in order to download Galleria.

3. Click the Download Galleria link.

Depending on the web browser you're using and the settings you have specified, the `.zip` file either downloads automatically or the Download Source dialog window opens and you can save the file to your hard drive.

4. Use a decompression program to unpack the contents of the file.

Most modern computers automatically unzip the contents when you double-click a `.zip` file. This step creates a folder named `galleria-1.2.3` (or whatever they named the most recent version). This folder contains a folder named `galleria`, and it contains subfolders with the script and theme files.

5. Copy the `galleria` folder into the main root folder of your website.

6. Create a new page or open the web page where you want to add the gallery in your favorite web design program.

We used Dreamweaver in the example shown in Figure 8-8, but you can use any program that lets you edit the code behind your pages.

If you like working in Dreamweaver, here's a tip: This gallery requires a script to work, and that isn't possible in the standard Design view window in Dreamweaver. When you add the code featured in this example to your page, your images appear in a row of large images, one above the other, until you preview the page in a web browser or click the Live View button, as shown in Figure 8-8. *Note:* Live View is available only in Dreamweaver CS5 and later versions.

7. Insert the code to load the Galleria theme into your web page:

```
<script>
Galleria.loadTheme('galleria/themes/classic/galleria.classic.min.js');
        $("#gallery").galleria({
            width: 500,
            height: 450
        });
</script>
```

The height and width in the preceding Galleria theme code can be edited to fit your images and designs.

The preceding bit of code works with the free version of Galleria, which comes with the Classic theme we use in the example in Figure 8-9. Though the theme is included in the current version of the site, you should check the most recent documentation on the Galleria website and review the contents of the `galleria` folder you download, to ensure that the names of the theme haven't changed and that the theme referenced in the preceding code is still current.

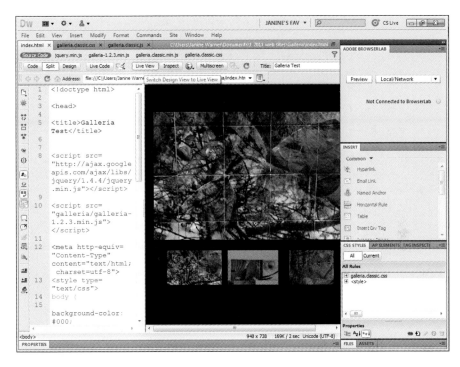

Figure 8-8: You can edit a Galleria page in Adobe Dreamweaver or in any other text or web page editor.

8. **Make sure the images you want to feature in your Galleria gallery are stored within the main root folder of your website.**

9. **Add the following code between the** `<body>` **tags on your website updating the image names and path for the images to match your site.**

   The HTML code looks like this:

   ```
   <div id="gallery">
           <img src="/images/photo1.jpg" alt="stained glass
           collage" title="Stained Glass Collage">
           <img src="/images/photo2.jpg" alt="museum instal-
           lation" title="Museum Installation">
   </div>
   ```

The Galleria script automatically resizes your images to fit the thumbnail and larger display sizes in the gallery. You can change the display size of the images by altering the code in the HTML file and the corresponding CSS. For best results, resize and optimize your images in Photoshop to match the display size you set for the gallery. Make sure you edit the height and width in the code in Step 7 to match the size of your optimized images. For best results make sure all your images are the same height and width.

10. **Add the link in the script to the** <head> **section of your web page using this code:**

```
<script src="galleria/galleria-1.2.3.min.js"></script>
```

When you download the script from Galleria, you may get a more recent version of the JavaScript file, so check the name. When we wrote this book, the instructions on the Galleria site specified galleria-1.2.2.min.js but the file in the .zip folder we downloaded was a newer version so we had to change the reference to galleria-1.2.3.min.js.

You can customize the way Galleria displays your photos in a variety of ways by editing the script and the CSS. For a complete rundown on the available options, visit the Galleria website at galleria.aino.se. To find out more on how to edit the CSS to change the look of a gallery created in Galleria, read Chapter 6.

Figure 8-9: The gallery script and themes available at Galleria are designed to work on the iPhone, iPad, and iPod.

The completed gallery page we used to create the design shown in Figure 8-9, looks like this:

```
<!doctype html>

<head>

<title>Galleria Test</title>


<script src="http://ajax.googleapis.com/ajax/libs/
        jquery/1.4.4/jquery.min.js"></script>

<script src="galleria/galleria-1.2.3.min.js"></script>

<meta http-equiv="Content-Type" content="text/html;
        charset=utf-8">
<style type="text/css">
body {
 background-color: #000;
}
</style>
</head>

<body>

 <div id="gallery">
          <img src="photo1.jpg">
          <img src="photo2.jpg">
          <img src="photo3.jpg">
          <img src="photo4.jpg">
 </div>

              <script>
 Galleria.loadTheme('galleria/themes/classic/galleria.
        classic.min.js');
          $("#gallery").galleria({
              width: 500,
              height: 450
          });
        </script>
</body>
</html>
```

When you're working with jQuery, you're working with a lot more than just the HTML shown in this code example. Remember that a complex CSS file is attached to this page that works with the JavaScript to create this gallery. You can add your own CSS to change the colors and positioning of the images within the gallery design and you can edit the CSS and other files in the galleria folder to make additional changes to the design or functionality of the gallery.

9

Adding Video and Audio

In This Chapter

▶ Designing pages with videos
▶ Comparing video hosting options on the web
▶ Hosting video on YouTube and Vimeo
▶ Optimizing audio for the mobile web

*E*ver since the days of the first portable TVs, video addicts have dreamed of ways to watch their favorite shows from any location. Their early attempts ranged from a suitcase-size monstrosity that weighed as much as a small child to the Sony Watchman and its rabbit-ear antenna that forced viewers to wrap tinfoil around it and stand in an awkward, yoga-like position to get good reception.

Although the advent of "TV anywhere" always seems a few years down the road, the rollout of high-speed, wireless data networks may finally bring the dream to reality.

As you might have figured out, video brings together all the most difficult challenges of designing for the mobile web: the plethora of screen resolutions on which to display the picture and the large file sizes burdening digital distribution networks. Video professionals trying to make the transition to the mobile space mutter darkly about dense technical specifications and toss around terms such as *back-haul* and *data packet prioritization* (words so obscure that we don't even bother you with their definitions). And, not to be repetitive, but one of the biggest challenges is that Flash, the most popular video format on the web, isn't supported on the majority of mobile devices.

If we were to shovel out the reams of data specifications and intricate formatting requirements you need in order to become an expert in creating your custom mobile video site, with high-quality audio podcasts, we would need all the remaining space in the later chapters of this book (and probably a couple others). Unless you're part of a dedicated, well-funded team working for a large media company, we would probably only confuse the issues, and, worse, you would be no closer to delivering audio or video clips to visitors of your websites. Therefore, we suggest (at least to start) that you leave the deeply technical issues to people who have already spent years working on this problem and concentrate instead on how best to take advantage of the fruits of their labors.

In this chapter, we introduce you to a few video hosting options; namely, content delivery networks (CDNs) and video sharing sites, such as YouTube and Vimeo. We then explain how to embed video into your mobile website from Vimeo and YouTube. We wrap up the chapter by describing some innovative ways to include audio on your site, and explaining the various audio settings and services that can make your designs sing (sorry — couldn't resist the pun).

If you want to use HTML5 to embed video on your pages when you host the video on your own web server, refer to Chapter 5 for information about the `<video>`, `<audio>`, and `<source>` tags.

Designing a Site for Video Views

Make no mistake: Video is a key ingredient in the success of Apple's devices. Industry experts dubbed Netflix as the killer app of the iPad because it offers the capability to stream movies in surprisingly good quality. Anyone who has whiled away the hours on a coast-to-coast flight has found that even the small iPhone screen is a great way to catch up on missed episodes of a favorite show.

When designing your website for mobile, remember that most savvy Internet users have watched at least some videos by now. That means they're likely to know how online videos are supposed to work— and how videos are *not* supposed to work. Your site design can assure visitors your videos are worth the download time and will deliver what you promise. If you combine well-designed pages with optimized video and add an exciting, well-written description, your users are much more likely to feel comfortable committing to watching your video.

When you add video to your mobile site, abide by these simple guidelines:

✓ **Deliver video in the right format.** If your visitors can't view your videos, you're in trouble from the start. The best way to make sure you deliver the best video to every device that may visit your site is to use a video hosting service, such as Vimeo or YouTube (covered later in this chapter). If you host the video on your own server, the MP4 format is a good choice for the iPhone, iPad, and iPod. (You find descriptions of the most popular video formats later in this chapter.)

✏ **Describe the value of videos.** Tell your users the benefit of choosing to invest their time and attention in your video. On mobile, even a video of modest length can take a long time to load and play. As you see in Figure 9-1, actor Yuval David hosts his video on the Vimeo hosting service (covered later in this chapter). When Yuval embeds the video with special code provided by Vimeo, the buttons in the top right of the preview frame automatically appear, adding the options to like, share, and embed videos.

✏ **Make the video easy to play.** Tapping on the right place on a small iPhone screen is hard enough — don't make your users fumble around for the link or control to make your video play. Make sure that Start, Stop, and Pause buttons are easy to activate with a fingertip on the iPhone and iPad.

✏ **Show the length and file size of the video.** Be upfront about your content; tell your users how long the video runs and the size of the file. When you use a hosting service, such as Vimeo shown in Figure 9-1, the length of the video is automatically calculated and made visible in the player. (As you can see, the actor's video clip is only 52 seconds long.) Better to have users bookmark your page to view later on a desktop than to frustrate them with a sluggish download — or to infuriate them by eating up their monthly data transmission allowance.

Figure 9-1: Actor Yuval David includes video clips of his work, hosted on Vimeo.

Mobile users are likely to be in a hurry, travel in and out of cell coverage, or pay by the byte for the data you send them (or all three). You should give them the confidence that you won't abuse their trust by sending them massively long and irrelevant material. (If you've ever had the experience of being *Rickrolled* — clicking a seemingly relevant link that reroutes you to Rick Astley's "Never Gonna Give You Up" video — you can appreciate why many web surfers have become cautious about clicking video links.)

Removing Flash from Your Site

If you've spent much time surfing the web on an iPhone or iPad, we probably don't need to tell you that Flash doesn't work on either device.

Sorry, but you cannot use Flash if you want your site to display well on an iPhone or iPad (although at the time we wrote this book, some apps were in the works that may allow you to view certain Flash files in the future).

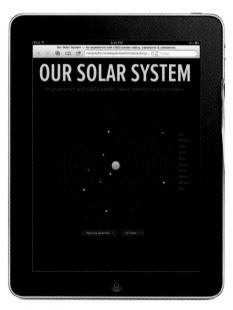

Fortunately, you can use CSS 3 to create beautiful, Flash-like effects, such as the planets orbiting the sun in the CSS 3 demo site shown in Figure 9-2. The app-like site is called Our Solar System, and it was created by the talented Alex Giron at http://neography.com.

As an iPhone/iPad designer, you should be on the lookout for the following four common ways that Flash is used on websites. Consider replacing the following uses of Flash with CSS 3 and JavaScript (covered in Chapter 7) to ensure that your site is optimized for these devices:

Figure 9-2: This Solar System demo shows how CSS 3 can be used to create the motion of the planets as they orbit the sun.

- ✔ **Whole-site Flash implementations:** The web is home to hundreds of thousands of Flash sites, many of which are being redesigned as we write these words. It's sad, really. Flash is ideal for web design. It scales well, and you can integrate animation and video in Flash files. Many restaurant owners, artists, and others were seduced into designing graphically complex, interactive features. Unfortunately, if you've designed your restaurant site in Flash, customers who want to find your address on the way to eat there or who want to review your menu on their iPhones or iPads are out of luck.

✔ **Advertising banners:** Advertisers fell all over themselves to design and insert Flash banners, for many of the same reasons that game developers and other site owners built all-Flash sites: It's a quick way to add animated characters who dance and sing to grab your attention on the screen. Flash also lets you add interactivity so that those characters can react to the movement of a cursor. The ad world is now in the midst of a major shift; in place of Flash, most designers are creating what they call *rich media* (usually, a combination of JavaScript, CSS 3, and HTML5).

✔ **Limited interactive features:** Some site designers have used Flash to add flair to a site, such as a little game or an animated image in their web pages. Although similar effects can be achieved using CSS 3 and JavaScript (covered in Chapter 7), many of us wish Adobe and Apple could work things out so that Flash would work on the iPhone and iPad.

Comparing Video Sharing Sites and Content Delivery Networks (CDNs)

When you look for a third party to deliver video content to your mobile users, remember that a dedicated *content delivery network (CDN)* provides high-end video hosting services for a price. A video sharing site such as YouTube, Vimeo, or Viddler offers free or low-cost services.

The essential trade-off between a CDN and a video sharing site is cost versus control. If you run a television network or produce video for a business or an organization that's willing to pay for high-end hosting, a CDN is definitely the way to go. The more you pay, the more control you have over your users' experience, access to analytics about how users interact with your video, and the freedom to run your own advertising and control access to your videos. A CDN also enables you to use more bandwidth than a free or low-cost service.

If budget is a driving factor or you want to tap into the built-in audience of a site like YouTube, keep in mind that the less you pay (and free is about as less as you can get), the more you're at the mercy of someone else's decisions. Free video hosting often comes with advertisements, links to related video, and other things you can't control on your pages.

You have to weigh the trade-offs of a CDN (covered in the next section) versus a video sharing site like YouTube (covered in the section that follows). To help you get started, the following sections provide a comparison of benefits and drawbacks.

Checking out CDNs

You can find many CDNs on the market, with specialized services to deliver mobile video. Increasingly, these services focus on delivering video to the iPhone and iPad, as well as the Android and other mobile devices. Dedicated CDNs offer many benefits. You can

- ✔ **Use the provided tools to customize the player:** Add your own logo or messages, for example.

- ✔ **Insert your own advertising:** CDNs sometimes maintain their own ad servers so that you can customize ads to appear depending on the user, time of day, location of user, or other criteria.

- ✔ **Track users by way of the CDN's performance metrics system:** Track who watches your videos and when and where they watch, and find all sorts of other data that's useful to you (and your advertisers).

- ✔ **Benefit from better customer support:** After all, if you're paying for the CDN's services, someone had better be there to fix annoying audio warbling or other common issues when you register a complaint.

- ✔ **Upload in batches:** Save time by publishing a collection of videos all at one time (rather than publish videos one at a time, as is often the case with free or low-cost services).

- ✔ **Take advantage of better copyright protection:** Many CDNs offer encryption and other Digital Rights Management (DRM) technologies designed to protect your content. Also, many of the free sharing sites require you to relinquish legal ownership of your videos in exchange for the free hosting.

- ✔ **Restrict the geographic region or domain:** Allow only certain users to access your videos.

- ✔ **Post videos of any length:** The length of your videos must be within reason, of course. Most free hosting services restrict video length to 10 minutes or less.

- ✔ **Rest assured that your video is delivered in higher quality:** CDNs spend more time tinkering with compression algorithms than free services, which take a one-size-fits-all approach to compression. A good CDN delivers better image quality yet smaller file sizes.

The drawback of using a dedicated CDN is that it can be quite costly: Hosting packages start in the hundreds of dollars for 200 gigabytes (GB) of videos served per month (the equivalent of about 50 full-length DVDs) and rise sharply after that amount.

Did we mention that CDNs are expensive? If your viral video is a hit, your CDN hosting bills can quickly skyrocket into the thousands (or tens of thousands) of dollars. High bills may be acceptable if you've worked out a beneficial advertising model or charge for your videos, but if not, a CDN probably isn't your best option.

Leading CDNs in the marketplace include the following:

- **Brightcove:** (www.brightcove.com/en/online-video-platform/mobile-devices) Brightcove, a larger player in the online video market, has rolled out a wide array of products to suit its high-end customers. A lot of its focus for the iPad/iPhone has been on delivering video for apps rather than for websites, but it has sophisticated content management, monetization, and syndication tools. If you're dealing with mission-critical videos and you need a bulletproof solution (and you have the budget), Brightcove is a good choice.

- **Kaltura:** (corp.kaltura.com) This open source video environment (online editing, management, player, and syndication) has been adopted by the Wikimedia site (www.wikimedia.org) to handle the delivery of its growing video assets. Kaltura serves many large sites, including Wikipedia, Coca-Cola, and CNET.

- **Limelight Networks:** (www.limelightnetworks.com) Like its competition, Limelight Networks has rolled out a product aimed at the mobile video market. The company claims that Limelight REACH can transcode video on the fly to adapt to whichever device receives the video stream.

- **Mobile CDN:** (http://mobilecdn.com) Mobile CDN laid claim to being the first CDN to launch a live streaming video application when it "mobilecast" the NBA All-Star game in 2009. Though this true boutique operation specializes in mobile video, it doesn't have the most polished offerings or customer service.

- **Ooyala:** (www.ooyala.com/videoplatform/mobile) The CDN with the funny name is serious about trying to find features the others don't have. Your visitors can use the Ooyala Playlist function to view multiple videos from within the same player and avoid having to reload web pages. The OoyalaDirect iPhone app lets users upload high-quality video to the web from their iPhones.

- **Sorenson 360:** (www.sorensonmedia.com/video-delivery-network) Sorenson is known more for its video compression engine. However, it has branched out into video hosting and delivery and was one of the first companies to make a big marketing push based on its ability to host and serve video specifically optimized for the iPhone/iPad platform.

Using video sharing sites

Whether you want to reach people who watch video on their desktop computers at home or work, on their iPads on their living room couches, or on their iPhones wherever else they may be, the simplest way to publish video on the Internet is to upload it to a video sharing site.

The most popular video site, YouTube (www.youtube.com), may serve you well, but before you set up a YouTube channel, consider the benefits of using sites such as Vimeo (http://vimeo.com), which provide more options and may better suit your video needs.

You can find step-by-step instructions for using YouTube and Vimeo in the following two sections, but first read a few reasons that you might choose one of these services instead of a CDN, followed by a list of sharing sites' most popular options.

Video sharing sites offer many benefits:

- **Low price:** Compared to CDNs, they're free, or at least inexpensive, to use.

- **Ease of use:** If these sites weren't easy to use, millions of teenagers around the world couldn't share their deeply held convictions that homework is, like, totally unfair.

- **Delivery infrastructure:** These hosting sites exist only to store and deliver video; they've spent millions (or more, in some cases) perfecting this technology. So, unlike with a CDN, when you use a video hosting service, the bandwidth costs and concerns are someone else's problem.

- **Easy-to-share content:** Your users can embed your videos on their sites, e-mail friends, leave comments, and post your videos to Facebook, for example.

- **Already existing traffic:** These sites already have plenty of visitors, so you don't have to go out of your way to do lots of search engine optimization (SEO) to get your video to appear in search engines.

And, here are some drawbacks of using video sharing sites:

- **Possible delivery of poor-quality videos:** Because video sharing sites process many thousands of videos every day, they can't pay much attention to the necessary details of making your project look its best. Common problems include *artifacting* (which makes solid backgrounds look like they're sparkling) and *audio warbling* (where it sounds like a choir of baby robots is singing in the background).

- **Putting *your* ads into your content:** If you're trying to monetize your content by inserting your own ads or if your video is just a blatant commercial for your business (such as MLM marketing come-ons), certain sites may yank it.

- **Putting *their* ads into your content:** While these sites may offer you free hosting, they still have to pay their bills. That means they may put ads in and around your content that detract from your user's enjoyment of your videos.

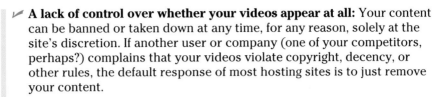

✔ **A lack of control over whether your videos appear at all:** Your content can be banned or taken down at any time, for any reason, solely at the site's discretion. If another user or company (one of your competitors, perhaps?) complains that your videos violate copyright, decency, or other rules, the default response of most hosting sites is to just remove your content.

✔ **Lack of ownership control over your video:** After uploading your content, you may no longer be the sole owner of the rights to control where, when, and how your video is displayed, packaged, advertised, or sold. Read the complete end user licensing agreement (EULA); don't just agree to it.

✔ **Limitations on video length:** Video length is limited to the length that the video sharing site dictates (usually, 10 minutes or fewer).

✔ **Limited analytics:** You probably don't receive much data to gauge user engagement or to see which sections of a video are the most popular or which ones the audience fast-forwarded, for example.

✔ **Traffic level that benefits the video sharing site, not yours:** Because your videos are hosted on the sharing site's servers, the video sharing site benefits from the value of the traffic that comes from *your* site. (The value of your traffic might be higher search engine rankings and advertising opportunities.) However, traffic can cost you hosting and bandwidth fees. If you're just getting started with video, using a video sharing site can help you build traffic without the fees. If your videos attract a growing audience, you may consider then moving your video hosting to a CDN in order to capitalize on that traffic.

Here's a brief introduction to popular video sharing sites, listed in order of popularity:

✔ **YouTube:** (www.youtube.com) The world's most popular video site is free and easy enough for any teenager to master. If you want to reach the largest possible audience, YouTube provides hosting and a wide range of ways to promote, and even make money on, your videos (if you attract a large enough audience). YouTube videos can be viewed either through the app that comes pre-loaded on the iPhone and iPad, or on mobile websites in the Safari browser.

✔ **Vimeo:** (www.vimeo.com) Vimeo combines a free video service, similar to the one at YouTube, with a professional level of service that includes the ability to customize the player (see Figure 9-3) and prevent anyone else from downloading or embedding your videos. The pro service costs $69 per year, which is a great deal when you consider that it includes high-definition (HD) video hosting and provides useful customization options.

- **Vid.ly:** (http://m.vid.ly) This new startup company appeared as this book was going to press. Vid.ly claims that it can take care of all your video needs. Just tell Vid.ly where your source video is stored, and it transcodes the video into all the formats you need for the mobile web. As with all just-launched start-ups, it is too soon to tell, but we're keeping an eye on Vid.ly, and we encourage you to give it a look.

- **Viddler:** (www.viddler.com) Viddler offers video hosting, ad revenue sharing, and detailed analytics.

- **Dailymotion:** (www.daily motion.com) Dailymotion is especially popular in Europe and features a broad range of media and entertainment and other categories.

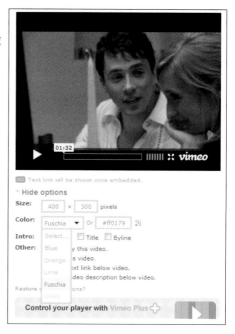

Figure 9-3: The Vimeo video service offers professional features, including the ability to customize the player.

Hosting mobile video on Vimeo

Vimeo delivers video to a wide range of devices, thanks to its universal player. As a designer, you simply add a single embed code to insert the video on a page. Vimeo does all the device detection for you, so that your video is optimized for a wide audience.

Whenever someone visits your site where you have used the Vimeo embed code to display a video, Vimeo determines which kind of device is being used to view the video and chooses the best format and player based on which features the device supports. A snippet of Java code is even provided that you can add to your sites to automatically upgrade the old embed codes, so you don't have to laboriously strip out the old embed codes and replace them with new ones.

In addition to delivering great video, you can embed the video directly into your web pages — a sharp contrast to the way most video is played on the web. If you simply link to a video on most hosting sites, an iPhone user who clicks your video watches the Safari browser close, the screen go blank for a moment, and then the video player launch to play the video. This process has been notoriously subject to crashing or causing long delays (although recent updates to Apple's iOS have mitigated this), which is why being able to play a video within a web page is a much better scenario.

Of course, on the iPad, the combination of the multitasking updates in iOS 4 and the larger screen size now provide a much different experience. Videos embedded on web pages play on those very same web pages (well, as long as they're in iPad-compatible formats), without your having to exit Safari to another screen.

Vimeo once required users to upgrade to a Pro account before they would transcode their videos for playback on mobile devices, but it now makes delivery to mobile available to everyone who uses its service. You can sign up for a free account and upload video to Vimeo by using its upload page, as shown in Figure 9-4.

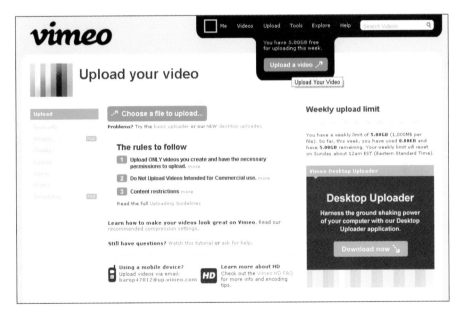

Figure 9-4: Vimeo helps you easily upload videos.

After you upload your video to Vimeo, follow these steps to embed a Vimeo video in your web page:

1. **Launch a web browser, log in to your Vimeo account, and choose My Videos from the Video menu, as shown in Figure 9-5.**

   The Your Videos page opens.

2. Select from the Your Videos page the video you want to add to your web page.

The video opens in its own page on Vimeo.

3. Click the Embed button in the upper right corner of the video window.

A window opens, containing the code for embedding the video on your web page, as shown in Figure 9-6.

4. Click the Customize Embed Options link at the bottom of the window.

The Embed This Video window expands to display several options, as shown in Figure 9-7.

5. Choose the pixel size for displaying the video, and type the numbers in the Size boxes in the Embed This Video window.

Choosing a size is one of the most difficult decisions that video designers wrestle with. Of course, the higher the resolution of the video, the crisper the picture and the better it looks — but the file being sent to the iPhone/iPad is, of course, larger and occupies more bandwidth.

The size you choose should depend on whether you want the video to be viewable on all the various Apple devices or have separate versions — a lower-resolution version for the iPhone and a higher-resolution version for the iPad. In Chapter 3, you find an explanation of the various video formats available to you.

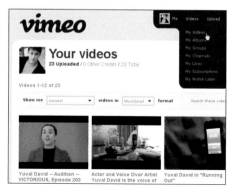

Figure 9-5: You can view all your uploaded videos at Vimeo on the Your Videos page.

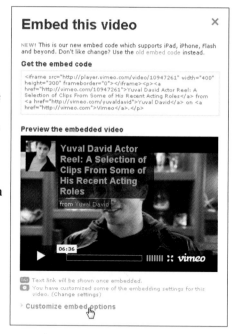

Figure 9-6: You can copy code from the Vimeo site to add a video to a web page.

One piece of good news: Vimeo automatically handles the math behind the screen resolution, so you shouldn't need a calculator for this one.

If you enter *640* as the horizontal size of the video, Vimeo fills in the appropriate size in the corresponding vertical box. In the case of 1280 x 720 high-definition video, the video is resized to 640 x 360 to preserve the widescreen format.

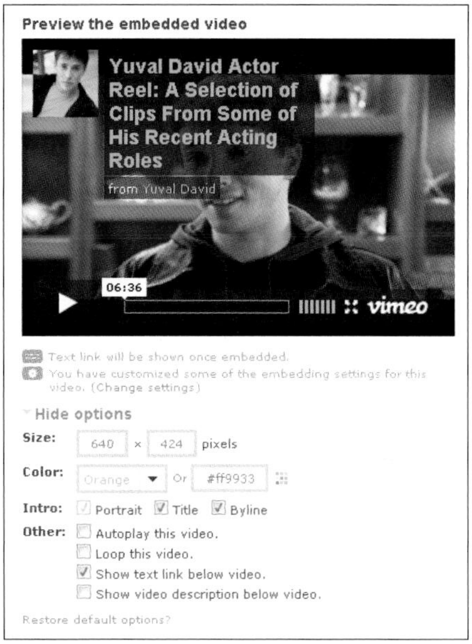

6. **Choose the color of the title of the video from the Color drop-down menu.**

You can also type a hexadecimal color code in the box next to the drop-down menu if you want to add a custom color for the title of the video (refer to Figure 9-7).

7. **Select the check boxes to choose which information appears on the screen before the video starts playing:**

- *Portrait:* Use a thumbnail from the video.

- *Title:* Display the title of the video in the color you set in Step 6.

- *Byline:* Display the creator's name below the title.

8. **Select any options you want from the Other section.**

We recommend against choosing Autoplay This Video or Loop This Video because we like to let visitors decide when a video starts and how long to play it. Having these options selected on a video that's being sent to the mobile platform can result in significant delays in page loading.

9. **When you have all the settings adjusted, click and drag to select all the code in the Get the Embed Code window and copy it.**

The text in the window is highlighted when it's selected. To copy the code, place the cursor anywhere in the code window and right-click (or Option-click on the Mac) and choose Select All⇨Copy, as shown in Figure 9-8.

Figure 9-7: Specify the size and text color and other options by using Vimeo embedding options.

Figure 9-8: Select and copy all the embed code from Vimeo.

10. **Open your web site in a web design program such as Dreamweaver, and paste the code you copied from Vimeo into your web page. If you use a blogging program such as WordPress, you can copy the code into Code view in the WordPress Dashboard editor.**

    In Figure 9-9, you see Adobe Dreamweaver being used to paste the embed code from Vimeo into a web page.

To see a broader range of options for how your videos display when hosted on Vimeo, click the Settings button in the upper right corner of the video page to see the Settings page shown in Figure 9-10.

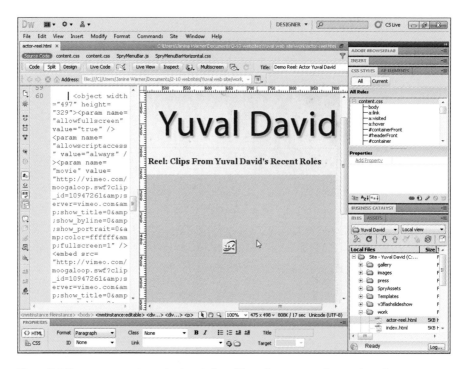

Figure 9-9: You can paste the embed code from Vimeo into your web page by using a program such as Dreamweaver.

Upgrading the embed code for your Vimeo video for the iPad and iPhone

Any new video you add using Vimeo will work across most devices, but if you added Vimeo videos to your website before Vimeo started supporting the iPhone/iPad, you need to change the embed code. Fortunately, you can upgrade all your embed codes automatically by inserting the following code into your web page just before the closing `</body>` tag on any page where you display Vimeo videos:

```
<script  src="http://assets.
vimeo.com/js/embedinator.min.
js"></script>
```

Figure 9-10: Vimeo offers, in its Settings window, more options for displaying your video.

Hosting mobile video on YouTube

For designers who don't want to struggle to figure out whole new lexicons of technical specifications, the simplest option is to let YouTube, shown in Figure 9-11, do all the work of hosting and delivering video.

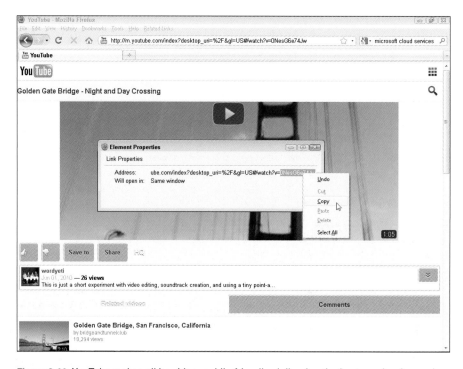

Figure 9-11: YouTube makes all its video mobile friendly, delivering the best version for each device.

When you upload a video to this popular website, you have two options for how to include the video on your website:

- **Link to a YouTube video.** If you add a link to a video on the YouTube site from your web page, when a visitor clicks the link, the YouTube site opens in Safari on both the iPhone and iPad.

- **Embed a YouTube video.** YouTube also makes it possible for you to copy a snippet of code from the YouTube site to embed a video directly into your web page, in much the way Vimeo does in the exercise in the previous section. When you use the embed code, the video plays in place in your page when viewed in an iPad. On an iPhone, when a visitor plays an embedded video, the iPhone video player launches and plays the video full screen. The visitor must then close the video window to return to your website in Safari.

Inserting video hosted on your server into a mobile web page

If you host your videos on your own web server, you can embed them into your pages by using the HTML video, audio, and source tags covered in Chapter 5. Whether you host your videos yourself, use a high-end content delivery network (CDN), or a video hosting service, such as YouTube, it's helpful to understand what formats work best on the web.

One challenge in working with video on the mobile web is choosing the best format. This list briefly describes the most common digital video formats and their file extensions.

These formats work on the iPhone, iPad, iPod:

MPEG-4: Fast becoming the standard format that users upload to video sharing sites like YouTube and Vimeo, MPEG-4 plays well on mobile devices. Also, users don't need a plug-in to play video in MPEG-4 format on desktop computers, even Windows machines. The MPEG-4 format, based on the QuickTime format, adds MPEG features that QuickTime doesn't support.

M4V: Most video distributed by way of iTunes is stored in the M4V format. It provides extra digital rights management (DRM) security protection so that files cannot easily be pirated and supports higher-quality audio than the standard MP4.

Motion-JPEG: Another format supported by the iPhone/iPad is M-JPEG. Before MPEG-4, Motion-JPEG was commonly used to capture video with digital cameras. This format is also supported by many game consoles, including PlayStation and Nintendo Wii.

MOV: Created by Apple, .mov files are typically associated with QuickTime (www.quicktime.com) because they play in the QuickTime player. This video format, which uses the .mov extension, has long been popular with Macintosh users because the player is built into the Mac operating system. (QuickTime files can be viewed on Windows computers by using the QuickTime Player.)

These popular video formats do not play on the Apple iPhone, iPad, or iPod:

Flash video: As of this writing, Flash doesn't work in the Safari browser on an iPhone, iPod, or iPad. Nothing. Nada. No video. In Safari on the Apple iOS, video in the Flash format doesn't even appear. It's an unfortunate turn for many video enthusiasts because the Flash Player is such a popular format on the rest of the web. Videos converted into the Adobe Flash Video format use the .flv extension. In the future, apps may play Flash video on the iPhone and iPad, but so far nothing has come along that looks like it will save Flash on the Apple iOS.

AVI: Created by Microsoft, the Audio Video Interleave (AVI) .avi format is one the most common video formats on Windows computers. Many video editing programs capture footage from digital cameras into the .avi format before rendering it into other formats.

Windows Media Video: Developed by Microsoft and popular on PCs, files in the Windows Media Video format use the .wmv extension.

Optimizing Audio for the Mobile Web

Getting sound to come out of an iPhone or iPad seems like a no-brainer, right? After all, they were designed to play sounds and even sync with users' iTunes audio libraries. If you haven't already added audio content to the mix on your website, take a look at some possible innovative uses for audio that mobile users might want to have at their fingertips — for convenience, to pass the time productively, to better answer a question, or to solve a crisis situation while they're away from the home or office, for example:

- **Nature:** Include examples of birdcalls or wild animal noises to help bird-watchers identify birds (or grouchy mama bears) by sound while in the field.

- **Travel:** A bed and breakfast might provide audio directions for motor-ists who are driving, who can't (and shouldn't) take their eyes off winding country roads to continually check the small print on a mobile screen.

- **Religious:** Members of a congregation can hear the latest sermon, hymns, or meditation.

- **Health:** Demonstrate exactly what a dangerous whooping cough sounds like as opposed to one resulting from the common flu.

- **Music:** Short teaser clips of musical works can incentivize fans to down-load higher-quality versions.

- **Health and fitness:** A personal trainer talks users through a special workout program that they can follow at the gym.

In the following sections, you discover the basics you need to know if you want to add audio to your mobile site.

Figuring out formats, file sizes, and more

As with any other multimedia, the biggest challenge arises from capabilities, bandwidths, memory, and wireless connection speeds that are uneven and unpredictable across different devices. The good news is that unlike some other common multimedia elements (such as Flash), the iPhone/iPad is a whiz at playing the industry standard audio format: MP3.

MP3 doesn't provide the best compression *codec* (the mathematical for-mula that reduces the size of an audio file). In fact, music engineers groan and rub their temples when forced to listen to the sound of highly com-pressed MP3s playing on tiny speakers. But MP3 is a universal standard just because of the number of people who have used it for many years. Thus, your biggest decision is how much to compress your MP3 to ensure that a mobile user can play it.

Essentially, you compress an audio file in an audio editor by setting the bit rate for the file. *Bit rate* — a measure of the file's audio quality — is the number of bits of digital information per second that are decoded and turned into a sound. In much the same way that reducing color depth in images (which we describe in Chapter 3) represents a trade-off between quality and file size, so too does bit rate work for audio files. Bigger is usually better — to a point. The following list explains the differences in bit rate for the desktop and mobile web:

- ✔ **On the regular desktop web, bit rates range from 96 to 320 Kbps.** Professionals consider 96 kilobits per second (Kbps) adequate for a file that contains human speech, such as an interview or a monologue. Until recently, 128 Kbps was considered standard for music, and the vast majority of songs sold on iTunes were at this bit rate; however, sites such as MOG (www.mog.com) are making a name for themselves by offering music at 320 Kbps or higher for true audiophiles.

- ✔ **For the mobile web, aim for 64 Kbps or lower.** The giant music-streaming service Pandora has found that 64 Kbps is the highest practical bit rate to deliver over wireless connections because of band-width and dropout constraints. However, as 3G networks become more stable, and as 4G networks get rolled out, we expect that number (and the quality of the audio) to start going up dramatically.

Comparing streaming audio versus downloads versus podcasts

You can enable mobile users to access your audio files in these three ways:

- ✔ **Streaming audio** refers to the process whereby the audio files are transferred continuously, bit by bit, to the mobile device while the user listens. The file isn't saved on the device but, rather, is sent to the user every time it's requested. However, to stream audio, you need to clear complicated technical hurdles (which we explain in the next section) to ensure that the audio files play as promised. Live concerts, press confer-ences, and sporting events are examples of situations where you might want to take on the challenges of streaming audio.

- ✔ **Downloadable audio** files are, not surprisingly, downloaded and then played on a mobile device without being connected to the web. This method allows your users to download a file before they get on a plane, for example, and then listen to it even when they're unable to connect to a wireless Internet connection.

✒ **Podcasts** are downloadable audio files with a Really Simple Syndication (RSS) tag that lets users subscribe to the podcast so that every episode of the podcast series downloads automatically. A description of how to create podcasts is beyond the scope of this book, but you can find free videos and tips for creating podcasts at www.dummies.com. For a more in-depth look at podcasting, check out *Podcasting For Dummies,* 2nd Edition, by Tee Morris, Chuck Tomasi, Evo Terra, and Kreg Steppe.

Linking to downloadable audio files

Providing a link so that your visitors can download an audio file is the simplest option, especially compared to streaming audio. We recommend linking to audio files rather than using the <object> tag, which is more common on the desktop web. Even some of the best-designed mobile sites that feature audio, including National Public Radio (www.npr.org), link to audio files rather than insert them directly into a web page.

Linking to audio from a mobile site works the same way it does on a desktop website: You upload the audio file to a folder on your web server (or to the CDN that you use). Then you simply insert a link to the audio file in any web page in your site. A link to an audio file looks like this:

```
<a href="http://www.YourSite.com/audio/YourSong.mp3"> Click
          to play my song!</a>
```

We strongly discourage any use of the <bgsound> command to play background music for a mobile web page. Similarly, using the <object> or <embed> tag with the autostart=true command to automatically play an audio file upon page load is a no-no. These commands either cause an error or force the mobile user to download the entire audio file to see the contents of your page.

Creating Mobile Commerce Sites

In This Chapter

▶ Comparing mobile commerce solutions

▶ Selling to the upscale iPhone/iPad demographic

▶ Looking at how users adapt to mobile commerce

▶ Understanding the basic building blocks of mobile commerce

▶ Comparing mobile commerce payment solutions

▶ Setting up commerce on a mobile site

*I*ndustry experts have long predicted that the "iPhone Mom" would become the most sought-after creature in the mobile world. Young mothers with iPhones would not only make the purchasing decisions for their families, but connect with each other using apps and social media on their phones to alert each other to special deals — and even take over shopping duties for their aging (and somewhat technophobic) parents.

The Black Friday online holiday shopping extravaganza was the iPhone's coming-out party. TV news broadcasts were full of stories about how shoppers were using their phones to find special discounts, check prices using barcode-scanning apps, and even pay for items.

One advantage of mobile commerce (or *m-commerce*) is that customers can impulse-buy wherever they are, whenever the urge hits them, not just on Black Friday or within the walls of your store. Your job as a web developer is to make that process as safe and as smooth as possible so that customers don't think twice about the purchase and abandon ship before they hit the Place This Order button. Think of m-commerce as the equivalent of having operators standing by to take your order; the only differences are that these operators never sleep or take breaks.

In this chapter, we explore how to add m-commerce to your website so that your users can buy your products and services, subscribe to your news feed, or pay to download digital goods, such as songs and videos, using an iPhone, iPad, or other mobile device.

Appreciating the Mobile Opportunity

Mobile commerce is growing fast, but you don't have to take our word for it. The team at the Morgan Stanley investment bank believe strongly enough in the power of m-commerce to conduct high-level business that they built an exclusive iPad app (different from the free Morgan Stanley Research app, available to everyone), which allows fund managers to monitor stock and bond markets, making decisions that affect billions of dollars in pension funds.

In Figure 10-1, you see a graph, from research conducted by Morgan Stanley, indicating that mobile commerce will grow much faster than traditional online commerce.

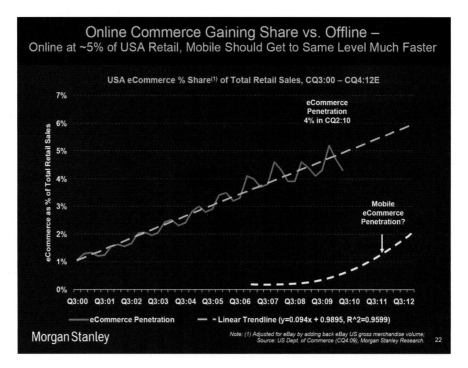

Figure 10-1: Exhaustive Morgan Stanley reports consistently highlight the growth of mobile commerce.

The rapid growth of m-commerce is staggering:

- Two-thirds of mobile phone owners use their devices while shopping; 62 percent to find deals, 32 percent to comparison shop, and 29 percent to take and send photos of products, according to a Yahoo! survey.

- Forty-four percent of smartphone users have accessed their bank account from their devices, and banks are rolling out apps that allow users to deposit checks to their accounts by using their cellphone cameras to snap pictures of the check.

- Thirty-five percent of smart phone users have redeemed a coupon they have received via text message, 41 percent have checked competitive prices on their smartphones while in a retail store by scanning the barcodes, 10 percent have bought movie tickets using their phones.

- Seventy-eight percent of the major retailers report that within the next three years, they want to sell items to their customers, using mobile phones to transfer the funds, according to IHL's Going Mobile study.

Comparing Mobile Commerce Solutions

When adding shopping carts and other e-commerce services to your mobile site, you can choose from many options. Many familiar brands, such as PayPal and Google, have made major efforts to migrate their online commerce technology to the mobile platform. And a crop of new companies is emerging, with dedicated mobile services that include everything from m-commerce to Short Message Service (SMS, or text messaging), mobile coupons, and other mobile features.

With mobile commerce, you have a wide range of options. The following helps you appreciate the four main ways you can add m-commerce to your site, each with its own pros and cons:

- **A Buy button or simple shopping cart:** Google and PayPal offer one-click Buy buttons that make it easy to sell one product, service, or digital good, such as a subscription or e-book, via your website.

  - *Pros:* You can complete this task in a few minutes without any upfront costs. Plus, everything you need is in one package, so you don't have to worry about setting up credit card processing or other transaction services.

  - *Cons:* You can sell only one item at a time, there are no shopping cart features, and you have few options about the way this button looks on your site.

✔ **A wide range of shopping carts combining mobile features with a payment service:** At the low end, Google and Paypal offer simple shopping carts in an all-in-one package. At the high end, the sophisticated shopping cart Magento (`www.magentocommerce.com`) has rolled out a custom mobile shopping cart with robust features. (See Figure 10-2.)

- *Pros:* You can better control how your merchandise is displayed, manage more products more easily, and even integrate online and offline inventory management. Some shopping cart services offer added features to help manage customers, product discounts, coupons, and so on.

- *Cons:* Using a shopping cart service requires considerable work to set up the software on your server and integrate it with your website. These services are also more expensive and generally worth the added cost and effort only if you sell at least a dozen products.

✔ **Dedicated mobile shopping carts:** More and more shopping carts and m-commerce services are designed specifically to work on the mobile web. Some of the newest m-commerce companies are set up to do all the work for you; others offer shopping carts you can design or customize and build into your site yourself.

- *Pros:* Designed from the start for the mobile platform, you can expect companies such as asknet (`www.asknet.com`) or 2ergo (`www.2ergo.com`) to provide solid support for mobile devices and understand the unique challenges of the mobile web.

- *Cons:* This is an exciting area of the mobile web, but like any new technology, you won't find much history behind some of these companies, so it can be harder to compare customer reviews or find third-party help or tech support.

Figure 10-2: Magento offers high-end m-commerce solutions.

✔ **A completely custom-built cart with your own back end:** This option is for the intrepid mobile web designer only. If you want complete control over the look and functionality of your m-commerce site, as well as control over how the checkout and money-transfer process is handled, you can build your own integrated solution from the ground up. Most likely, you would need a team of experts to handle all the complex issues involved in such an undertaking.

• *Pros:* You have total control over the look and feel of the shopping cart. If something goes wrong, you can take matters into your own hands to fix it, rather than relying on someone else's customer service to pick up the phone or respond to e-mails. All the data about your customers and what they buy is under your control.

• *Cons:* You have to take care of every little nitpicky detail. If you miss something, only you can fix it. And if you're away and the site goes down while you're on vacation, you're out of business (at least until you can access your site again). You will need to have your own mechanism for transferring the funds and maintain your own secure database for your customer's financial data.

Mobile commerce is evolving so rapidly that the companies listed here may well have added new features by the time you read this. Visit `www.digital family.com/mobile` for updates to the providers and services featured in this chapter and elsewhere in the book.

In this chapter, we provide detailed instructions for two of the simplest shopping cart options and include references to some of the most sophisticated options.

No matter what route you choose, m-commerce sites have some basic elements in common, and the key points in this chapter about how mobile commerce works, and what it takes to add e-commerce functionality to your website, applies to both the high end and low end of web services.

Understanding the Basic Building Blocks of an M-Commerce Solution

Whether you sell just one thing or have a site chock-full of thousands of items of all shapes, sizes, and prices, each store must have some of the same elements. The following sections guide you through the basics of how online commerce services (both for mobile and for the desktop web) work so that you can better understand your options. We also tell you what to look for when you design a shopping system for your web-based business.

Creating a mobile shopping experience: The front end

This *front end* of your site is where your customers shop and pick out what they want to buy. Whether you sell one item with a simple Buy Now button or you design a sophisticated shopping cart, think of your m-commerce site as your virtual showroom.

Everyone has wandered through a warehouse-style store at some point: You can easily get lost, the prices aren't always marked clearly, and no one's around to help you when you need assistance. Few things cost you more sales online than getting your customers lost in a sea of poorly organized links. You also don't want visitors to question your credibility because they feel they've wandered into a crummy junk shop with the merchandise piled in heaps. Even if they find something they like, they can't wait to get out.

Good m-commerce design is about making the site attractive and easy to use.

The following two sections help you imagine how customers might use your site so that you can design with these uses in mind. The sections also introduce you to mobile design do's and don'ts that clarify how to design a commerce site that's easy to use.

Imagining your target customers

One of the most valuable things you can do before creating your store is to step back for a second and imagine your target customers (the people most likely to spend money on your products). Don't just try to visualize who your target customers are — put yourself in their shoes. Where are they, and what are they doing when they come to your site on an iPhone or iPad? People who are going to spend money while browsing a store on their mobile devices are likely in one of these five situations:

- **They're looking for a special deal while they're out and about.** For example, a couple on a date just found out that the restaurant they planned on eating at is closed and the movie they wanted to watch is sold out. Now they just want to order some takeout, go home, and snuggle in front of the TV. So they do a GPS-enabled search and find that your place is within two blocks and will have their food waiting by the time they arrive.

- **They're in a critical situation.** They absolutely need to buy your product and close the deal as soon as possible. For example, diehard sports fans may have just received your text alert that an entire section of seats to the Super Bowl has just become available. However, the tickets are selling fast and probably will be gone by the time they can rush home — unless they can place a bid on your site *this instant* via their mobile phones.

✔ **They're shopping on impulse:** Maybe they've trudged through snow-drifts past your billboard advertising tropical cruises for the last month. Today, the bus splashed them with a wave of freezing slush and muck. Shivering in their seats, they pull out their phones and punch in your travel agency's web address.

✔ **They're in-store bargain-hunters.** Retailers are starting to notice that shoppers are whipping out their mobile phones and punching in product names and details to make sure that they're getting the best deal.

✔ **They're bored and killing time.** Stuck in detention, a group of 15-year-olds decide to see what the new super-exclusive designer sneakers you just got in look like and how many chores they may have to do to earn themselves a new pair.

In each case, *immediacy* is one of the driving factors behind customers making a purchase with their iPhones. People buy things for all sorts of reasons, but when it comes to m-commerce, a lot boils down to just being in the right place, at the right time, with the right offer.

Following mobile design do's and don'ts

What makes m-commerce so exciting is that the mobile web puts your store in your customers' pockets wherever they go. Before you get too excited by visions of 'round-the-clock shoppers, here are a few deadly design errors you need to avoid:

✔ **Don't cram too many items on your page.** The screen size is small, and even if you have hundreds of things you want to offer, if you try to put them all in one space, your customers can't figure out what they're supposed to click.

✔ **Don't use gimmicks, such as hokey animations and music, to try to grab users' attention.** If they've made the effort to hit your mobile site, they're already interested. But they're also skittish — mobile shopping is still a new experience for most people. If your site looks like a 13-year-old girl's MySpace page, they're probably not going to trust that their financial information is safe with you.

✔ **Don't get cute and hide prices.** Maybe your mobile customer is running up stairs, rushing into a meeting, or stopped at a traffic light. If they have to go through the whole checkout process only to find that your price isn't what they thought it was, they may never come back.

Guide customers by using just a few options per screen until they're ready to make a buying decision. eBay provides a particularly useful example of how efficient mobile web design can boost sales and profits. By designing for the mobile web, eBay encouraged millions of users to shop using their mobile phones — and they've added hundreds of millions of dollars of sales.

TIP

The differences between the desktop experience and the mobile web experience come into sharp focus when you look at how eBay appears when you navigate to the regular desktop site on a iPhone, as shown on the left side of Figure 10-3. Note how tiny the icons all look, how they all seem jumbled together, and how you can't really read any of the links. On the right side of Figure 10-3 is eBay's site as it appears when you go to the version that's optimized for the mobile platform. Note how having fewer choices makes it easier to figure out how to navigate the site.

Figure 10-3: The eBay desktop website (left) and mobile site (right) as they appear on the iPhone 4.

Exchanging money with a checkout system

If everything goes well, you ultimately guide your shoppers to the *checkout:* the place where the key action — money moving out of shoppers' accounts and into yours — happens. As you might expect by now, this is also where most of the second thoughts (or *cart abandonment*) happen. If you've designed your site well, you will overcome your customer's initial reservation to make a purchase and close the sale.

Your checkout must be as smooth and frictionless as possible; studies show that every 15 seconds of delay increase the chances of cart abandonment by as much as 25 percent. That is, if a whole minute passes for a user on an iPhone (who moves around and has a short attention span) to get a response after clicking the Pay Now button, the odds of him just chucking the whole process approach 100 percent.

 If your customers don't see what's happening, their fear overcomes their desire. You must not only use Internet-based security measures that use Secure Sockets Layer (SSL) technology (see the later section "Securing transactions with your customers"), but also prominently reassure your customers that their financial information won't get stolen or misused. Nobody wants to risk virtual credit card theft just to buy a vintage concert T-shirt. We discuss this in a little more depth in the upcoming sections regarding the back end of a site.

A good checkout system needs to

- ✔ **Total the cost of all the items in the potential customer's shopping cart, including any tax and shipping costs.**

- ✔ **Allow the customer to choose shipping options.** Customers like shipping options — FedEx, delivery vans, in-store pickup, friendly kayakers, whatever.

- ✔ **Send the customer tracking information and a confirmation e-mail.** Pay attention to that confirmation e-mail because it's a great way to entice customers to come back and shop again, rate their transaction efficiency, or receive discounts by referring their friends.

 Do some research. Go to your competitor's online stores and go through the buying process. Go to big online sites that have invested millions in perfecting the shopping experience, such as Amazon, eBay, Dell, and so on, and ask yourself questions every step of the way. Do you like the way the product's pictures are displayed and how the ad copy is written? What can you do better? What do you need to include? Take careful notes. If you start out armed with a clear vision of what you want and how you want to do it, you have a much better chance of coming out with a store that you like.

Amazon's shopping cart, shown in Figure 10-4, is a good model. This cart has both a large image of the item and a link to more images. The price is prominently displayed with a link to immediately check out and pay. And, at the bottom of the cart is a suggestion to try to sell the customer other items that complement selection. All the links are clear and easily understood, and the navigation at the bottom of the screen is unobtrusive.

Working behind the scenes: The back end

Broadly speaking, the *back end* of your m-commerce site includes all the things that your customers don't see. Think of this as your stockroom where you store all your stuff on shelves, next to filing cabinets and order sheets. You use the back-end features of your m-commerce solution to:

- Enter product and pricing information
- Manage shipping and tax options
- Configure any other features provided by the m-commerce service you use

Figure 10-4: The Amazon m-commerce site as it appears on an iPhone 4.

The back end of your m-commerce site also has to integrate smoothly with your payment solution. If you choose a service like the Google Merchant (which is part of Google Checkout), you get everything you need in one easy package. If you want a more customizable shopping cart that offers mobile services, consider a shopping cart such as ZenCart, www.zencart.com, a free, open-source option, or Magento, www.magentocommerce.com, a premium service. Keep in mind that you have to integrate the cart features with a transaction service yourself. (See the earlier section "Comparing Mobile Commerce Solutions" for more on these options.)

Google and PayPal offer many levels of service, so you can use Google or PayPal as an all-in-one solution for simple shopping sites, or you can use Google or PayPal just to handle the transactions if you use a more sophisticated shopping cart, such as ZenCart or Magento.

Securing transactions with your customers

We hate to sound like a broken record, but security is one of the biggest hurdles that m-commerce has to clear. Your customers watch TV ads about having their identities and credit card numbers stolen (particularly the ones that show little old ladies chortling in a gruff, male voice, bragging about all the expensive stuff they scammed by stealing Granny's identity).

Above all, make sure your site is secure and reassure your customers by explaining what you've done to protect their security.

Here are the three main goals of security:

- **Protect your customer.** Customers who don't get robbed are much more likely to come back — and still have money in their pockets when they arrive.

- **Protect the merchant.** You want to keep your site from being used to launder money or having all your products drop-shipped to a P.O. Box in some prince's name in some far away land.

- **Protect yourself.** If you're a web designer creating m-commerce sites for clients, you don't want an angry customer coming after you with a lawsuit because someone hacked the system you designed.

If you're a designer and don't take security seriously, you could face legal ramifications. If credit card numbers and personal identities are stolen, expensive lawsuits could result. Depending on the kinds of contracts you develop with clients, you may be liable. Consult an attorney for the best way to protect your business and consider investing in a business insurance policy that covers online commerce.

The standard technology to protect transactions is *Secure Sockets Layer* (SSL). All the information sent between a computer or mobile phone and the payment site is encrypted. Options range from 128- to 256-bit encryption, but 128-bit is more than enough for most businesses. Banks and brokerage houses that transfer billions of dollars around the world use 256-bit security, but they pay a high price for that level of security, as well as the bandwidth and computing power that go along with a site built to securely manage such high-end services.

Think of mobile security this way: You don't need to hire a helicopter gunship to hover over your business to fend off robbers, but an alarm system and a good insurance policy are well worth the expense. Be safe but not so paranoid that you blow all your potential profits on security.

To set up a secure website, you also need to get a Secure Sockets Layer (SSL) certificate to provide protection when you transfer vulnerable data, such as credit card numbers, online. SSL certificate prices vary depending on where you purchase the certificate and whether you complete the setup task yourself or use a service that handles it for you. Many web hosting services offer SSL certificates as add-ons to their regular hosting fees; others make it possible for you to set up your own SSL, which can be purchased from a number of different sources, including VeriSign, as shown in Figure 10-5. One advantage of using an all-inclusive e-commerce service, such as Google Checkout or the Yahoo! Store services, is that they take care of the SSL certificate for you.

Figure 10-5: VeriSign offers a wide range of services for conducting more secure transactions online.

Calculating taxes, shipping, and handling

After your customers buy your goods, the back end of your system needs some way of getting that merchandise to them. Whether you offer digital downloads, package your products in bubble wrap and cardboard boxes, or use a pizza delivery scooter, make sure it's clear to your customers what, if anything, you're charging them for delivery. If you offer multiple choices, such as rush services, make sure the m-commerce service you choose includes features to handle different shipping options (some are directly connected to common services, such as UPS and FedEx, to make things even easier).

Developing a custom system for mobile commerce

If you truly want to create your own custom-built site, look for more advanced books or other training specific to developing shopping carts, or consider paying for one of the services described in the "Comparing Mobile Commerce Solutions" section or hiring a contractor to take care of it for you.

To create such a system, here's what you need:

↙ You need to know how to use sophisticated functions in a dynamic programming language or technology, such as ASP.NET or PHP.

↙ You need the ability to integrate your system into a payment system in ways that require managing a secure server, SSL certificates, and other settings on your web server.

Because setting up your own m-commerce system gets complicated quickly, a range of online services combine all of these features for you.

Another charge that you need to be able to track and record is the amount of sales taxes you collect. Trust me, if you ignore this step, your accountant (not to mention the IRS) will have some very interesting things to say to you. And charging taxes isn't as easy as you might think because in most cases, you need to charge taxes only to those who live in your same state, and depending on your state, those taxes may vary from county to county. This can get complicated fast, and to ensure you're in compliance in your state, check your state business and sales tax requirements.

Checking Out Mobile Commerce Payment Solutions

Most sites are best served by the latest online m-commerce tools, which combine the flexibility of displaying merchandise on your own site with offloading the heavy-duty banking and money-transfer functions to close the deal. Most web designers agree that the best ways for individuals and small to mid-size businesses to add m-commerce are to use a company that includes a shopping cart and transaction service or to combine a dedicated shopping cart with a transaction service. In the following sections, we introduce you to companies that offer m-commerce services.

Amazon Payments

```
http://payments.amazon.com
```

This powerful and flexible payment engine allows users who are already familiar with, and trust, the Amazon brand to purchase goods from your website by using their Amazon customer ID. The advantage is that Amazon has established itself as one of the biggest retailers on the web, and its techno-logical backbone is very strong.

The downside, however, is that your customers have to already have an account with Amazon; otherwise, they're forced to create one when they make their first payment. As you can see in Figure 10-6, the Amazon brand is all over every page (on the buttons, in the colors, and in the typography), which helps your customers know they're dealing with a reputable firm — but that also means Amazon promotes itself all over your site.

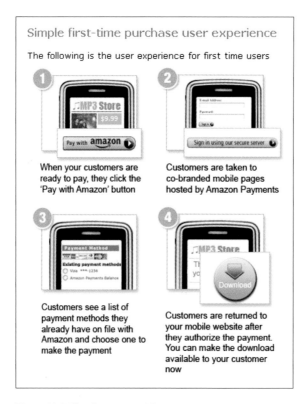

Figure 10-6: The Amazon mobile payments solution.

Still, if you sell digital downloads, such as ringtones, MP3s, videos, or pic-tures, Amazon's payment and pricing system is innovative and robust. And if you already sell your stuff on Amazon, it's very easy to integrate the links and payment system on your website because customers who have already paid with Amazon at your m-commerce store can buy with just one click. The Amazon site has detailed instructions for both amateurs looking for the sim-plest solution and seasoned developers looking to customize.

iTunes

```
www.apple.com/itunes
```

As of this writing, iTunes is still limited in what it sells, restricting anyone using the service to music, videos, and iPhone/iPad applications. You must submit your digital goods to iTunes for review before they can be listed on the site, and Apple's approval process can take a few days or even weeks.

But with more than 100 million credit card accounts on file (outnumbering even the 94 million Amazon customers or the 75 million PayPal customers), speculation is rife that Apple will extend its iTunes checkout processing technology to allow merchants to sell their stuff to customers who want to pay via their existing iTunes accounts. And iTunes provides digital goods for the iPhone, iPod touch, and iPad, so the combined audience is significant.

PayPal

```
www.paypal.com
```

PayPal is highly customizable and offers a wide range of services, broad international e-commerce support, and everything from simple one-click buttons to high-end transaction services that you can integrate into most of the popular shopping cart services.

At the high end, you need quite a bit of technical coding skills to tweak PayPal's API to work with third-party shopping carts, but PayPal has been around for a long time, so you can draw on a large international developer network when you need help. At the low end, you can easily add PayPal buttons. See the section "Creating a simple PayPal Buy button," later in this chapter.

As with Amazon, the PayPal brand is the one your customers see on each Buy button when it comes time to make their payments.

PayPal has also created some extremely powerful and extensible technology to allow people to transform their cellphones into wallets. And because PayPal is owned by eBay, the integration between the two services is quite good. If you're selling your items through your eBay store, this may be all you need.

PayPal is developing interesting extensions on its iPhone app. Not only can users transfer money directly from one phone to the other by bumping together the two phones, but a new service also uses GPS location data to allow users to find businesses on a map and send money directly to those businesses.

Google Checkout

https://checkout.google.com/sell

Google has spent enormous amounts of time and money developing a whole host of other products and services to go along with its core business of being the top search engine on the planet. We discuss setting up Google Checkout later in this chapter because of the wide panoply of other products and services that Google has — most especially Google's recent acquisition of the mobile advertising company AdMob for $750 million. Spending that kind of money is a clear indication that Google takes the mobile web seriously, and that it's going to continue to devote significant time and resources to ensuring that its existing products are mobile-friendly.

Google Checkout is easy to set up, and because it piggybacks on Google's massive network of server farms, it loads quickly — no matter where on Earth your user accesses your m-commerce site from (not an insignificant consideration as billions of people come online via their mobile devices).

Like PayPal, you can use Google Checkout to add a Buy Now button to your site, to set up a simple shopping cart and transaction package in one, or to use Google for the transaction processing in combination with any number of shopping carts that are designed to work with Google. (Some shopping carts can be integrated with PayPal, Google, or both if you want to give customers the option.)

If you use Google Checkout, the downside, similar to Amazon, is that your customers have to already have an account with Google; otherwise, they're forced to create one when they make their first payment. The Google brand is what your customers will see when they make their payments; the buttons will have the Google logo on them, the color scheme will look like the color scheme that is used by Google, the words "Fast checkout through Google" will appear on the screen, along with a link that says "What is Google Checkout?" and leads to a page that's all about Google Checkout. Another possible downside for you may be that Google Checkout doesn't support currency in as many countries as PayPal. What Google Checkout does is to use the conversion rates of the major credit cards to perform the currency conversion, primarily to U.S. dollars, euros, and British pounds sterling. If your buyers are in one of the supported countries (and the list of countries has grown significantly in just the last year), a currency conversion calculator from Citibank pops up to show them what the price actually is in their local money.

Dozens of e-commerce shopping cart providers have made a special effort to ensure that they integrate cleanly with Google Checkout. If you want to use a more sophisticated shopping cart than the one provided by Google, you can view Google's recommended list of third-party vendors in the Integration Partners section on its website at https://checkout.google.com/seller/integrate_cart.html.

If you use Google Checkout, Google offers a couple other features that can tie into your Google Checkout system:

✔ Google also has a wizard that allows you to easily convert a Google Docs spreadsheet into a shopping cart and even an embeddable store. If you have a Google ID, you can use Google Docs to create a spreadsheet via the web. Basically, in Google Docs, you fill the spreadsheet with any data you want to include about your products, including descriptions, pictures, pricing info, and so on. Then, run the wizard at `https://storegadgetwizard.appspot.com/storegadgetwizard/` to convert your spreadsheet into a shopping cart.

✔ Google Analytics allows you to track page traffic information, such as how many users come to your site, which items are most popular, and how much time visitors spend on each page.

Magento

`www.magentocommerce.com`

The sophisticated e-commerce platform Magento has rolled out a highly customizable mobile shopping cart with robust features. (See Figure 10-2 earlier in this chapter.)

High-end shopping cart services like Magento can be complex to install and set up, but if you sell a lot of items, want to track sales across many channels, or need your online system to be integrated with your brick-and-mortar inventory system, you may find Magento well worth the cost. Magento supports many transaction services, including Google, PayPal, and most banks that offer online merchant services.

asknet

`www.asknet.com`

This large, international e-commerce company, based in Germany, offers custom-built mobile sites and high-end m-commerce.

Partnered with many Internet security companies and software retailers, the company specializes in handling m-commerce across international boundaries. asknet provides support for multiple currencies, tax laws, delivery of goods, and customer tracking. Videos on its site explain how its service works.

The asknet network of warehouses can handle fulfillment, so you can use asknet to store your merchandise and handle shipping around the world. It even burns CDs/DVDs, applies your labels, sticks them into jewel cases, and delivers them to your customers if you sell digital merchandise. As you might expect, asknet is far from the cheapest solution; it doesn't even list its prices on its site, but you can contact asknet for more information.

CardinalCommerce

www.cardinalcommerce.com

CardinalCommerce, shown in Figure 10-7, has partnered with Sprint to provide the back-end payment solution for the new Sprint Mobile Wallet. Although CardinalCommerce formerly specialized in handling large transactions for major multinational corporations, it has made a concerted effort to reach out to small- and medium-size businesses, and its partnership with Sprint is intriguing.

Figure 10-7: This mobile commerce solution has partnered with Sprint.

Unlike AT&T's entry into the mobile commerce space (covered in the next section), Sprint and CardinalCommerce are not trying to force merchants and shoppers to buy things by adding the sales price to the user's existing cellphone bill. Instead, the Sprint Mobile Wallet aggregates your existing payment methods — PayPal, Amazon Payments, MasterCard, and Visa, for example — in one place, and allows you to choose which one you want to use to pay for something.

As of this writing, the Sprint Mobile Wallet is brand-new and mostly untested. However, Sprint claims it has designed this payment system so that mobile developers can process transactions quickly and easily on their sites, and the Sprint handsets available as of late 2011 will all come preloaded with the Sprint Mobile Wallet. Sprint also plans to make its Mobile Wallet service available to users on other phone carriers, such as AT&T and Verizon, by creating apps and web-based plug-ins that allow designers and developers to access the service. Check the CardinalCommerce site for the latest developments and offerings if you're considering this service.

Boku and AT&T

www.boku.com

Not to be outdone, days after Sprint announced its partnership with CardinalCommerce, AT&T announced that it would team up with startup company Boku to provide mobile payments. The difference is that rather than charging transactions to a credit card or bank account, Boku (shown in Figure 10-8) utilizes the user's cellphone account to pay for the transaction. That is, rather than getting a bill from Visa at the end of the month, the charge shows up on your phone bill.

Figure 10-8: Boku provides mobile commerce solutions for publishers.

Although most users in developed countries are probably not in favor of anything that actually makes their cellphone bill bigger, the advantage of Boku is that it has massive worldwide coverage, via partnerships with carriers in more than 60 countries. Boku even allow users with prepaid phone cards and accounts (pretty much the standard in Third World countries) to pay for goods and services via mobile transfers. If you're marketing around the world, Boku is a strong competitor. Boku is moving aggressively to line up deals with carriers in the United States; it signed an agreement with

Verizon, using the BilltoMobile service, to add carrier billing (although it's also working on direct integration with the giant mobile phone company).

However, the disadvantage to Boku is similarly large. Although credit card companies take between 2 and 6 percent of the transaction as their fee, Boku and the carriers carve out 35 percent. They claim that because the conversion rate for transactions with Boku is 60 percent compared with 7 percent for credit-card transactions, vendors will actually come out ahead. This figure is hotly disputed by credit card companies.

Setting Up an M-Commerce Site with PayPal and Google Checkout

In this section, we guide you step by step through the process of setting up m-commerce with popular and easy-to-use services. You begin with the simplest option — adding Buy buttons with the popular PayPal service. You also discover how to create a basic shopping cart with Google Checkout. We then guide you through the process of adding your Buy button or shopping cart to your mobile website by using Dreamweaver and WordPress.

Both Google Checkout and PayPal offer simple Buy buttons, as well as shopping cart features, making it easy for anyone to sell products on a website with no upfront costs and a competitive transaction fee. Why would you choose Google over PayPal or vice versa? Two key differences: Google has a nicer interface design, but it doesn't support as many foreign currencies as PayPal. The PayPal interface is a bit clunky: Every time users add products to their shopping carts, they're sent off to the PayPal site and have to navigate back to your site to add more products. However, on the positive side, you can send products to more countries by using PayPal.

Creating a simple PayPal Buy button

The simplest and quickest option if you want to sell only a few products or services on your website is to create a PayPal button for each item you want to sell. (See Figure 10-9.)

To add PayPal buttons to your web pages, follow these steps:

1. **Open your browser and navigate to** `www.paypal.com`.

   If you have a PayPal account, log in here. If you don't have an account, click the Sign Up link to establish an account and then follow PayPal's easy online instructions. Depending on what level of account you want to sign up for, you need a valid credit card and your merchant account information handy.

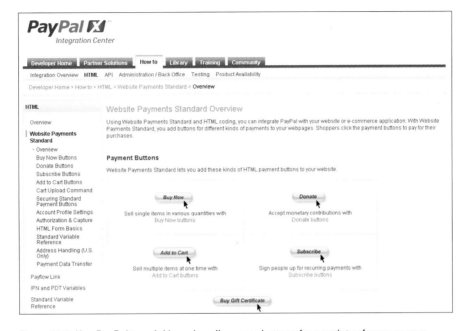

Figure 10-9: Use PayPal to quickly and easily create buttons for a variety of uses on your m-commerce site.

2. Click the Merchant Services tab.

A page opens with many links to all the various actions you can take with your PayPal account, as well as links to various resources to help you run your online business.

3. Click the Website Payments Standard link in the box on the left side of the page.

The Website Payments Standard: Overview page opens. (Refer to Figure 10-9.) This page allows you to choose from a couple other options, but for now, stick with creating a button for just one item at a time. PayPal also offers a Website Payments Pro service, but you must register for a business account with PayPal and use an integrated shopping cart or build one with PayPal's APIs.

4. Below the Sell Single Items heading, click the Create One Now link.

The Create PayPal Payment Button page opens with blank fields on which you type the description of your item.

5. Choose a button type and select Buy Now from the drop-down list.

You can also create a payment button to sell your services, set up a sub-scription or recurring billing process, collect a donation, or buy a gift certificate. In this example, we make a simple button to sell one item.

6. **Type the item name in the Item Name field.**

   The optional Item ID field allows you to enter a tracking code for the item you're selling, if you want to use that number in your spreadsheets or inventory programs.

7. **In the Shipping section, fill in the amount you charge for the shipping and handling of your item.**

8. **In the Tax section, fill in the amount of sales tax and other applicable taxes you charge.**

9. **Choose how you want to be notified when someone has bought your item.**

   You can be notified through your secure merchant account. If you select this option, your e-mail address doesn't appear in the button's HTML code. This may or may not be important to you. Some merchants want to appear as transparent and open as possible; others are afraid of having their e-mail inboxes overflow with spam.

   If you choose to use your PayPal e-mail address, you receive a notification in your e-mail inbox every time someone buys something from you with this PayPal button.

10. **Click the Create Button button.**

    A page labeled You've Created Your Button opens. In a panel in the middle of the page is the code for your PayPal button. Don't worry that the code looks like a lot of gobbledygook. You don't have to type this in anywhere.

11. **Click the Select Code button to select the button code.**

    The code is highlighted.

12. **Press Ctrl+C (on a Mac, Command+C) to copy the code.**

    You aren't done yet. . . .

13. **Add the code to your web page.**

    Depending on what you use to create your website, skip to the section "Adding a shopping cart to WordPress," or "Adding a shopping cart with Dreamweaver," later in this chapter. Start with Step 1 in each section.

Creating a simple shopping cart with Google Checkout

Because so many people already use Gmail, Google Docs, or some other web-based Google product, Google Checkout (shown in Figure 10-10) is a popular and trusted solution for adding m-commerce to your site. We've tested the shopping cart features, and they work great on the iPhone and iPad. If you already have a Google account, you're halfway there. Also, Google Checkout has a special integration with Google AdSense, so you can easily advertise your products.

Figure 10-10: Google Checkout lets you sell items with multiple options.

Make sure that you have handy basic information about your products before you proceed further. You need to know the names of your items, their prices, what options are available (size, color, weight, materials, and so on), and the URL where the picture of that item appears on your website. When you have that info, follow these steps:

1. **Open your browser and navigate to** `http://checkout.google.com/sell`.

   The sign-in page opens.

2. **Type your Google e-mail address and password.**

   If you've used Gmail, your username may already appear; if so, just type your password.

3. **Click the Sign In button and then follow the steps to either use an existing account or create a new one.**

   The Google Checkout page opens.

4. **Click the Tools tab.**

   The Integrate Your Website with Google Checkout page opens.

5. **In the Google Checkout sign-in screen, enter your e-mail address and password and then click the Sign In and Continue button.**

   The Tell Us about Your Business page opens. One of the somewhat annoying tics of Google Checkout is that it prompts you to enter your username and password at every turn. You may be prompted during several steps along the way to re-enter this information. Some of that is because Google times-out of the sessions with Google Checkout to prevent you from leaving the screen open on your computer when you walk away from it and allowing someone else to quickly drain your accounts or hijack your site.

6. **Type the contact information, public contact information, and financial information for your business into the boxes provided on the page.**

7. **Scroll down to the bottom of the page and select the I Agree to the Terms of Service check box.**

   The Signup Complete page opens.

   Note: Read through the Terms of Service. You must agree to them if you want to continue and use the service.

8. **Click the Google Checkout Shopping Cart link on the right side of the page.**

   A page opens (refer to Figure 10-10) with fields for you to enter the details of your product.

9. **Choose from the following product types:**

   - *Simple* means that there's only one product, with no other options or prices, such as an antique vase.

   - *With Multiple Options* enables you to let your customers choose multiple options that are all the same price for a product, such as a T-shirt that can be white, blue, or black.

   - *With Multiple Prices* enables you to take a basic item and charge different prices, depending on the options that the customer chooses.

10. **Enter a product name in the Title field.**

11. **(Optional) Enter the URL where the image of your product appears on your website.**

Adding the image's URL causes a small thumbnail of the item to appear next to the item title and price in the shopping cart when your customer clicks to purchase it. Because this is just a little extra flourish, don't feel like you have to do this if it becomes difficult or time-consuming.

> *a. To get the URL, navigate to where the item appears on your site and then right-click (on a Mac, Command+click) the photo of the item.*
>
> A menu opens with options that allow you to do many things with the photo.
>
> *b. Select Copy Image Location from the drop-down list and then navigate back to the Google Checkout page.*
>
> *c. Click in the Image URL field and press Ctrl+V (on a Mac, Command+V) to paste the image URL into the field.*

12. **(Optional) Enter the options in the fields next to the words Option 1 and Option 2.**

    The default fields are Small and Large, but you can type whatever you want. If you have many options for the item, click the Add an Option link and keep typing until all the sizes, colors, time lengths, or whatever other variables your item has are covered.

13. **Enter the price.**

    Next to each option is a field for the price associated with that option. Click the fields and then type the prices.

14. **Test your changes in the Preview box.**

    You can see what your shopping cart will look like by clicking the buttons in the Preview box. If you spot an error, go back through the previous steps and re-enter the correct information.

15. **When you have the description the way you want it, select the Yes, I Have Configured My Account to Accept Unsigned Shopping Carts check box and be sure to configure your account at some point.**

    If you haven't yet configured your account, you can return and do it later; just be sure to select the check box here.

    Because the Google Checkout shopping cart works entirely in the web browser, a visitor to your site can alter the pricing in Google Checkout when placing an order. You can prevent this problem if you complete the process of registering for a digitally signed shopping cart — though the steps are subject to frequent updates. To be sure that you're following the correct procedure, we recommend following the instructions at

```
http://code.google.com/apis/checkout/articles/Posting_
         Signed_Shopping_Cart.html
```

The simplest solution, and the one we recommend if you're just getting started, is to use an unsigned shopping cart and monitor the orders that come in to ensure that customers aren't doing anything shady. According to Google, the orders are secure —you just can't prevent customers from altering the pricing and total sales values when placing orders.

To use the Google Checkout service and connect it to your bank account, you must verify to Google that you understand and agree to use an unsigned shopping cart:

  a. *Click the Settings tab and then click the Integration link on the left side of the page.*

  b. *Deselect the My Company Will Only Post Digitally Signed Carts check box and then click the Save button.*

16. **To generate the code to add to your web page, click the Create Button Code button.**

A page opens with two boxes of code generated by Google, as shown in Figure 10-11. The top box contains the code that needs to be copied into your page where you want the button to appear.

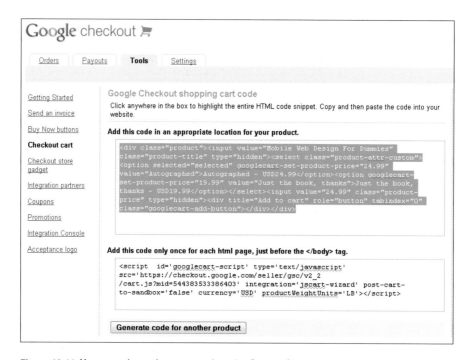

Figure 10-11: You copy the code generated on the Google Checkout site and paste it into the code on your own site.

17. Select the code and press Ctrl+C (on a Mac, Command+C).

The next step depends on whether you sell your items from a blog, such as WordPress, or from a static web page that you've designed with a program, such as Dreamweaver. The bottom box contains the code that creates the cart; it needs to be pasted into the bottom of each HTML page, which we address in the two following sections. (In the sections that follow, you find instructions for adding code to your site using WordPress and Dreamweaver.)

18. Repeat these steps for each item in your store.

Adding a shopping cart to WordPress

Many site owners are migrating away from having a collection of static pages or using expensive, custom-made content management systems. Instead, they're opting for open-source solutions like WordPress. Yes, WordPress started as a free blogging-software solution; however, its widespread use has spurred legions of developers around the world to customize its source code to make it do all sorts of wonderful things.

When you use WordPress for your shopping cart, you need to know the pros and cons:

- ✔ **Pro:** WordPress allows a site owner to quickly and easily update the site's content; as the saying goes, "If you can type an e-mail, you can write a blog post." Adding the shopping cart buttons you create in the previous two sections to a WordPress blog is as easy as cutting and pasting.

- ✔ **Con:** Adjusting the look and functionality of a WordPress site can be tricky and requires expert knowledge of the programming language PHP.

To copy and paste button code into a WordPress blog post, follow the steps here. (If you use another CMS, such as Joomla!, Drupal, Movable Type, or Blogger, you can still use the basic concepts explained here to make the buttons show up next to your items.)

1. Open a new tab in your browser and navigate to your blog's Dashboard.

This is the page where you compose new posts, control which widgets appear in your sidebars, or adjust your site's theme.

2. In the Posts heading, click the Posts link.

3. Scroll until you find the post containing the item you want to sell, and either the PayPal button or Google shopping cart you just created.

When you run your mouse pointer over the title of the post, a menu appears with the options for editing that post.

4. Click the Edit link.

The post opens in the familiar window that you use to type text and upload photos.

5. In the upper right corner of the editing window, click the HTML tab.

In the editing window, the text changes to the code view of the blog post.

6. Click in your post where you want to insert the button for the item you want to sell and then press Ctrl+V (on a Mac, Command+V) to paste in the code for the button.

This is the code you copied in Step 12 (for the PayPal button) or Step 17 (for the Google Shopping Cart) in earlier sections. See Figure 10-12 for an example of what inserting this code looks like.

7. Click the Visual tab to see where the button appears in your post.

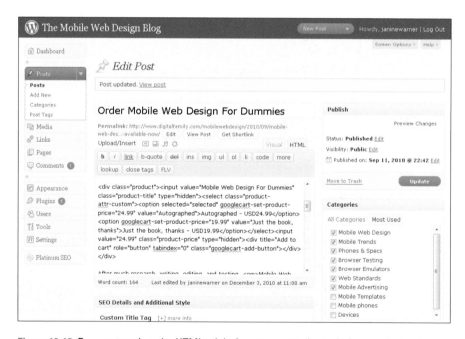

Figure 10-12: Be sure to select the HTML tab before you paste the code for your button into your WordPress post.

8. **If you don't like the button's placement, switch to HTML view, delete the button code from where you've placed it, and then repeat Step 6 to put it in the new location.**

9. **When you have the button where you want it to appear, click the Publish button on the right to publish the page.**

   If you're editing an existing page, the Publish button changes to an Update button.

10. **(For Google Checkout) Click to return to the tab in your browser where you got the code you just placed in the blog post.**

    This is the page where you got the code for your shopping cart. You're going to have to get one more piece of code to make this work in your WordPress blog.

11. **Select the code in the bottom box on the page and press Ctrl+C (on a Mac, Command+C); click to return to the tab where your WordPress blog's Dashboard is still open in your browser.**

    The bottom box is the one with the heading that reads "Add this code only once for each html page, just before the </body> tag."

12. **In the Appearance panel on the left side of your Dashboard, click the Editor link.**

    The Edit Themes page opens in your browser. In the middle panel is the code for your blog. On the right are the various templates controlling how the elements of your blog (such as the header, the sidebar, or the comments) appear.

13. **On the right side of the page, click the Footer link.**

    The PHP code for your blog's footer appears in the middle panel.

14. **Scroll until you see the </body> code and then click the line above and press Enter (on a Mac, press Return).**

15. **Press Ctrl+V (on a Mac, Command+V) to paste the code here.**

    This code enables every page on your blog to handle the buttons and Google Checkout shopping cart. This piece of code has your Merchant ID number in it and the currency you use.

16. **Click the Update File button and then test your work by clicking the name of your WordPress blog at the top of the Dashboard page.**

    Test how well your button works by going through the order process — right up to placing an order to yourself from your site.

Adding a shopping cart with Dreamweaver

If you sell your merchandise through a static site, insert the button(s) by using whatever tool you used to construct the site. In the example here, we show you how to use Dreamweaver, the industry-standard tool used to create custom websites. To insert a button with Dreamweaver, follow these steps:

1. **Open the page of the item using Dreamweaver and then click the Split button at the top of the workspace.**

   This opens the dual-panel view, where you see the underlying code and the page's design.

2. **Click the page where you want the button to appear and then press Ctrl+V (on Mac, Command+V) to paste the code for the button into your page.**

   Again, this is the code that you copied in Step 12 (for the PayPal button) or Step 17 (for the Google Shopping Cart) earlier in this chapter.

3. **Return to the tab in your browser where you created the shopping cart code, and then select and copy the code in the lower panel.**

   Press Ctrl+C (on a Mac, Command+C) to copy the code.

4. **Return to Dreamweaver, scroll to the bottom of your page, and find the `</body>` tag.**

5. **Click just above this tag and press Ctrl+V (on Mac, Command+V) to insert the code.**

   This code needs to be added to each HTML page where the shopping cart button appears. (See Figure 10-13 for an example of what inserting the code in Dreamweaver will look like.) If you have multiple pages, put this code at the bottom of each page. It's helpful to use Split view when you paste in the code for your button, so that you can control exactly where it's placed among other page elements and gain a sense of how it fits into the rest of your page design.

   If, however, you have multiple items on one HTML page, return to your browser to generate the other buttons for the other items on your page.

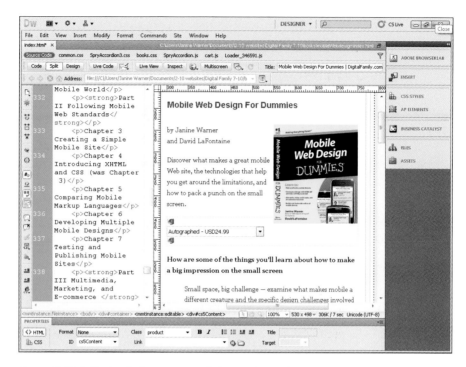

Figure 10-13: Split view in Dreamweaver helps you insert the code for the shopping cart.

Part IV
Publishing Your Site

The 5th Wave   By Rich Tennant

"Other than this little glitch with the landscape view, I really love my iPad."

efore you publish a site for the iPhone or iPad, this part will help you make sure you've tested everything thoroughly. In Chapter 11, you discover great places to validate your code and some of the best Dreamweaver features for testing links and other aspects of your site. You also find out how to use Dreamweaver's built-in FTP features, as well as stand-alone FTP tools. In Chapter 12, you find tips for optimizing your designs so that they load quickly and find an introduction to device detection and mobile switchers to make sure your visitors find the right version of your website. In Chapter 13, we cover how to make a blog work well on an iPhone or iPad by using some of the free themes and extensions available for Joomla! and WordPress.

iPhone not to scale

11

Testing and Publishing Your Designs

In This Chapter

▶ Comparing testing options

▶ Testing with computer web browsers

▶ Using web-based testing services

▶ Validating HTML and CSS code online

▶ Creating a mobile testing plan

▶ Using the Dreamweaver testing features

▶ Publishing a mobile website

"**T**esting, 1, 2, 3. Testing, 1, 2, 3." If you've ever witnessed a sound system being set up, you've probably heard these words spoken into a microphone. Most people realize that you shouldn't start a concert or a speech, or even make a toast at a wedding, without making sure the microphone works.

If only it were as easy to test the design of a website.

The biggest challenge for most designers who create sites for the World Wide Web is having to test it in many different web browsers and on different operating systems and devices. If you're worried only about testing the iPad/iPhone, you're a lucky web designer.

One huge advantage of focusing on the iPad/iPhone as you design a website is that you can relatively easily test your designs. Even if you have only the desktop version of Safari (available on both the Mac and Windows operating systems), you can adequately approximate the way your website will display on an iPhone or iPad.

Of course, the best way to test your designs is to use a physical iPad or iPhone device, but if you don't have one (or you don't have every version of these devices), the emulators and other services in this chapter can help.

This chapter explains several testing methods, ranging from free and open source options to an expensive, complex device farms, such as the one offered by Device Anywhere, which features an array of mobile devices, activated data plans and connections that you can control using a desktop computer and a web browser to form a complete picture of what your website looks like on the mobile web. We also introduce you to testing tools that help ensure that your code is clean and error free.

If you're working on a relatively small site (fewer than 25 pages or so), a simple testing plan may be all you need, but if you're building a large site or a site with many interactive features, databases, and advanced programming, you may need to develop a plan for how you will test before, during, and after you build your site. On a site with complex interactive features — such as the ability of users to upload their Flicker photos from their computers or cellphones — you must do rigorous testing on the iPhone and iPad (shown in Figure 11-1) as well as on many other devices.

You find in this chapter some suggestions for how to conduct a variety of different tests for small and large sites. At the end of this chapter, you find tips for publishing your mobile web pages, using FTP programs, and using the built-in testing and FTP features of the popular web design program Adobe Dreamweaver.

The testing and validating services featured in this chapter can help you test your pages on more than just the iPhone and iPad, but if you face the ultimate challenge of the web — designing for the oldest browsers and low-end mobile devices, you have to take quite a different approach to development and testing than you find in this book. This book talks about designing for the high end of the mobile web, the iPhone and iPad, and the most recent web browsers on desktop computers. If you're looking for a guide to help you design for a wide range of mobile phones, pick up a copy of *Mobile Web Design For Dummies,* written by Janine Warner and David LaFontaine.

Figure 11-1: Interactive websites, such as Flickr.com, test different versions of their sites for the iPhone, the iPad, and other devices.

Comparing Site Testing Solutions

The most important principle to understand when testing your website can be summed up in one well-worn aphorism: "In theory, there is no difference between theory and practice — but in practice, there is." And so it is with the mobile web. Although simulators and emulators and the numerous testing services we describe in this chapter *approximate* how your designs will look, you can never fully replicate the quirks of using a real iPhone or iPad over a Wi-Fi or mobile connection, even with the best mobile testing tools on your desktop computer.

Here are five ways you can test your mobile sites (you find more detailed descriptions of each of option in the sections that follow):

⮑ **View your site in every version of the iPhone or iPad:** In an ideal world, you have a desk full of devices, all connected to the Internet and ready to test every page on your website thoroughly.

- **Use the Safari browser on a computer to view your pages:** The next best thing to Safari on the iOS is Safari on the Mac operating system. You can also download the Windows version of Safari to test designs on your computer — a handy way to do preliminary testing as you develop on your computer.

- **Browse your site in online mobile simulators:** A few websites offer mobile emulators. These are the simplest but most limited options for testing how websites will appear on mobile devices. We don't recommend them, and we explain why in the later sidebar "The limitations of online mobile simulators."

  The difference between a mobile emulator and a mobile simulator is that a *simulator* is an application that tries to re-create the display of the device in a manner similar to how it would appear on a physical device. In contrast, an *emulator* is a program built to display web pages just as the physical device would display by executing code in the same, not similar, way.

- **Download and install mobile emulators to test on your local computer:** Many device manufacturers, including Apple, offer emulators of their devices, as well as more complete software development kits (SDKs) that can be downloaded and installed on Windows and Macintosh computers.

- **Use more advanced options:** It's difficult to categorize all the testing options in the ever-changing world of mobile web design, so we lump several services into this category of high-end options (including DeviceAnywhere, which lets you remotely control hundreds of mobile devices around the world).

Testing with the iPhone and iPad

Every mobile designer worth his salt admits that you can do only so much with tools on a desktop computer to simulate what users do on a live iPhone, iPad, or iPod touch. The following list describes only some of the problems that might not show up on your computer but can arise when your web designs are viewed on a portable iOS device:

- Your color scheme is unreadable under harsh daylight conditions.

- Tapping your navigation links is frustrating, or even impossible, given the limited interface options of a touchscreen device. (Remember that thicker fingers need more room to tap.)

- Having your highly interactive page open may drain the battery more quickly.

You can't know these things sitting in a comfy chair in a safe, air-conditioned office with all the power of your desktop computer and the interface options of a mouse and keyboard.

True mobile gurus say that the best option is to have shelves, drawers, or closets overflowing with testing units, but most settle for a representative sampling of the most common devices. If you don't have the resources to keep all versions of the iPhone and iPad on hand for testing, consider these options:

- ✔ **Use the "friends and family" plan.** Ask all your friends and family members what kinds of phones they use, and then enlist them as testers for your site or sites.

- ✔ **Use social networks.** The next stage in assembling an ad hoc mobile testing network is to start reaching out to people on social networking sites, such as Facebook, Twitter, MySpace, and LinkedIn. You can send messages to your connections in the networks and ask people to visit your site and describe any problems they see.

- ✔ **Join professional associations.** Join Mobile Monday (`www.mobile monday.net`) or any other group of web designers, and attend (or organize) gatherings where you get together and test each other's sites.

- ✔ **Visit an Apple Store in person.** Make frequent trips to the Apple Store, but remember that it generally has only the latest devices and isn't able to help if you want to ensure your designs work in the iPhone 1.0.

Using developer tools in Safari on iOS

Enabling the Debug Console in Safari on iPhone, iPod touch, or iPad allows you to see HTML, CSS, and JavaScript errors directly in the device. This is the most reliable way to ensure that you have no surprise issues to resolve when you do your final testing.

To enable the Debug Console in Safari, follow these instructions.

1. **Tap the Settings icon on the iPhone or iPad desktop.**

   The Settings screen opens.

2. **Tap to choose Safari from the list of software available on your device (see Figure 11-2).**

Figure 11-2: The Settings screen on the iPhone 4.

The Safari Settings screen opens, as shown in Figure 11-3.

3. **Scroll to the bottom of the screen and then tap Developer (see Figure 11-3).**

The Developer screen appears.

4. **Touch the On button to activate the Debug Console (see Figure 11-4).**

After the Debug Console is enabled, Safari reports any errors it encounters when accessing a website. At the top of every web page, just under the address bar, the Debug Console reports any HTML, JavaScript, or CSS errors.

 Long log entries are now truncated to fit the space available in the Debug Console. For best results, when using the Debug Console to track JavaScript log events in Safari on iPhone or iPod touch, keep your log entries short.

Figure 11-3: The Safari Settings screen.

Testing with a Browser on a Computer

Sometimes it's easier to work with what you have. If you already have Safari or Chrome installed on your computer, you're in luck. They render mobile sites similarly to how they would be rendered on an iOS device, and they have development tools built in that can help you troubleshoot your code.

Testing iPhone and iPad designs with the Safari web browser on a computer

The closest you can come to having Safari on an iPhone or iPad is Safari on a computer. It has a few notable differences, including the larger screen size that most people use on computers and the fact that Flash works in Safari on a Mac or Windows computer but not on an iOS device.

Figure 11-4: The Developer Debug Console screen.

The Safari web browser, shown in Figure 11-5, is available for free for both Windows and Macintosh computers from the Apple Safari website, also shown in Figure 11-5. Safari is definitely the best browser to use when testing designs for the iPhone or iPad on a desktop computer. You can download Safari by visiting www.apple.com/safari/download.

Figure 11-5: You can download the Safari web browser for Mac or Windows computers.

The desktop computer version of Safari is different from Safari on your iPhone and iPad. Sites don't always have the same displays across all devices and operating systems, which is why you must test your pages in a variety of ways, and why being able to change the user agent, covered in the next section, can come in handy.

Changing the Safari user agent to view pages the way they're sent to the iPhone/iPad or another device

A *user agent* is a snippet of text sent from a web browser to a web server to inform the server which version and type of device, operating system, and browser are being used to visit a website. We like to think of it as a virtual introduction. First impressions are important on the Internet, which is why sending the right user agent is one of the biggest challenges of testing mobile sites on a desktop or laptop computer.

Many mobile-optimized websites use device detection to identify visitors, and content adaption to deliver the best version of the site to each device. (Find out more about how this topic works in Chapter 12.) What matters when you're testing a website is that if the device detection script on a server recognizes that you're using a browser on a computer, it doesn't show you the phone version.

That's where user agent switching enters the picture. Safari includes special features that make it possible to change the user agent.

 If you're working on a site with a special URL for the mobile version of your site, or you know the specific mobile URL of a site, you can sometimes open the mobile version without changing the user agent. (For a list of common mobile URLs, such as www.bbc.com/mobile, see the later section "What is the best mobile URL?")

To activate the User Agent Switcher, in Safari, follow these steps:

1. **Click on the Gear shift icon, shown in the top right corner of the Safari web browser, in Figure 11-6, to open the General Menu.**

2. **Choose Preferences, also shown in 11-6.**

3. **Click to select the check box labeled Show Develop Menu in Menu Bar. (The cursor is pointing to it at the bottom of Figure 11-7.)**

   The Develop menu option is added to the top menu bar (see Figure 11-8).

Figure 11-6: You can change the user agent in the Developer settings in the Safari web browser.

 If you don't see the menu at the top of the Safari web browser, be sure to select the Show Menu Bar option from the general menu (refer to Figure 11-6). When this option is selected, the name changes to Hide Menu Bar and the menu is visible at the top of the browser, as shown in Figure 11-8.

Figure 11-7: To access the user agent switcher in Safari, select the bottom most check box in the Preferences Advanced Settings.

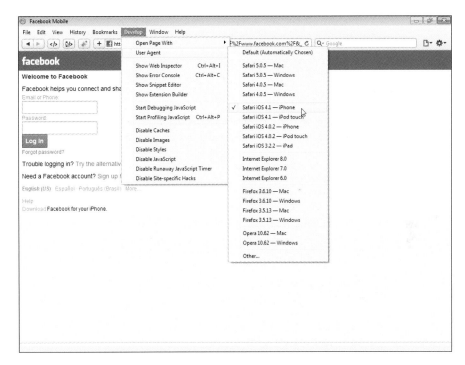

Figure 11-8: The Develop menu in Safari includes a user agent, complete with iPhone and iPad profiles.

4. **Click the Develop menu option and select User Agent⇨*user agent* to open a list of profiles (refer to Figure 11-8).**

5. **Open any web page to see how it displays with the selected profile.**

In Figure 11-8, the iPhone profile is selected and the Facebook web page displays in a narrow column aligned to the left — the version of the page that's optimized for the iPhone. In Figure 11-9, you see how to resize the browser window in combination with the user agent to create a general idea of how the page will display on an iPhone.

Enhancing Safari's testing features with extensions

The Safari Extensions Gallery has program add-ons that can help you test your iPhone/iPad site more accurately on your desktop. In the following list, we review our favorite Safari extensions for iPhone/iPad web testing:

✔ **ReSize Me** adds a toolbar that automatically resizes the Safari browser window to six preset sizes, including 640 x 480 and 1024 x 768. Unfortunately, ReSize Me doesn't yet support the smaller 320 x 480 size of the iPhone. (We hope that it's added soon, and you can always resize the window yourself in the meantime.)

Combine the User Agent Switcher with Resize Me to get a good idea of how a site will look on a variety of different mobile devices using Safari on a desktop computer.

✔ **SafariSource:** Using the Safari Source extension, you can view the source code behind any page on the web with the benefits of line numbers and color syntax highlighting. You can even open the source code in a new tab with this plugin. Adding colors and line numbers makes it easier to find errors and conflicts in your code.

Figure 11-9: The iPhone version of the Facebook web page, displayed in Safari on Windows 7 with the window resized.

✔ **Firebug Lite:** If you're a veteran web designer, you probably already have the Firebug extension. In case you don't have it, it's a powerful set of tools for viewing and debugging HTML, CSS, and JavaScript. With this extension installed, you can easily edit the code for any page you're viewing in the browser — a helpful way to test and learn.

✔ **Unicorn:** The Unicorn extension adds the W3C validators for CSS and HTML to the Safari web browser. Although you can test any web page online with the online validators from the W3C (covered in "Testing Your Site Code with the W3C Tools," later in this chapter), this extension makes the process faster and easier.

Most Safari extensions are free, although some developers ask that you donate money if you like how they work. We encourage you to support their efforts.

Installing Safari extensions

Safari extensions are super simple to add to your browser. You don't even have to download them before you install them, as you do with Firefox. With Safari, follow these simple steps to install an extension:

1. **Visit the Safari Extensions Gallery at `http://extensions.apple.com`.**

2. **Find the extension you want.**

   You can find any extension listed in the preceding section by typing its name in the Search field on the Safari Extensions Gallery page or by clicking the Developer link to display all the extensions shown in Figure 11-10.

Figure 11-10: You can install extensions on the Safari web browser with a simple click of a button (and you don't even have to restart Safari).

3. **Click the Install Now button (refer to the bottom of Figure 11-4).**

   You don't even have to restart Safari to make the extension active. After an extension is installed, the blue Install Now button (shown in Figure 11-10, below the Alexa traffic statistics), changes to the green Installed icon (shown below the Better Source extension).

Testing with the Chrome web browser

In the Chrome web browser, you can launch the developer tools by clicking the Wrench icon in the top right corner of the browser window and choosing Tools⇨Developer Tools or by choosing the key command Control+Shift+I in Windows or Command+Option+I on the Mac (see Figure 11-11).

Figure 11-11: You can open the developer tools from the Tools menu.

The Developer Tools window in Chrome (shown in Figure 11-12) has many tools to help you find detailed information about any page you open in the browser. Using the Elements panel, shown in Figure 11-12, you can view the source HTML or CSS styles, browse the Document Object Model, and manipulate each of them in real time. After the window is open, you can leave it connected to the main browser or allow it to float independently.

Figure 11-12: The Developer Tools window opens in the Chrome web browser and displays the page's HTML and CSS.

The limitations of online mobile simulators

Although they seem to offer the simplest option for testing mobile web designs, most simulators that work within a web browser suffer from two major limitations:

✔ **They run on your computer:** Your computer almost certainly has a much faster processor and many other capabilities you don't find on mobile phones.

✔ **They display desktop, rather than mobile, versions of a site:** Unless you're using a

User Agent Switcher, as described earlier in this chapter, all you're doing is opening the desktop version of a site in a small window within a web browser.

Indeed, in our most recent testing of the sites `www.iphonetester.com` and `www.testiphone.com`, we found that they were almost useless because of their inability to properly render pages as an iPhone. We no longer recommend either of these services.

The Resources panel shows resources that have been loaded, such as HTML, CSS, JavaScript, Images, Fonts, HTML5 Databases, and other elements related to a web page. The interactive panel makes it possible for you to make changes to the code and see their impact (without changing the live web page because the tools are only temporarily altering the code that's cached in the browser.)

The developer tools include several tabs, including the Network panel, which shows the components a page is requesting from web servers, the length of requests, and the bandwidth that's required. The Scripts panel shows a list of scripts requested by the page and comes with a full-featured script debugger.

Using Mobile Emulators and SDKs

You can preview mobile designs and get a good idea of how they will look in many different mobile devices by using mobile *emulators*.

Although it takes time and effort to download, install, and use mobile emulators and SDKs, these tools generally do a better job of showing you how a mobile device will work on a desktop computer than do most of the simulators you find on the web. These emulator tools are designed for programmers creating applications for mobile devices. However, web designers may also find these tools useful.

Mobile emulators are designed to work the way the physical device would work, and they generally work better than the mobile simulators covered in the nearby sidebar "The limitations of online mobile simulators."

- ✔ **iPhone:** You can download the SDKs, simulators, and other support tools for free from the iOS Developer Center at `http://developer.apple.com`.

- ✔ **Android:** Although the focus of this book is the iPhone and iPad, most sites created to work well in the Apple iOS also work well on cellphones and tablets that run on the Google Android operating system. Just reaching the iPhone and Android audience will gain you a large share of the mobile web. Download the Android SDK, which includes a mobile device emulator, by visiting `http://developer.android.com`.

Testing with High-End Online Services

If you have the money and testing your mobile website across a wide variety of devices is critical, the high-end services may be worth the cost.

DeviceAnywhere

Our favorite option for testing mobile designs on a wide variety of devices using a desktop computer, DeviceAnywhere (`www.deviceanywhere.com`) lets you access more than 1,500 handsets and test them as they would perform on carriers in the United States, Canada, England, Spain, Germany, France, and Brazil.

The electronic innards of all the devices are wired into long racks connected to the Internet; when you sign up for the service, you can choose a device (see Figure 11-13 for a glimpse at available devices) and then use your computer mouse and keyboard to manipulate it. For example, you can type a URL into a browser on any phone directly to see how it will display in that phone's web browser, on its operating system, as it should be delivered by the carrier you selected. You can also click a simulated keypad to send a Short Message Service (SMS, or *text*) message, and even connect a microphone and speaker to your computer to test audio-related features, such as listening to music or using the microphone to leave a short voice message.

Using DeviceAnywhere works as described in this list:

1. Sign up for an account and then download and install the special software on your hard drive.

2. After you launch the software, you access the DeviceAnywhere service over the Internet.

3. Scroll a list of available phones (refer to Figure 11-13). Sometimes, devices are busy or out of commission, but after testing extensively, we found the service to be remarkably reliable, especially considering the wide range of devices it supports.

4. When you find a device you want to use, right-click (Command-click on the Mac) to acquire and open the device.

5. After a device opens on your screen, you can use your mouse to click the buttons on the image of the phone to interact as though you were pressing the keys on the phone's keypad.

   It can take a little trial-and-error to figure out how to use some devices, especially limited-feature phones that you may never have used, but DeviceAnywhere includes a few special tools to help you enter URLs and interact with each phone.

6. Disconnect the device when you're done testing on it.

   The quickest way to "burn" your minutes is to get carried away with the cornucopia of devices that are available to play with at DeviceAnywhere. Always right-click (on a Mac, Command-click) to disconnect the device as soon as you're done testing.

Figure 11-13: DeviceAnywhere shows the list of available devices and what they look like when you have your website loaded.

The first three hours of testing are free (albeit limited to eight of the most popular devices), but after that, the testing packages can get expensive. The time spent testing the devices is measured in 6-minute (one-tenth of an hour) increments, and the devices have a built-in failsafe mechanism that shuts them down and disconnects you if you forget and leave one running in the background for 30 minutes. Additional testing hours cost about $16 per hour, with package deals reducing the cost.

Keynote

Keynote (www.keynote.com) offers a high-end service that includes testing your mobile websites, applications, and other services for you. Keynote, shown in Figure 11-14, serves big companies and is a premium (by that, we mean not cheap) service that provides testing and monitoring using real devices on a broad range of mobile carriers all over the world.

Figure 11-14: Keynote provides high-end mobile testing and monitoring services.

If you need the highest level of testing for your site, Keynote not only tests on many devices but also performs load testing over many different operator networks, one of the best ways to ensure that your site works well on a broad range of mobile devices. If you can justify the expense, the best way to test the speed and other capabilities of a website is by using Keynote.

Testing Your Code with the W3C Tools

Testing your web designs with the World Wide Web Consortium (W3C) validation tools has always been a good idea, but it's even more important for mobile web design. Desktop web browsers, including Internet Explorer, Firefox, and Chrome, are surprisingly forgiving of common errors in HTML code. Mobile web browsers are not. That's because mobile web browsers are much smaller applications than their desktop counterparts and lack the capacity to handle even the most common mistakes in coding.

The W3C, long revered for its work on developing and encouraging the use of standards on the web, offers the new mobileOK Checker, shown in Figure 11-15, which checks for known issues on mobile phones.

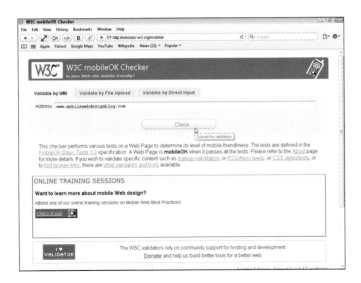

Figure 11-15: The W3C online mobileOK Checker.

Here's how it works:

1. **Point your browser to** `http://validator.w3.org/mobile`.

2. **Enter the URL of the site you want to test into the Address box on the Validate by URL tab.**

3. **Click the Check button.**

   The tester reviews your site, checking your code for known conflicts and errors, and then returns a report on what you need to do to clean up your site.

Compressing code for faster download speeds

If you want your site to download as fast as possible, it's good practice to optimize it by compressing it and removing extra spaces. The more compressed your code, the faster it will download, which is especially important to anyone using a slow mobile connection.

You can get the best of both worlds by using a CSS minification compressor such as YUI. The Java version can be run on your computer, and

you can get it from `http://developer.yahoo.com/yui/compressor`.

If you prefer, you can use an online version and compress code by entering the URL of any page into `http://refresh-sf.com/yui`. As a bonus, YUI also compresses JavaScript. On the YUI site, you see what compressed CSS code looks like with all the spaces removed.

While you're at it, test the markup language on your site at `http://validator.w3.org` and then test the Cascading Style Sheets (CSS) on your site at `http://jigsaw.w3.org/css-validator`.

Your pages work better in web browsers when they're error free, and search engines like them better, too. By resolving errors before you publish a site, you help ensure that site visitors have a positive experience and don't abandon your site because of an unexpected error.

Creating a Mobile Testing Plan

Test early and test often — iterative (repetitive) testing is the key to developing a site quickly and with confidence that your resulting site will work well. If you're working on a small website, a little testing of your code and design display before you publish your pages may be all you need, but if you work on a large or highly complicated website, you may need to develop a more comprehensive testing plan. This section provides suggestions for creating a detailed testing plan, an important addition to any good project development plan (covered in Chapter 2).

We recommend seven types of testing before, during, and after you launch a website (we cover each type in more detail in the sections that follow):

- Preliminary testing
- Developmental testing
- Quality assurance testing
- Performance and nonfunctional testing
- Load testing to gauge site speed
- Regression testing after updates
- Usability testing

Preliminary testing

As you start developing a site, do some preliminary testing, to ensure that all the initial framework and design elements work before you add more complicated features.

When you want to try out a specific new feature or enhancement, good practice mandates testing it on a blank page before you start integrating it into a website. Testing a new feature on a page with nothing else on it enables you to check the functionality without interference from other elements on the site.

Preliminary testing can often be done well enough with Safari on a desktop computer or using an online emulator, but before you advance too far into the development (or rabbit hole) of your site, be sure to test the basic design and most important feature on a physical iPhone/iPad device, to ensure that it works as it should. (Find tips and suggestions for testing your designs on a computer in the section "Testing with a browser on a computer," earlier in this chapter.

Developmental testing

As you're developing a website, you need a quick way to test your pages regularly. Sometimes, it requires setting up a testing server on a remote site or on your own computer.

As you're developing a site, you can test your work using an emulator or, even more simply, by using the Safari web browser on the computer you're writing code on. Being able to test your pages in Safari on a Windows or Macintosh computer (covered in the section "Testing with a Browser on a Computer," earlier in this chapter) can save you from having to upload pages every time you make a change just to test them on your iPhone or iPad.

Quality assurance testing

Before you launch a new site, always fully test its design and functionality on the iPhone or iPad, to ensure that the site looks and works the way you think it should. Using a simulator is never a substitute for completing a final checklist on a physical device.

As part of your final test, we recommend that you complete these tasks:

- ✔ Review every page and test every function.
- ✔ Submit every form, look at every image, and click every link.
- ✔ Test the device indoors and outdoors, in both bright and dim lighting.
- ✔ Test in Portrait and Landscape modes.
- ✔ Test in the car (when you're a passenger) and on a bus or train. (Each environment provides a somewhat different perspective on the places and situations where visitors may view your content.)

✔ Test your site on older iPhone versions (as this book goes to press, versions 1, 2, and 3) and on the most recent iPhone to see how your site looks on older devices.

✔ Examine how your images and videos and other media types look on the faster iPad and higher-resolution iPhone 4.

Regression testing after updates

Every time you revise an existing web page, be sure to complete *regression testing,* in which you rerun earlier tests to ensure that your updates don't break functions that were previously working.

The amount of regression testing you should do depends on how complicated your site is and your estimation of the risk of adding defects to a site that was working previously.

A helpful approach to regression testing is to develop a series of tests of the most important features of your site and then run that same series of tests every time you update your site. As you further develop your site, maintain a running list of new features you add and include them in the checklist.

Performance and other nonfunctional testing

The term *nonfunctional* describes the type of testing required in order to measure the characteristics of systems and software that can be quantified on a varying scale, such as response times for performance testing.

Nonfunctional testing measures the way the system works, or performs. The goal of performance testing is to determine how well your server handles large amounts of traffic to your site. Performance and other types of nonfunctional testing are especially important if you

✔ Expect a lot of traffic to your site

✔ Use complex scripting or databases

✔ Use e-commerce to sell products or services on your site

✔ Include audio or video files, high-resolution images, or other types of large files

Load testing to gauge site speed

Load testing helps you gauge the impact of having many site visitors at one time, and services that help you do so are much easier to use than, say, coordinating all your neighbors to visit your site at 1:37 p.m. on a Thursday.

For example, Load Impact, at `http://loadimpact.com`, offers a free service that simulates as many as 50 users at a time visiting your site (see Figure 11-16). The service provides a quick measurement of how well your site would respond if 10, 20, 30, 40, and then 50 people simultaneously used their mobile phones to visit your site.

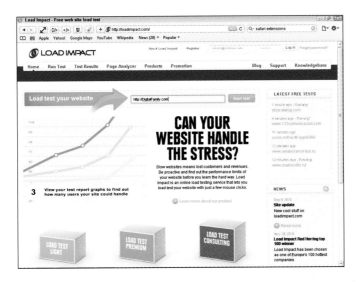

Figure 11-16: Using the online service Load Impact, you can test your site's ability to handle multiple simultaneous users.

While the test is running, you see what the 51st person would see by visiting the site with your iPhone or iPad.

If you're hosting your site on a good hosting company, the resulting curve should be flat, showing the same speed of response for at least 50 people. If you're expecting more than 50 people at any particular moment, you may want to pay for a more thorough test to ensure that everyone can see your site in a reasonable amount of time.

Usability testing

When investing a lot of time developing a site, you get to know it quite well — so well that you may overlook elements that are obvious to you. Usability testing tests a site by watching how actual users (other than you) use the site. Usability testing doesn't test users to determine how well they can use your site; it tests the site to see how well your visitors can use it.

Because everyone has different abilities and perspectives, you should perform usability tests on a minimum of five people. If three or more run into trouble with the same element, you know that you need to change your site to better accommodate your users. Test users who already have iPhones. That way, users who are unfamiliar with how to browse on an iPhone won't skew your results.

Start by asking a friend to review your site. If you have a deep site with a lot of functionality, you may want to ask your friend to talk out loud while reviewing so that you can understand what they are thinking.

The following tips can help you gather information about your site's usability as other people explore your site:

- **Using the finger pointing trick:** No, we don't mean finger pointing as in blaming someone else. This trick is useful when watching someone test your site: Ask the person to use their finger to point at what they're looking at while they make their way through the site. Adding a little finger-pointing to their running monologue will help you see the site through their eyes.

- **Assigning specific tasks:** Ask the user to accomplish a task that satisfies a goal of the site. If you have a blog site, for example, you may ask the person to make a comment on a post. To do this, state the task and then keep quiet — the hardest part of usability testing is not helping the user navigate the site — that would nullify the test!

- **Spying from a distance:** Sometimes, it's better to be out of view and ask a friend to test in a room alone, using a list of tasks you want them to try. In these cases, set up a discreet video camera to record what they say and do — just make sure that they know they're being recorded. (In many states, recording someone without their knowledge is illegal.) Even when people are aware of being videotaped, getting out of the room can help take the pressure off testers who may be influenced by your reactions when they get lost or when things don't work as well as you'd hoped. When you find things that don't work, don't take it personally — it's a great chance to make your project better.

Testing Your Code with Dreamweaver's Site Reporting Features

If you've used Dreamweaver to build your mobile website, you can check your work using the Dreamweaver Site Reporting features. It lets you create a variety of reports and even customize them to identify problems with external links, redundant and empty tags, untitled documents, and missing alternate text.

You can easily miss problems — especially when you work on a tight deadline — and common problems in web design are magnified on the mobile platform.

Follow these steps to produce a site report of your entire website:

1. **In the drop-down list in the top left corner of the Files panel, select the site you want to work on.**

   If you already have open the site you want to test in Dreamweaver, you can skip this step. *Note:* Your site appears in the Files panel list only if you've completed the site setup process. See "Setting up Dreamweaver's FTP features," later in this chapter, for more on this topic.

2. **Make sure any documents you have open in the Dreamweaver workspace are saved by choosing File⇨Save All.**

3. **Choose Site⇨Reports.**

   The Reports dialog box appears, as shown in Figure 11-17.

4. **In the Report On drop-down list, choose Entire Current Local Site.**

   We most commonly use this feature to test an entire site just before publishing it to the web, but you can choose to check only a single page by opening the page in Dreamweaver and then choosing Current Document in the Report On drop-down list. You can also run a report on selected files or on a

Figure 11-17: You can select any option, or all of them, in the Reports dialog box to run tests on your website.

   particular folder. If you choose Selected Files in Site, you must first click to select the pages you want to check in the Files panel.

5. **In the Select Reports section, select the check boxes for the reports you want.**

   You can select as many reports as you want.

6. **Click the Run button to create the report or reports.**

   If you haven't already done so, you may be prompted to save your file, set up your site, or select a folder.

   The Results panel appears, displaying a list of problems found on the site. To sort the list by category (such as filename, line number, or description), click the corresponding column heading.

Using a dedicated FTP program

If you prefer to use a dedicated FTP program rather than Dreamweaver's built-in features, you can download FTP programs for the Mac and PC at these web addresses:

- `http://fireftp.mozdev.org`: This nifty little add-on to Firefox is a useful alternative to Dreamweaver's FTP features. FireFTP is ideal for fixing problems when you're on the road and don't have Dreamweaver or don't want to use it to view the files on your server. This program can be added to any version of Firefox (for free).

- `http://filezilla-project.org`: The popular open source option FileZilla works on computers running the Windows, Mac, or Linux operating system.

- `www.ipswitch.com`: A popular FTP program for the PC, WS_FTP is so sophisticated (and popular) for the PC that many

web designers pay to use it; it also offers a free trial version.

- `www.cuteftp.com`: The popular Windows program CuteFTP can be downloaded from its website.

- `www.fetchsoftworks.com` and `www.panic.com/transmit`: If you use a Macintosh computer, popular options are Fetch, available for download at the former web address, and Transmit, available for download at the latter address.

- `http://cyberduck.ch`: Web designers working on the Mac platform are singling out for praise the freeware program Cyberduck because it handles FTP, SFTP, WebDAV, and Cloud files.

7. **Double-click any item in the Results panel to open the corresponding file in the document window.**

   The file opens, and the error is highlighted in the workspace.

   You can also right-click (Windows) or Control-click (Mac) any line in the report and choose More Info to find additional details about the specific error or condition.

8. **Use the Property inspector or another Dreamweaver feature to correct the identified problem and then save the file.**

For more on how to maintain a site and fix its design problems, consult a book on web design, such as *Dreamweaver CS5 For Dummies* (which Janine wrote).

Publishing a Website with Adobe Dreamweaver

After you create and test your website so that it's ready to publish on the web, you can use Dreamweaver's publishing tools to upload your site to your web server. Which features you use depends on the kind of web server you use. If you use a commercial service provider, you most likely need

Dreamweaver's FTP features, which we cover in detail in the following section. (If you prefer to use your own FTP program, see the earlier sidebar "Using a dedicated FTP program.")

You need information from your web hosting service, as described in the following list, before you can configure Dreamweaver's FTP features. Most service providers send this information in an e-mail message when you sign up for an account. If you don't have this information, request it from your service provider because it's unique to your account on your web hosting service. Here's what you need:

- **The FTP hostname:** A human-readable nickname used by the Internet to locate a particular server; for example, `ftp.domainname.com`.

- **The path to the web directory:** A path that looks similar to `/web/ htdocs/slightlyusedcats`. (The path is optional but highly recommended.)

- **Your FTP login or username:** Your personal username, which you created or which was assigned to you when you established your web hosting account.

- **Your FTP password:** You know this one (and if you don't, you can get it from your web hosting service).

- **Special instructions from your server:** Instructions indicating whether you need to use passive FTP or any other advanced settings covered in the following section, for example. Instructions vary from server to server, so ask your web hosting service. (If you're having trouble connecting and you aren't sure about these options, you can always experiment by selecting and deselecting the options to see whether a setting enables you to connect.)

Setting up Dreamweaver's FTP features

After you gather your FTP information, you're ready to set up Dreamweaver's FTP publishing features. This process can seem daunting and often takes a few tries to get right, but the good news is that you have to do it only once. (Dreamweaver saves these settings for you so that you don't have to set them up every time you want to upload new pages to your site.)

Follow these steps to set up Dreamweaver's FTP features and publish files to a web server:

1. **Open Dreamweaver and choose Site⇨Manage Sites.**

   The Manage Sites dialog box opens.

2. **In the list of defined sites, select the site you want to publish and then click the Edit button.**

The Site Setup dialog box opens. If your site isn't listed in this dialog box, you haven't set up your site.

3. **Select Servers from the categories listed in the left panel of the Site Setup dialog box.**

   The server list appears. If you haven't yet set up a web server in Dreamweaver, the list is blank, as shown in Figure 11-18. Any servers you have set up properly are listed in this dialog box.

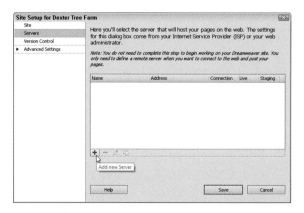

Figure 11-18: Click the plus sign at the bottom of the Server category in the Site Setup dialog box to set up a new server.

4. **Click the small plus sign in the lower left corner of the server list area (refer to Figure 11-18).**

   The Basic tab opens in the Servers dialog box and FTP is selected automatically (see Figure 11-19). If you need to use an option other than FTP, look ahead to the list at the end of these steps.

5. **Enter a name in the Server Name field.**

   You can name your server any-thing you like. Choose a name that lets you easily choose among the servers you've set

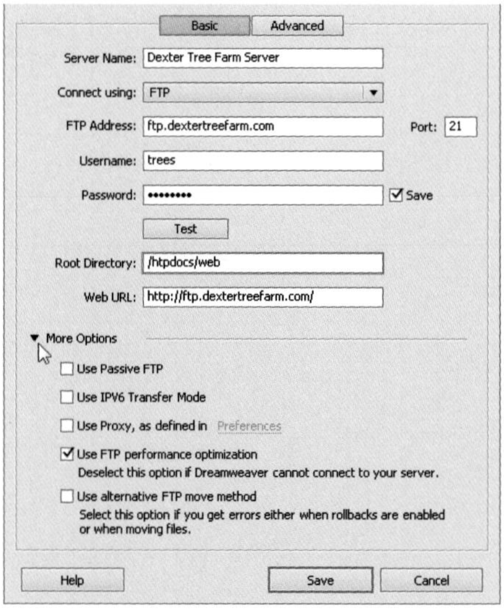

Figure 11-19: Enter your login information for web hosting, including name and password, in the Basic Server Setup dialog box.

up. (If you use only one web server to host your site, the name doesn't matter as much as if you host your site on multiple sites, which is generally done only by large or international sites.)

6. **Enter the FTP address for your web server account.**

   Again, this information depends on how your web server is set up, but most use ftp.*servername*.com, ftp.*yourdomainname*.com, or simply *yourdomain*.com with nothing at the beginning of the domain.

7. **In the Username and Password fields, type your username (or login name) and password, respectively.**

   Again, this information is unique to your account on your web server.

8. **Select the Save check box to the right of the Password field if you want Dreamweaver to store your access information.**

   This action is handy because you can then automatically connect to the server anytime you want to upload or download pages. However, selecting the Save check box could enable anyone with access to your computer to gain access to your web server.

9. **Click the Test button to make sure you've entered everything correctly.**

   Making a mistake is easy, so the ability to test the connection and make any necessary adjustments before you close this dialog box is helpful. If you connect with no problems, Dreamweaver responds with the message Dreamweaver connected to your Web server successfully. (**Note:** You must save the password in order to use the test feature, but you can deselect the Save box after you test, if you prefer not to save the password in the program.)

   If you have trouble connecting to your site, skip to Step 11 for a few advanced options that may help.

10. **In the Root Directory (also known as the local site folder) field, type the directory name of the remote site in which documents visible to the public are stored.**

    The root directory usually looks similar to public_html or www/htdocs. Again, it depends on your server.

    If you upload your files to the wrong directory on your server, they aren't visible when you view your site in a browser.

11. **Click the small arrow to the left of More Options.**

    You may not need to change any settings, but if you have trouble connecting to your server and are sure you've entered your username, password, and FTP address correctly, adjusting these settings may enable you to connect.

Select and deselect each of these options and then click the Test button after each change to see whether any of the adjustments make the difference and enable you to connect to your server.

A little experimentation with settings before waiting on hold with tech support personnel is usually worth the effort. But if you're truly having trouble establishing a connection with your server, call or e-mail the tech support staff at your web server. The only people who can help you are those who run your web server, because the settings are specific to your service provider and can vary dramatically from one hosting company to another. We've done our best to give you the most common options here, and with a little trial and error, these suggestions should help you connect to most web hosting companies. If you're stuck, though, ask for more help from the people who run your server.

12. **After you fill in all the information, click the Test button; if you successfully connect to your server, click the Save button to save your settings.**

   Dreamweaver saves all your FTP settings (assuming that you opted to save the password). The beauty is that you never have to enter these settings again after they work properly, and you can access your web server from the Files panel in Dreamweaver, as you can read about in the next section.

Dreamweaver provides five access options. If you work at a large company or university, you're likely to use one of the following options rather than FTP. The options available from the Connect Using drop-down list (see Figure 11-20) are described in this list:

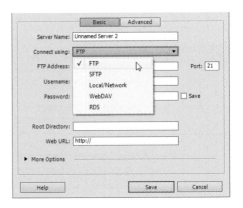

Figure 11-20: Most FTP programs, including Dreamweaver, support multiple ways of connecting to a web server.

  🖝 **FTP:** Provides basic File Transfer Protocol connection and transfer features.

  🖝 **SFTP:** Provides a more secure FTP connection. If you can use a secure connection, it's definitely the preferred choice, and it's required by certain web servers to maintain higher levels of security.

  🖝 **Local/Network:** Select this option if you're using a web server on a local network, such as your company's or university's server. For specific settings and requirements, check with your system administrator.

✔ **WebDAV:** Select this option if you're using a server with the web-based Distributed Authoring and Versioning (WebDAV) protocol, such as Microsoft IIS.

✔ **RDS:** Select the RDS (Rapid Development Services) option if you're using ColdFusion on a remote server.

Publishing files to a web server with FTP

You can upload pages to your server and download pages from your server using the built-in FTP capabilities of Dreamweaver.

To transfer files between your hard drive and a remote server (after you've successfully set up the FTP features we cover in the preceding section of this chapter), follow these steps:

1. **Make sure the site you want to work on is selected in the Files panel in Dreamweaver.**

2. **In the upper left corner of the Files panel, click the Connects to Remote Host button (which looks like a blue electrical cable plugging into itself).**

   If you're not already connected to the Internet, the Connects to Remote Host button starts your Internet connection. If you have trouble connecting this way, establish your Internet connection as you usually do to check e-mail or surf the web, and then return to Dreamweaver and click the Connects to Remote Host button after you're connected. When your computer is online, Dreamweaver should have no trouble automatically establishing an FTP connection with your host server.

   If you still have trouble establishing a connection to your web server, refer to the earlier section "Setting up Dreamweaver's FTP features" and make sure that you specified the server information correctly.

3. **After you establish a connection between your computer and your web server, click the Expand/Collapse button (which looks like stacked horizontal lines at the far right end of the top of the Files panel).**

   When you click this button, Dreamweaver displays both the local folder with your site on your hard drive and the remote folder with the site on your server. We prefer this dual view because seeing both folders side by side makes moving files from one place to another easier. This dual view also helps you visualize the structure of the site on the server.

   The row of buttons across the top control FTP functions, making it easy to connect to your web server and upload or download files. You can also view your local site folder by choosing Local View from the drop-down list in the upper right corner (see Figure 11-21). Or, choose Remote View to see only the files on the server.

4. To *upload* a file (transfer it from your hard drive to your web server), select it from the Local View panel, which displays the files on your hard drive, and click the Put Files button (the up arrow) in the Files panel.

The files are copied automatically to your server when you transfer them. You can select multiple files or folders to be transferred simultaneously.

Always test your pages after you upload files to your server, by viewing the new files in a web browser. For more complete testing recommendations and resources, refer to the earlier sections in this chapter on testing the page display and validating code.

FILES	ASSETS	
🗀 Dexter Tree F. ▼	Local view ▼	

Local Files	Size	Typ
⊟ 🗀 Site - Dexter Tree Fa...		Folde
⊞ 🗀 images		Folde
⊞ 🗀 Templates		Folde
⊞ 🗀 trees		Folde
🗀 untitled		Folde
📄 2008-growing-se...	6KB	HTMl
📄 about-dexter-tre...	5KB	HTMl
📄 about-robin-warn...	5KB	HTMl
📄 contact-us.html	4KB	HTMl
📄 how-we-grow-tre...	5KB	HTMl
📄 index.html	4KB	HTMl
📄 main.css	3KB	Casc
📄 whats-new.html	3KB	HTMl

Date: 12/29/2009 2:29 PM [Log...]

Figure 11-21: The buttons across the top of the Dreamweaver files panel make it easy to upload and download files.

5. To *download* (or transfer from your web server to your hard drive) files or folders, select the files or folders from the Remote View panel (which displays the files on your server) and then click the Get Files button (the down arrow) in the Files panel.

The files are copied automatically to your hard drive when you transfer them.

When you copy files to or from your server, the files you transfer over-write the files already at the destination. Dreamweaver notifies you about the overwriting if it notices that you're replacing a newer file with an older one, but it can't always correctly assess the proper time differences. Take note of these warnings, but keep in mind that warnings aren't always accurate when they're based on file age, especially if you use more than one computer to work on your website.

When the transfer is complete, you can open the files on your hard drive.

6. To close this dual panel dialog box and return to the main Dreamweaver workspace, simply click the Expand/Collapse button again.

Choosing a Mobile Domain

You can upload your mobile web page files to your web server using FTP, just as you would upload the files of any desktop website (as you can see in the section that follows). The real challenge is deciding where to put your mobile version. At least eight (at last count) domain variations are commonly in use for mobile websites. Some mobile web designers publish their mobile sites to a new domain with the `.mobi` domain ending. Many other designers are using the *subdomain,* a version of a regular domain that shares the same basic address.

Table 11-1 describes what the full URLs would look like in some common subdomain examples.

Table 11-1	Common Mobile Subdomains
Subdomain Prefix	*Example*
mm	m.slightlyusedcats.com
mobile	mobile.slightlyusedcats.com
pda	pda.slightlyusedcats.com
xhtml	xhtml.digitalfamily.com
wap	wap.artesianmedia.com
wml	wml.hardnewsinc.com
wireless	wireless.sipsfromthefirehose.com

Some mobile designers prefer to use folder names to add mobile addresses. In this case, you simply upload the mobile version of your site to a special folder with a name such as `/m`, `/mobile`, `/i` or `/iphone`, `/gmm`, `/portable`, or `/wireless`. If you set up this folder at the main, root directory level of your site and name the home page of your mobile site `index.html`, the URL looks something like this: `www.digitalfamily.com/m`.

Our testing has shown that entering the slash (`/`) character on low-end feature phones is often difficult. If you're designing a site for these basic devices, you might want to consider setting up a subdomain that uses a prefix, such as those included in Table 11-1, rather than a folder name.

After you set up your mobile site (or sites) at one or more special URLs, you can link directly to those addresses and promote the addresses in your advertising. If you want to route the traffic from mobile sites directly to these addresses, you have to use a mobile detection and redirection system. For more on this subject, see Chapter 12.

12

Using Device Detection to Target iPhone and iPad Designs

In This Chapter

▷ Understanding device detection

▷ Detecting and directing content to an iPhone or iPad

▷ Setting up simple browser detection with PHP

▷ Using open source detection scripts

A restaurant must get the right meal to the right table while the food is still hot, or else it won't stay in business long. To meet this goal, well-informed wait staff must first write the order correctly and staff members in a well-organized kitchen must prepare variations of the same meal quickly, without compromising quality.

Similarly, if you want to deliver tailored versions of your website to the iPhone/iPad or another device, you must properly determine the kind of device each visitor is using (device detection, similar to turning in the right order) and then deliver the best version of your site for each of these devices (content adaptation, or preparing each meal to order).

As you consider how best to design your website, consider these three options:

↳ **Create a single version of your site.** To simplify the updating and managing of your website, you can create a single version of your website and use CSS to tailor its design on each device (and device orientation). We cover how to target the iPhone and iPad with CSS in Chapter 6.

✔ **Use a relatively simple script.** PHP can filter content and change the design for each device. A good example is the script we use in the Jelly Rancher contact page: We used PHP to remove a section of the page that's sent to an iPhone, which makes the page size smaller and removes information that's useless to an iPhone user. To detect several devices, try the PHP script created by Andy Moore, which we cover in the later section "Detecting and Directing Mobile Devices."

✔ **Set up a highly complex device detection system and create multiple versions of your content to best meet the needs of all devices now on the market.** If you need your website to work on older "feature phones," such as the Motorola RAZR, as well as on the latest version of the iPhone, you need this advanced strategy. We offer, at the end of this chapter, a few tips to get you started down this path.

In this chapter, we help you explore all three of these approaches to designing a site with mobile support. In the following section, we discuss the trade-offs of using each development approach.

Developing a Device Detection System

The basic concept behind *device detection* is straightforward: The website identifies the visitor's device when it arrives, then sends the visitor the optimal version of a web page based on what the server knows about the device. (For a more technical explanation, see the nearby sidebar, "User agents and device detection.")

The challenge with device detection — and the subsequent redirection of visitors — is that more than 8,000 devices are now in use, and more are added all the time. Although the various categories of mobile phones have similarities, the specific support information for each device varies.

Successfully delivering the right version of a site to the right phone is the "secret sauce" of many high-end mobile web design firms. They build up libraries of device capabilities to determine the optimal content to deliver to each device. Some capabilities are simple and address common difference, such as screen size and multimedia support. Others are highly complex and describe capabilities based on combinations of attributes from each device.

Open source solutions are available, as they are for most common problems with the web, thanks to the generosity of programmers who share their work and offer applications for free (or a donation). We cover a few of these solutions at the end of this chapter. In the next section, we focus on relatively simple ways to target designs for the iPhone and iPad.

Setting Up Simple Browser Detection

Using CSS, you can apply different rules to iPhones and iPads to optimize how your site looks. As we describe in Chapter 6, you can alter how a page appears in landscape or portrait view, and you can hide certain parts of a page when viewed on specific devices. Using CSS to target your designs is the simplest route, but when you take this approach, you're still delivering the entire content of your page to each device, which means that you may make your audience download more content than necessary. This issue is especially problematic if visitors are viewing your pages over slow connections or if you include a lot of large image, video, or audio files.

In this section, we explore how to use a relatively simple PHP script that delivers different content to an iPad than it does to an iPhone. This kind of script is useful if you want to block videos, images, or other types of content from being downloaded to an iPhone.

As shown in Figure 12-1, we used the Jelly Rancher contact page as an example. In this case, the PHP script delivers more content to the iPad than the iPhone because we removed the QR code and Microsoft tag in the right sidebar before delivering the page to the iPhone. See the nearby sidebar "Using QR codes and Microsoft tags" to find out more about these scannable tags that work with mobile devices.

The PHP code featured in this section provides a handy way to tailor the content delivered to an iPhone or iPad on a specific page. The contact page (refer to Figure 12-1) displays more information on the larger iPad screen than on the iPhone screen. In this example, we use a little PHP code to remove the second photo, as well as the QR code and Microsoft tag, from the contact page before the page is sent to an iPhone.

When you use PHP code in an HTML document, you must change the extension of the file from `.html` to `.php`. You can mix pages with `.html` and `.php` extensions in the same website.

The first step in being able to send only the data that each individual browser needs is to detect which browser is visiting the page. You can use any server-side language, such as Java, .Net, or PHP.

The PHP used in this example works fine for a simple example, but you're better off with a more comprehensive device detection script, such as the one created by Andy Moore, which we cover in the section "Detecting and Directing Mobile Devices," later in this chapter.

iPhone not to scale

Figure 12-1: You can use a script to deliver different content to the iPhone than to the iPad.

Determining the device type

In the contact page example (refer to Figure 12-1), and in the following code sample, we show you how to check the user agent for key terms that indicate which type of browser is being used to visit your site. The *user agent,* which is sent with the request from a browser to a web server, is a text description that identifies the browser version and operating system. Here's the current user agent for an iPhone:

```
Mozilla/5.0+(iPhone;+U;+CPU+iPhone+OS+4_3_2+like+Mac+OS+X;
        +en-us)+AppleWebKit/533.17.9+(KHTML,+like+Gecko
        )+Version/5.0.2+Mobile/8H7+Safari/6533.18.5
```

Using QR codes and Microsoft tags

You can scan QR codes and Microsoft tags by using the camera in your iPhone or iPad 2. QR codes and Microsoft tags are increasingly being added to print publications, billboards, and on products to provide scannable, updatable information to anyone with a capable mobile phone. A recent study by Compete reported that 39 percent of iPhone users have tried a bar code scanning application.

These codes make it easy to save contact information, link to a web page, or provide additional resources. Adding a QR or Microsoft tag to a contact page, as we did in the example used in this section, makes it easy for people viewing your site on an iPad or computer screen to scan the web page with their phones and automatically save your name and number, and any other information you want to provide, directly into their Contacts list on the iPhone. We cover QR codes and Microsoft tags in more detail in Chapter 15.

Here's the user agent for an iPad:

```
Mozilla/5.0+(iPad;+U;+CPU+OS+4_3_2+like+Mac+OS+X;+en-us) +App
        leWebKit/533.17.9+(KHTML,+like+Gecko)+Version/5.0.
        2+Mobile/8H7+Safari/6533.18.5
```

You insert the following code into your web page to detect the user agent and deliver the optimized version of the page to each device. (Note that the line numbers on the right aren't a required part of the code. They're included only for your reference as we examine a few lines of code in detail in the next paragraph.)

```
<?php                                                    1
        $ua = $_SERVER['HTTP_USER_AGENT'];               2
        $iPhone = strpos($ua,"iPhone");                  3
        $iPad = strpos($ua,"iPad");                       4
        $iPod = strpos($ua,"iPod");                       5
        $Mac = strpos($ua,"Mac OS X");                    6
?>
```

The following list explains what's happening in the preceding code block:

✔ **Line 1:** Tells the web server to process the following as PHP code before sending the page to the browser.

↙ **Line 2:** Retrieves the user agent from the browser's request for this page. You create a variable named $ua and assign it the value of $_SERVER['HTTP_USER_AGENT'. Now the variable ($ua) has the value of the user agent string. If an iPhone visited the site, $ua would have the value of the iPhone user agent.

↙ **Line 3:** Creates a variable named $iPhone. Then using the function strpos(), PHP finds the position of "iPhone" in $ua and assigns its starting position to $iPhone.

```
$iPhone = strpos($ua,"iPhone");
```

If $ua doesn't contain "iPhone" strpos() returns FALSE. Later in the page, you can recognize whether a iPhone is requesting a page by testing the value of $iPhone.

↙ **Lines 4, 5, 6:** Detect other systems in the same way as Line 3.

Sending the right content to an iPhone

After you determine whether a visitor to your site is using an iPhone or an iPad, you can hide content from either device as you deliver each page. In the contact.php page used in this example, you can see that we deliver different information to the iPhone with the PHP code in the header:

```
<?php if ($iPhone == true) {// it's an iPhone ?>         1
    <h3><a href="tel:+12345678901">Call Mark</a> or     2
        <a href="mailto:mark@jellyrancher.com"> Email
        Mark</a></h3>                                    3
    <?php} else {// it's not an iPhone ?>               4
    <h3>Call Mark at +1 (234) 567-8901 or               5
        <a href="mailto:mark@jellyrancher.com"> Email
        Mark</a></h3>                                   6
<?php } ?>                                              7
```

The first line shows an if statement; it checks to see whether the variable $iPhone is true. (The = operator is used to assign a value; == evaluates whether two elements are equal; and === determines whether two elements are exactly alike.) If $iPhone is true, an H3 section on the page offers two options the user can act on: Call Mark, which initiates a phone call on the iPhone, or Email Mark, which creates an e-mail message. If the visitor to this page isn't using an iPhone, the phone call link is removed and only the e-mail option is offered. That way, an iPad or a desktop browser doesn't display a click-to-call that fails on a device with no phone. We keep the e-mail option for anyone with an Internet connection.

We show one type of content and not another by using an `if/else` statement. Its format resembles the `if` statement but adds, at the end, the `else` clause, which replaces the content in the first block — in this example, `Call Mark` or `Email Mark`, with a single option, `Email Mark`, in the second block if the device is not an iPhone. ***Note:*** This example is focused on the iPhone and iPad; to target other devices specifically, you may need to add additional code.

Using the built-in iPhone capabilities

When you include a phone number on a web page, the iPhone recognizes it and automatically makes it possible for a user to place a call by touching the number. If a user touches *and holds* on a phone number for a second, the iPhone offers four options: Call the number, send a text message, create a new contact, and add to existing contact, as shown in Figure 12-2.

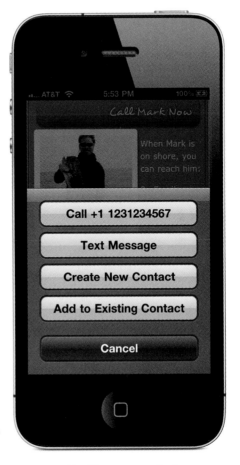

Figure 12-2: The iPhone automatically opens this list of options whenever a user touches and holds a phone number.

All iOS devices with phone capabilities include these options, but not all users understand that if you tap on a number with your finger you initiate a call and if you touch and hold for a second, you see a list of options. If you want to help less experienced users who may not be aware of this feature on an iPhone, you can add a simple message to bring it to their attention.

The code in the following example includes a message that displays only on iPhones. On any other browser, the page shows just the phone number (without the touch and hold tip for the iPhone).

```
<?php if ($iPhone == true)  { ?>                              1
<p>By phone: <a href="tel:+12345678901">+1 (234) 567-8901</a>
          (you can create a contact by touching and holding
          a phone number)</p>                                 2
<p>By text message: <a href="sms:+ 12345678901">Text Mark</
          a></p>                                              3
<?php } elseif ($iPad == true || $iPod == true) { ?>          4
<p>Add Mark to your contacts: +1 (234) 567-8901 (on an iPad
          you can create a contact by touching a phone
          number)</p>                                         5
<?php } else { ?>                                             6
<p>By phone: +1 (234) 567-8901</p>                            7
<?php }?>                                                     8
```

This bit of code is similar to the example we show in the previous section. Now you're checking to find true statements twice. The first block is an `if` statement, but rather than use the `else` statement, you use `elseif` to evaluate the next statement. Keep in mind that if the first block is true, the `elseif` isn't even evaluated. Finally, you can use the `else` clause for any situation that falls outside the first two scenarios.

To create your own contact page, just replace all Mark's contact information with your own and integrate it into the code.

Detecting and Directing Mobile Devices

Before delving into the details of the most complex ways of managing device detection, this section begins with an overview. If you want to deliver different versions of a website to the thousands of different devices now in use on the web, follow these general steps:

1. **Develop device groups based on device capabilities.**

   Determine which devices you want the design to look good on. Thousands of mobile phones and other devices are used by visitors. Categorizing devices into manageable groups based on factors such as screen size and the level of multimedia support enable you to focus on one group at a time. For example, you may want to send the same image to an iPhone and iPod touch because their screen sizes are similar, while sending a larger image to the iPad to take advantage of its larger screen.

2. **Develop (or acquire) a device database or a configuration file.**

   To deliver the right version of your site to the right device, you need a configuration file or database that contains detailed information about every device. Many private companies create their own device databases, but you can also use the open source Wireless Universal Resource FiLe (WURFL), described in the section "Using open source device-detection scripts and services," later in this chapter.

3. Write (or acquire) a program that can deliver the right version of your site to the right device.

The challenge in this step is to develop an application that can match the contents of the device database with the different design options (device profiles, special URLs, or other parameters) you've created for your site. Though top mobile design firms create their own solutions, a great place to get a head start is Andy Moore's device detection script. (See Figure 12-3.)

4. Develop a design that you can adapt to the needs of different devices on the fly, or create multiple designs, each optimized for a different device or device profile.

When you use either approach, expect to spend a significant amount of time creating designs that display well within the constraints of each device.

5. Test, test, and test again, making adjustments as needed.

The many variations among devices and the sheer number of devices in use on the mobile web make it almost impossible to deliver a perfectly optimized page to every device every time. Even if you get your mobile design strategy right, the mobile web is a moving target. Develop a strategy that best meets the needs of your site users now (and works within the limitations of your time and budget), and make refinements to keep your strategy up-to-date later. Chapter 11 provides details on testing.

Figure 12-3: Andy Moore's device detection script provides a helpful head start in case you want to detect and redirect mobile visitors to a separate mobile version of your site.

User agents and device detection

When you open a web page, your web browser sends a *user agent string* to the server that hosts the website. This string essentially introduces your browser to the server, describing which browser version you're using and relating other information about your computer or mobile device, such as the operating system. You can see your browser's user agent by going to http://whatsmyuseragent.com.

Device detection systems are designed to recognize user-agent strings and direct visitors based on the capabilities of each device. Because many websites use device detection to direct mobile visitors, you can't just open the mobile versions of certain sites in a desktop browser on your computer. That's where the User Agent Switcher comes in

handy. This plug-in for Firefox (available at https://addons.mozilla.org/en-US/firefox/addon/59) enables you to change the user agent of your web browser, effectively tricking the server into thinking that you're using an iPhone or any other user agent you can load into the plug-in.

Because the User Agent Switcher makes it possible to visit the mobile version of a website by using a browser on a desktop computer, the switcher also makes it possible to view the source code behind those pages. This feature is especially valuable because browsers on mobile devices don't offer an option to view the source code, which is standard in desktop browsers such as Chrome, Firefox, Internet Explorer, and Safari.

Using open source device-detection scripts and services

Although you can create your own configuration file or device database with the specifications of every mobile device you want to support and you can write your *own* device detection scripts (if you're an experienced programmer), you're almost certainly better off starting with one of the open source options included in this section. However, even using these helpful resources, you'll need some programming experience to get these solutions to work on your server.

WURFL

```
http://wurfl.sourceforge.net
```

The oldest and most common mobile device detection project: the Wireless Universal Resource File, or WURFL, is a freely available configuration file created by many contributors with the goal of providing a comprehensive list of all mobile devices now in use and which web design standards they can support. Although no one claims that the list is all-inclusive all the time, it's regularly updated and well respected in the mobile development community.

Tera-WURFL

```
www.tera-wurfl.com
```

Built on WURFL (and linked to from the WURFL site), the Tera-WURFL application was created using PHP and MySQL. The Tera-WURFL application detects and matches mobile devices by first collecting user agent information from every site visitor and then passing the information to the Tera-WURFL library, where it's evaluated and assigned to a UserAgentMatcher. Each UserAgentMatcher is designed to work with a device profile, made up of a group of devices with similar capabilities. Essentially, the Tera-WURFL helps you complete most of the device-detection and -redirection process, but you still need to use a script that redirects visitors to the right version of your site based on the results.

Device Atlas

```
http://deviceatlas.com
```

If you don't want to maintain your own device database, Device Atlas will keep your device database up-to-date. You can look up the specific features supported by nearly any mobile phone, including the markup languages, multimedia types, and image formats that each phone supports. Device Atlas also offers an API you can use if you're developing your own device detection solution.

Andy Moore's device detection solution

```
http://detectmobilebrowsers.mobi
```

Andy Moore has the simplest method we've found for setting up an automatic detection and redirection solution for your site. Note, however, that you still need at least basic PHP skills to set up and install the code.

The solution, a PHP function, has eight parameters, which you can easily define to handle common devices. You can use the drop-down menu options on Moore's web page to alter the settings for each option.

For an introduction to PHP, check out *PHP 5 For Dummies,* by Janet Valade.

13

Creating iPhone/iPad Designs for a WordPress Blog

*B*logging is one of the simplest and most popular ways to publish on the web. If actors and politicians can run their own blogs, well, then just about anyone should be able to pull it off, right?

But how do you make sure your blog posts can be read on an iPhone or iPad? Fortunately, that part is easy as well. Just download and install a special theme, and you'll be all set.

In this chapter, we review the most popular WordPress themes for the iPhone/iPad, (and offer a few tips for Joomla! users) that make your sites mobile friendly.

Making Your Blog Mobile Friendly with Plug-Ins

A *plug-in* is a software package that you can add to a blog to enhance its features. You can use plug-ins to fight off spammers, add your Twitter feed to a sidebar, integrate Google Maps into your blog, and much more.

You can find thousands of WordPress plug-ins at `http://wordpress.org/extend/plugins`. You can spend hours browsing the myriad ways that programmers around the world have tried to customize the functions of WordPress blogs. If you have any PHP programming skills, you might even come up with some new ways on your own. Some plug-ins that were intended for use with WordPress (such as Akismet, Cincopa, Lightbox, and others) have proven to be so useful that developers have made versions of them that can work on other websites or blogging platforms.

Not all plug-ins are available for blogs hosted on WordPress.com (as opposed to hosting WordPress on your web server or a commercial hosting service). WordPress.com limits the plug-in options on its free service because of security concerns, but you can request that any plug-in be added. Search the Themes section at `www.wordpress.com` to find themes that support the iPhone.

For the majority of bloggers who host their own WordPress blogs, here are a few of the WordPress plug-ins for the iPhone/iPad that we recommend you consider using on your blog. In the sections that follow, we offer more specific instructions on how to use some of the more popular plug-ins:

- ✔ **WordPress Mobile Pack:** The most sophisticated of the mobile plug-ins, the WordPress Mobile Pack adds a suite of tools, including a mobile switcher, themes, widget, and mobile admin panel. That means you can take care of everything you need in order to optimize your blog for mobile devices with this single handy plug-in. It redirects mobile devices to a simplified theme that displays a version of your blog correctly on smaller screens, and adds other mobile design touches. In addition, this plug-in adds analytics to help you track mobile traffic, and it even has a mobile ad widget that's integrated with Google AdSense and the AdMob advertising network. (Look for instructions for installing and using this plug-in in the next section.)

- ✔ **WPtouch:** One of the most popular plug-ins for the iPhone and other mobile devices, this add-on solves several problems at once. It converts the look of your blog into something akin to an iPhone app by adding a special theme. It enables you to customize your blog's appearance. And the developers promise that it won't change a single line of code in your main WordPress theme. If you upgrade to the pro version, you can customize the design even further.

- ✔ **iPhone Control Panel:** This plug-in makes it possible to add custom CSS, designed specifically for the iPhone, and directs iPhone devices to display those styles instead of main styles for your WordPress theme. In addition, you get a bookmark icon and the ability to redirect visitors to a distinct URL.

- ✔ **iPhone-WebApp-Redirection:** As its name implies, this plug-in detects whether visitors are using the iPhone, iPad, or iPod touch and then directs them to a specified URL. This detection makes it easy for you to direct visitors to any page or special version of your site based on their devices. This plug-in can also detect phones that run the Android operating system, as well as some Blackberry phones and other devices.

- ✔ **iPhone Theme Switcher:** This plug-in lets you automatically change the theme used in your blog when someone views the blog with an iPhone.

- ✔ **iPhone Countdown:** Use this plug-in to add a countdown counter to your blog — a great way to remind visitors how many shopping days they have before Christmas, how many days before the next election, or any other date you want to make sure your visitors don't miss.

Adding the WordPress Mobile Pack

If you're looking for a single simple tool that can take care of everything you need to make your blog mobile-friendly, the WordPress Mobile Pack is the plug-in for you. Just add the plug-in through the WordPress Dashboard, and you're most of the way there.

In Figure 13-1, you see how our Mobile Web Design Blog displays in the Firefox browser on a desktop computer running Windows 7. In Figure 13-2, you see the same blog as it displays on an iPhone 4 thanks to the Mobile Pack plug-in.

Figure 13-1: The Mobile Web Design Blog looks like this when displayed in Google Chrome on a Windows computer.

Although your results may vary based on the design and complexity of your blog, the WordPress Mobile Pack transforms most blogs in the following ways:

- ✓ **Simplifies the banner and color scheme.**

- ✓ **Stacks blog post headlines in a long row.** iPhone users like to scroll up and down through easy-to-grasp headlines, rather than the traditional blog format, where long posts may require scrolling through a dozen screen-lengths on the iPhone.

- ✓ **Moves sidebars to the bottom of the page.** Because the iPhone screen is narrow, having content appear on the sides means that either the design looks squeezed and unreadable or users have to scroll from side to side as well as up and down to access the content.

After you install the plug-in, you can adjust several settings so that your blog displays your content and design elements as logically and attractively as possible. Although we cannot anticipate every situation or need, the following sections help you start creating a mobile-friendly design

Figure 13-2: This page is on an iPhone 4 using the WordPress Mobile Pack plug-in.

for your visitors who are using iPhones or similar devices. After you follow the steps for creating the basis of the design, you can test and refine the settings on your own.

Installing the Mobile Pack plug-in

The steps in this section walk you through the process of installing the WordPress Mobile Pack plug-in on your WordPress blog.

One risk of installing complex plug-ins, including this one, is that when WordPress periodically updates its software, the update sometimes conflicts with your plug-ins. If this happens, you may have to deactivate or uninstall the plug-in until it's updated as well.

Now that you know what the gotchas are, you're prepared to look out for them and are ready to install the plug-in as follows:

1. **Open a new tab in your browser and navigate to** `http://word press.org/extend/plugins/wordpress-mobile-pack`.

   The WordPress Mobile Pack page appears, as shown in Figure 13-3.

2. **Click the Download button on the right of the WordPress Mobile Pack page (*not* the Download button in the WordPress.org header at the very top right).**

3. **In the window that appears, choose where you want to save the Zip file containing the WordPress Mobile Pack plug-in. Click Save to download the file.**

4. **Log in to your WordPress blog and click the Plugins button in the sidebar on the left of the page.**

5. **From the drop-down list that appears, select Add New.**

   The Install Plugins page appears, as shown in Figure 13-4. You can use this page to browse all kinds of plug-ins. The tag cloud in the center of the page gives you a snapshot of the most popular plug-ins that bloggers are searching for and using. This page is also where you upload plug-ins you want to add to your blog.

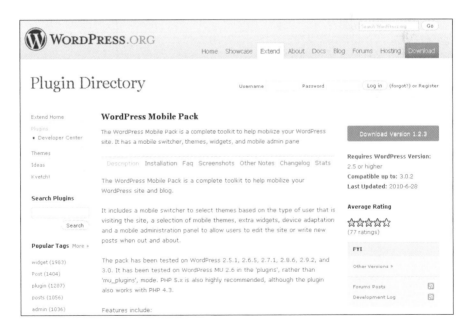

Figure 13-3: The WordPress Mobile Pack page in the Plugin Directory of WordPress.org.

6. **Click the Upload link near the top of the page.**

   The Upload page opens and allows you to easily upload the Zip file containing your plug-in to your blog database without having to use an FTP program.

   The Featured, Popular, Newest, and Recently Updated links can keep you up-to-date on the latest plug-ins that bloggers are using.

7. **Click the Browse button.**

   A window opens and lists your default directory.

8. **Navigate to where you just saved the WordPress Mobile Pack Zip file. Select it and then click the Open button.**

9. **Click the Install Now button.**

   Your computer automatically uploads the plug-in to the proper directory in your WordPress blog and unzips the contents of the file.

10. **Click the Return to Plugins Page link.**

    The Manage Plugins page opens.

11. **Click the Activate link under WordPress Mobile Pack.**

    Your blog activates the plug-in, and *Plugin Activated* appears at the top of the page. If a conflict exists between this plug-in and one of your other plug-ins, or with your blog's theme, you receive an error message. If this happens, you have to troubleshoot by systematically deactivating and reactivating the conflicting plug-ins or features of your blog.

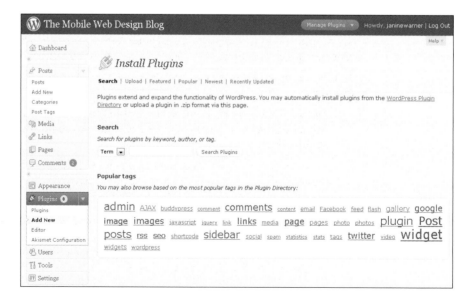

Figure 13-4: The Install Plugins options make it easy to add new features to WordPress.

At this point, you can sit back and let the automatically selected settings take over and determine how your blog will look on mobile devices, or you can dig a little deeper into the various settings to try to customize the look. We lead you through some of the options in the upcoming sections. You don't have to know any real computer programming to adjust these options, although you have to invest time and effort in testing the various settings.

If you have PHP and CSS skills, you can really take matters into your own hands and edit the files to completely customize how this plug-in makes your blog look.

Tweaking the mobile switcher

With the WordPress Mobile Pack plug-in installed, the first thing that greets your visitors is the mobile switcher. Before we get into customizing how this nifty bit of code works, here's a brief explanation: The mobile switching agent identifies what kind of device is visiting the page and delivers the design that is optimized for that device. For more on user agents and how mobile switchers work, see Chapter 12. Follow these steps to adjust the settings:

1. **Open a browser and navigate to your WordPress blog's Dashboard.**

2. **Click the Plugins button in the left sidebar.**

   The Manage Plugins page appears.

3. **Scroll to the WordPress Mobile Pack plug-in and click the Switcher link.**

   Alternatively, you can access the Mobile Switcher by selecting it from the Appearance tab, as shown in Figure 13-5.

   The Mobile Switcher page opens, as shown in Figure 13-5. This page contains various drop-down lists that you can use to adjust the settings.

4. **On the Switcher Mode drop-down menu, choose from the following options:**

   • *Disabled:* Choose this option to disable the switching feature, perhaps because you have a site that is designed to be seen only on mobile devices.

   • *Browser Detection:* When users access your blog, their browser sends a little information to your server, telling it what kind of browser and operating system are making the request. (Think of polite guests knocking on your door and announcing who they are.) This mode is effective, although the WordPress mobile switcher may not recognize very new or nonstandard browsers, in which case users would be sent to your desktop site. (To guard against that kind of error, see Step 9.)

Figure 13-5: Use the Mobile Switcher to control what content iPhone users see when they visit your blog.

- *Domain Mapping:* This option identifies whether the visitor to your blog is trying to access a mobile domain (say `m.mobilewebdesignblog.com`, `mobilewebdesignblog.com/m`, or `mobilewebdesignblog.mobi`) or just the regular desktop site. This is quite effective if your users are typing in the complete address. However, you must create a completely separate mobile site at that address.

- *Both Browser Detection and Domain Mapping:* The advantage of using this setting is that it covers almost all possible mobile user access scenarios and flashes a warning message when your user tries to access the mobile site through a desktop browser or vice versa.

5. **In the Mobile Theme drop-down list, select the theme you want your mobile users to see.**

   The defaults are limited to the base color scheme, as well as blue, green, or red. If you customize and save a mobile theme of your own, it appears here, too.

6. **In the Browser Detection drop-down list, select User-Agent Prefixes, if you like.**

   This drop-down list is available only when you choose Browser Detection or Both Browser Detection and Domain Mapping in Step 4. If you're not using Browser Detection, the choices here are not available.

   As this book goes to press, the only option on the Browser Detection menu is User-Agent Prefixes. However, updates to this mobile pack may provide more options.

7. **In the Desktop Domains text box, change the text only if you have a complicated or custom-built site.**

   The default is your primary web address where users visiting your site from traditional desktop or laptop computers are sent. If you don't know what you're doing with this text box, leave it alone.

8. **In the Mobile Domains box, enter the names of any custom mobile domains you've created.**

   As we mention in Step 4, you can create a completely different site at an m.*whatever*.com or *whatever*.mobi domain. However, just filling in a variation of your existing domain address doesn't magically create this site. Creating subdomains like these requires a fair amount of specialized knowledge and access to server-level functions that not all web hosts offer.

9. **(Optional) Select the Footer Links check box to allow your users to override the mobile switcher.**

   This places a link on the bottom of the page that allows users to defeat the switcher in case it sends a desktop user to a mobile page, or vice-versa. If you're confident in the switcher and want to save space on your page, don't include the link, but most people choose to just in case.

   Allow your users to choose which version of your blog they want to see; maybe a desktop user is on a particularly slow connection and just wants to access the simplest version of your site.

10. **Click the Save Changes button when you are done.**

Customizing your mobile theme

Although you can choose the basic color scheme of the existing mobile themes when you configure the mobile switcher (see the preceding section), the Mobile Theme page allows you to further customize what your mobile users see when they access your blog.

1. **Open a browser and navigate to your WordPress blog's Dashboard.**

2. **Click the Plugins button in the left sidebar.**

   The Manage Plugins page appears.

3. **Scroll to the WordPress Mobile Pack plug-in and click the Themes link.**

   Alternatively, you can click the Mobile Theme link under the Appearance tab, as shown in Figure 13-6.

   The Mobile Theme page opens, as shown in Figure 13-6. This page contains various drop-down lists you can use to adjust the settings.

4. **If you have a dedicated page for your blog, deselect the Show Home Link in Menu check box.**

   If you have a dedicated home page for your blog (such as a big picture, a video, or an animation), deselect this check box. Otherwise the plug-in places two Home links on your mobile page. If you don't have a dedicated home page, leave this check box selected.

5. **Choose the number of posts to display on your home page or archive page.**

   The default is five. If you want your blog to load quicker, type a smaller number. If you want your readers to see more items and aren't worried about load times (or believe that your readers mostly have fast phones or a lot of patience), then increase the number. Experiment with this setting until you're happy with how your blog downloads and displays in a browser. (Chapter 11 is all about testing and publishing.)

6. **From the Lists of Posts Show drop-down list, select one of the following options:**

   - *Title Only* causes the mobile version of your blog to display only the title of your blog posts. Again, this is a tradeoff between detail and loading speed.

   - *Title and Teaser for the First Post, Title for the Rest* is a good compromise setting. Your readers see the title of your most recent post and the first few words of the post; after that, readers see just the headlines.

   - *Title and Teaser for All Posts* displays as much information as possible to get your readers to click through to the full posts. Of course, when this setting is selected, the pages load slower. Your readers may get frustrated and abandon your blog.

7. **Select the Display Metadata for Posts option if you want to display additional information about your posts.**

   If you select this option, each post also shows the name of the author and any tags you've chosen.

Figure 13-6: Further customize the switcher settings by using the Mobile Theme page.

8. Choose the teaser length (if any).

The default is 50 characters. If you want a longer teaser, type a larger number. Again, experiment until you're happy with the display and download time.

9. Type the number of widget items you want to display.

The default is five. Your widgets display on your mobile blog not in a sidebar, but in a bar at the bottom of the page. If your widget contains a lot of information, only a short teaser and a link to the full list appear.

10. Select the Remove Media option if you want remove all rich media content from on your blog.

When you choose Remove Media, the plug-in removes the object, embed, marquee, script, frame, and iframe HTML tags and their content.

Depending on what you blog about, removing media can be one of the most crucial decisions you make. If you use a lot of audio, video, or animations in your blog posts, then removing all your audio, video, or animation files may leave you with little content to offer mobile visitors. However, if you mostly post text and photos on your site and occasionally have audio or video, removing these elements may be in your best interest. Rich media elements are usually large in size; users may not want to wait around — or burn up their limited data plans — waiting for your home page to download. And, of course, as noted many times in this book, Flash content doesn't display on the iPad/iPhone.

11. **Select the Partition Large Pages option to break up your content into bite-size pieces.**

    If you tend to write long posts (if your post requires the user to scroll through more than four screens of content, it's long), you might want to give your audience a break with this option. If, however, you want people to load only one page at a time and avoid clicking repeatedly to load page after page, leave this check box deselected.

12. **Select the Shrink Images option to resize your pictures to fit on mobile screens.**

    Shrinking images might not be a good idea in some circumstances. If you're a photographer and are afraid that the resizing engine in this plug-in might add noise or distortion to your photos, or you prefer to handle the resizing yourself, leave Shrink Images deselected. Otherwise, it doesn't make much sense to have a poster-resolution image on a postage-stamp-size screen.

13. **Select the Clear Cache Now option if you want to ensure that the resized images are the ones that appear for mobile users.**

    Sometimes, WordPress caches images locally so that it doesn't have to keep going into the database to retrieve them. If you chose to resize images but haven't cleared the cache, your blog could continue to deliver the large image files.

14. **Select the Simplify Styling option.**

    This removes any little flourishes that have crept into your posts and pages, such as having ornate initial capital letters or having unique styles as frames around pictures. On the mobile web, these kinds of elements are referred to as "drag," as in "All the fancy typography and design on that blog are dragging it down like an anchor thrown into bottomless quicksand."

15. **Click the Save Changes button when you're done customizing your settings.**

    Call up your blog on your mobile device to see what your changes have done to your blog's appearance.

Choosing which widgets to display

If you're a blogger, you've probably added a widget or two (or ten). After you set up your WordPress blog for the mobile web using WordPress Mobile Pack, follow these steps to display widgets for your readers:

1. **Open a browser and navigate to your WordPress blog's Dashboard.**

2. **Click the Plugins button in the left sidebar.**

   The Manage Plugins page appears.

3. **Scroll to the WordPress Mobile Pack plug-in and click the Mobile Widgets link.**

   The Mobile Widgets page appears, as shown in Figure 13-7. This page contains various check boxes that allow you to winnow your widgets to just the ones that are absolutely essential to your blog. You can enable your widgets on the regular Widgets page, where you can drag and drop the elements to add, subtract, or reorder the content.

4. **Select which widgets you want to display on the mobile version of your blog.**

   Accepted wisdom is that no more than three widgets should load when you hit a mobile page. (Purists say anything more than three is pushing it.) Consider carefully what information absolutely, positively has to be on your mobile blog. Widgets for stock tickers, Twitter feeds, Flickr slide shows, or MP3 players can severely clog page load times.

5. **Click the Save Changes button.**

Figure 13-7: The Mobile Widgets page.

Blogging from an iPhone or iPad

The world seems to demand ever faster updates to blogs, so it's a good thing we can now post from our iPhones or iPads no matter where we are (from a bus, a fishing boat, or even a bicycle — if you're coordinated enough).

You can find dozens of ways to post to a blog from an iPhone or iPad; the App Store is overflowing with custom-built tools to empower bloggers to capture every waking second of their lives in words, pictures, and video. We encourage you to check out these apps to find the one that best suits your needs.

If you don't want to tie your blogging future to the whims of an app developer, some free and easy tools enable you to add and update posts using the most basic skills and setup — namely blogging via e-mail. Admittedly, sending an e-mail does not allow you to format the post with precision or to preview how it looks — but posting to your blog via e-mail delivers the content into your blog immediately from any device that is capable of sending an e-mail.

In the sections that follow, we explain how you set up a WordPress blog to accept blog posts via e-mail. If you use a blogging platform other than WordPress (such as Blogger or TypePad or if you use Joomla! or Drupal), the specific steps you follow vary, but the basic idea is the same.

Creating a secret e-mail address

Before you start blogging via e-mail, you have to create a unique e-mail address to send your blog posts to. The creation process will vary depending on the way your web-hosting service or e-mail is set up. Essentially, you can use any e-mail address, but there are significant risks to doing this with a Gmail, Hotmail, or Yahoo! account because so many spammers and noxious advertisers randomly blanket every possible address with messages that would then wind up as content on your blog.

Don't use your regular e-mail address. If you do so, then all the e-mail you get in your inbox (including secret love notes and chain letters from your crazy uncle) posts automatically and immediately to your blog. WordPress recommends you create a really obscure e-mail address (see the examples that follow) and keep this e-mail address as secret as possible. If the e-mail address becomes known, spammers can then hijack your blog by sending whatever noxious material they want to that Inbox, and your blog will automatically post it.

So before you start down this path, make sure that you have a safe and secure e-mail address that's dedicated only to receiving e-mails that will then be converted into blog posts. You can share this e-mail address with (very) trusted friends, such as a group on a vacation or at a big concert, so they can post their impressions to your blog as quickly and easily as possible.

To make your special blogging e-mail address safe and secure, WordPress prompts you to use semi-random strings of letters and numbers, such as `4lrp59qs@yourmail.com`. Because nobody sane has a name like 4lrp59qs, the automated programs that spammers use to guess common names won't hit upon this combination for their unwanted messages.

Converting e-mails into WordPress posts

Here's how to set up your WordPress blog to accept your e-mails and turn them into content:

1. **Open a browser and navigate to your WordPress blog's Dashboard.**

2. **Click the Settings button in the left sidebar.**

   Depending on how you have set up your own blog, your Settings button may be in a different location, such as at the bottom of the sidebar.

3. **Click the Writing link.**

   The Writing Settings page opens, as shown in Figure 13-8. This page enables you to adjust many of the settings for creating new posts. Skip the first two sections because they have nothing to do with creating posts via e-mail; make changes to them only if you know what you're doing.

Figure 13-8: The Writing Settings page opens your blog to publishing content sent by e-mail.

Under the Post via E-Mail heading is a paragraph containing three suggested "random strings," which look like this: 23anir8r2c. These are for you to use as usernames to send your blog posts to. That is, you send your e-mails to 23anir8r2c@*yourdomain*.com, and they automatically publish.

4. Enter the mail server for your e-mail account.

If you have a self-hosted WordPress blog, the mail server probably looks similar to mail.*yourblogname*.com.

5. Enter the secret e-mail address in the Login Name box.

6. Enter the password you established for this e-mail account.

7. Select a category from the Default Mail Category drop-down list.

If you want the posts from your mobile device to be in a special category (such as Out and About), you choose it in this step. This setting assigns this category to all e-mail messages you send to the secret e-mail address.

8. Click the Save Changes button.

After you complete this process, all you have to do to post to your blog is send an e-mail to the secret address you specified in Step 5. The Subject line of your e-mail becomes the title of your blog post, and whichever elements you have in the message area (text, photos, or even video) become the content of your post.

Creating an iPhone Design for a Joomla! Site

Similar to WordPress, you can find extensions you can add to a Joomla! site that help automate the process of making a site more mobile friendly. The most popular of these is MobileJoomla!, and you can download it for free from www.mobilejoomla.com.

You can use the Joomla! Extensions Manager to install the extension just as you would install any other Joomla! extension. For this extension to install properly, however, you must have directory write access for the components, modules, templates, and plug-in directories.

Part V
The Part of Tens

The 5th Wave   By Rich Tennant

©RICHTENNANT

CELL PHONES

"Of course your current cellphone takes pictures, functions as a walkie-talkie, and browses the Internet. But does it shoot Silly String?"

The Part of Tens features a collection of great Web 2.0 resources and marketing tips. In Chapter 14, you find a collection of online resources that you can use to extend the features in your websites. From Google Maps to Picasa slide shows, this chapter shows you some of the fastest and easiest ways to trick out your site. Best of all, the resources in this chapter are all available for free! In Chapter 15, you discover ten ways to market your site. After all you've done to make your site look good on an iPhone and iPad, you want to make sure that people find you so that they can appreciate your handiwork.

14

Ten Web 2.0 Opportunities: Google Maps, Facebook, and Beyond

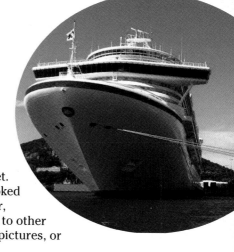

*T*hough some people maintain that *Web 2.0* is one of the more nebulous "buzz phrases" ever inflicted on the unsuspecting populace, it generally refers to the art of including in your web pages interactive elements from other sites on the Internet. If Web 1.0 was built from static pages that users looked at and scrolled through, Web 2.0 goes a step further, enabling users to share, save, or send your content to other people — and even to contribute their own words, pictures, or videos to your site.

Web 2.0 features enable your biggest fans to become your best allies in popularizing your content via social networking sites and in helping you build out content that other users may find valuable. Determining how much control you want over the content on your site is a philosophical question that you will have to work out for yourself. In order of the decreasing amount of control that you would exert over the contents of your website:

1. You can have a completely static page, where the only content that appears is text, photos, videos, or audio that you create and/or choose.

2. You can have a page that is mostly your content but include a comments section where your audience can include their thoughts and even have a conversation with each other.

3. You can have a page where you pose a question or announce a contest, and where your audience contributes their written thoughts, photos, videos, or audio, and then argues with each other about which one they like best, and then votes to determine which contribution is most prominently featured.

The risks attendant to entrusting the contents of your website to your audience are obvious to anyone who has spent time reading the comments section underneath controversial political videos on YouTube. Not all the members of your audience are going to behave themselves. That downside is counterbalanced by the opportunity presented by empowering your users to express themselves creatively in the space you have provided, in delightful ways that you could never have anticipated.

That, in a nutshell, is the Web 2.0 ethos: Provide a space for your audience to participate on their terms. If you've done your job as a designer to block obvious spam messages and weed out online trolls, users will pitch in and help police the site themselves. A 2009 study by the Nielsen company shows that allowing your audience to interact with your content increases the time they spend on your site and makes it 1,000 percent more likely that they will recall what your content is after they leave.

Perhaps one of the best aspects of Web 2.0 is that it's all about leveraging the great work and helpful resources of other sites on the web by integrating their features into your own sites. This chapter explores ten of our favorite Web 2.0 features and how you can use them in your designs for the iPhone or iPad. We have presented these Web 2.0 tools using the Web 2.0 criteria of "interestingness" — a somewhat hard-to-define concept that is used on sites like Flickr. In the case of Flickr, recommended photos appear on the home page or login screen that users will see when they first visit the site. These pieces of content that are deemed by the site administrators or community managers to have a high degree of interestingness are ones that are not only artistically beautiful to look at but also require a degree of technical skill to produce and have an innovative quality to them, where the user has demonstrated that they have a unique or quirky vision that they want to share with the rest of the world.

So in the following sections, in decreasing order, we have listed tools that we think have a certain interestingness — or "cool factor," or whatever hip New Media term you would like to use to describe them — that we have found effective in reaching out to engage users and inspire them to contribute their skills, content, or attention to your site.

Finding Yourself on Google Maps

`http://maps.google.com`

A fun way to engage users and take advantage of the unique powers of the mobile web is to create a photo gallery integrated with a Google map that automatically places geolocated photos on a map, to show where they were taken. Consider these examples:

- ✔ If your website serves a community, such as a travel club, a group of marathon racers, or another group that likes to share photos, the nifty features at Picasa let you, or anyone, easily upload photos from a cellphone and automatically create photo galleries. If the phone model includes geodata (such as the iPhone does; on other models, it depends on the privacy settings), you can add photos to a Google map automatically. Then, when your travel club members are taking photos out their windows on the group's next road trip, everyone on your site can see the photos in real time and track where club members visit by following the photos across a map.

  Geodata is the precise longitude and latitude of your location on the planet, expressed in degrees, minutes, seconds, or radians; the raw numbers look a bit like this 38° 53' 55.133" N by 77° 02' 15.691" W. A computer mapping program takes these coordinates and produces a point on a map — in this case, the location of the White House in Washington, D.C.

- ✔ Adding photos to maps is a helpful way to improve the directions on your website. For example, if you're creating a site for a restaurant located down a tricky side street, with a blind entrance from the parking lot, just use this process to create a map that potential customers can follow on their mobile devices to show not only the restaurant's location on the map but also a picture (or a series of pictures) that shows the street-level view of where customers should park and any other useful details.

You can build this functionality by hand-coding scripts that use the GPS data that mobile devices encode into digital photos. But Google has already built sites and scripts that do this for you for free, so why reinvent the map? Combining the power of Google's free Picasa photo-sharing service (see Figure 14-1) with Google Maps is a powerful, easy, and cost-effective option. (Did we mention that it's free? All you have to do is sign up for a free Google account.)

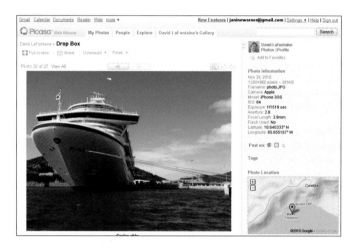

Figure 14-1: Because Picasa and Google Maps are integrated, you can upload images from your phone to Picasa and have them automatically appear on your Google maps.

If you have a Gmail account, you're already signed up for Picasa and Google Maps. If you don't have a Gmail account, sign up for one at `http://picasa web.google.com` before following the next set of steps.

To set up Picasa so that you (and anyone you share your account with) can automatically upload photos from a phone, follow these steps. (To then add your photos to a map, continue with the instructions in the second set of steps.)

1. **Log in to your Picasa account with your Google user ID and password and then click the Settings link in the upper right corner.**

   The User Settings page opens.

2. **Click the General tab and specify the options you want.**

   You can specify your nickname, upload a profile picture, and change the URL for your photo gallery.

3. **Select the Allow Me check box to upload photos by e-mail.**

   You must select this check box if you want to send photos directly from your phone.

4. **In the Enter a Secret Word field, type a secret word.**

   This secret word is used as part of the e-mail address for you or your users to send photos to Picasa. The secret word must be from 6 to 15 characters long and look like this when you use it in an e-mail: *YourName.Secretword*@picasaweb.com. You can see the address appear below the Secret Word box as you type it.

   Be sure to use a secret word that's hard to guess and to give this address only to people you trust. Any photos sent to the e-mail address you create are published automatically in your Picasa photo feed, which opens the possibility that a prankster could upload objectionable photos.

5. **Click the Save Changes button and then e-mail a photo from your mobile device to the address you generated from Picasa that includes the secret word.**

   The Subject line of your e-mail is the headline. Just attach the photo or image to the e-mail as you normally would from your mobile phone.

Because the latest models of the iPhone have GPS receivers that add geodata to your images, you can add your photos to a Google map by continuing the Picasa setup process. Follow these steps:

1. **Click the My Photos tab in Picasa.**

   The page with your photo albums opens.

2. **Click the Drop Box album and then choose Edit⇨Album Properties.**

   The Edit Album Information window opens. You can edit the title and fill in a description of the gallery.

3. **In the Share drop-down list, choose Public and then click the Save Changes button.**

4. **On the right side of the screen, right-click the RSS link and choose Copy Link Location.**

5. **Open a new tab in your browser and navigate to** http://maps.google.com.

   The Google Maps page opens.

6. **Press Ctrl+C (or Command+C on a Mac) to paste the RSS link into the Search Maps field.**

   This step causes little pins to appear on the Google map that correspond to the places where you took the photos. Refer to Figure 14-1 for an idea of how they're displayed on a map. Clicking a thumbnail opens a larger version of the image, along with its latitude and longitude, its title, and the option to view it at full size.

7. **In the upper right corner of your Google map, click the Link link.**

   The Link dialog box opens.

8. **Do either of the following with the code:**

   • Send the link to this map to your friends via e-mail.

   • Embed the code that allows you to add to any blog or website this live map of all the places where you take photos.

Adding a Facebook Like Button to Your Site

`http://developers.facebook.com/docs/reference/plugins/like`

In the summer of 2010, Facebook announced that it had more than 150 million mobile users. At about the same time, surveys showed that the most popular use of the mobile web on iPhones, after checking e-mail, is to access Facebook to update friends, share interesting discoveries, and see what the people in your social group are up to. With that much attention now being paid to Facebook, it makes sense that, after you've gone to all the effort of building a sparkling new iPhone or iPad site, you should take advantage of the opportunities Facebook offers to drive traffic and recruit new users to see what you've done.

Adding a Like button to your page enables users who enjoy your content to do your bragging for you — with just the click of a button. Facebook lets you easily generate the code you need in order to embed this button on your site. Simply use the Facebook "configurator" series of drop-down menus and text-entry boxes (see Figure 14-2 for an example of what the configurator screen looks like).

To find the configurator section, navigate to the URL provided at the beginning of this section. The series of text boxes that you type information into, as well as the drop-down menus on this page are called the "configurator" by Facebook. By entering information into these text boxes and clicking on the drop-down menus to choose options, you will configure how the Like button will appear on your web page. Configuring the Like button means that you are determining some of the characteristics of how it will look on your website, as well as choosing some of the functions that your users can access by using this Like button.

Detailed instructions for generating the code appear below the configurator section. The only variable you need to pay special attention to is the Layout Style drop-down menu. In the standard configuration, the default width of a Like button is set to 450 pixels, which is probably too wide for a site that users view on an iPhone (although it's just right for an iPad). You can manually adjust the width of the button to 225 pixels or choose another option under Layout Style to generate code for a button that's 90 or 55 pixels wide (but doesn't include pictures). Experiment with the settings here to see which combination of sizes, fonts, and color scheme meshes best with your mobile site.

Figure 14-2: Add a Facebook Like button to help visitors to your site easily "like" your Facebook page.

Asking Users What They Think with a Poll

www.polleverywhere.com

People love to see what other people are thinking and then chime in with their two cents' worth. Embedding a poll on a web page has long been a quick and relatively easy way to engage your users with your content, to allow them to give you feedback about what you've done, and to spark discussions in your comments section.

Poll Everywhere (see Figure 14-3) takes this process to another level, allowing your users to not only vote on a question or statement you choose but also to see the results of the voting in real time, on their phones. On your mobile website, you can embed an animated bar graph that displays which response is in the lead.

The basic level of Poll Everywhere is free but restricted to only 30 users. If you find that you have more than 30 users trying to respond to your polls, you can choose from six levels of service upgrades, ranging from $15 to $1,400 per month and able to accommodate as many as 20,000 users. If you're allowing users to submit text responses to polls, consider the Presenter level of service, which enables you to moderate comments (and remove any obscenities or spam) before they appear on your site.

Figure 14-3: Add a poll to your site to gather feedback and collect opinions from your visitors.

Building Slideshows with Flickr Gallery

`www.flickr-gallery.com`

As the most popular photo-sharing site on the web, Flickr has a useful mix of both proprietary and third-party tools to allow designers to insert photo galleries and slideshows on their sites. Unfortunately, the Flickr tools for generating slideshows and galleries use Flash, a technology that neither the iPhone nor iPad supports.

However, the third-party Flickr Gallery tool (see Figure 14-4) uses iPhone/iPad-friendly jQuery or the Prototype/Script.aculo.us to display the images, and has other neat features, such as zoom effects, rounded corners, and automatic thumbnail creation. The non-commercial use of Flickr Gallery is free. If you're using Flickr Gallery for business purposes, you pay from $49 to $69 per year, depending on the number of sites you use it on. The business-level Flickr Gallery allows you to replace their watermark with your own logo.

Although Flickr Gallery makes it possible to display a photo gallery of all images uploaded to Flickr that are tagged with the word *cheeseburger,* the pictures that are then fed into your website may come from Flickr users who might have reserved some of the rights to their images.

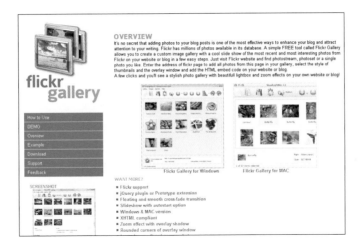

Figure 14-4: Flickr is the most popular photo sharing site on the web and, thanks to Flickr Gallery, you can include your images on your mobile site, too.

Displaying the Latest Information with a Twitter Feed Widget

http://twitter.com/about/resources/widgets

The microblogging service Twitter has been taking over the world, 140 characters at a time. All kinds of iPhone/iPad apps exist to allow the "twitterati" to update their profiles, customize which Twitter updates (or *tweets*) they see, and keep up on Justin Bieber's latest choice in hair care products. If you're active on Twitter, you can also bring its immediacy to your site by displaying your Twitter updates on your mobile site. Here's how:

1. **Log in to your Twitter account and navigate to the Widgets page.**

2. **Select Resources on the left side of the Home screen, and then select Widgets.**

3. **In the Widgets For column, shown in Figure 14-5, click My Website and select the Profile Widget.**

4. **Type your name, and then complete the process of customizing the various settings.**

   For example, you can choose whether to display a scroll bar, specify the number of tweets you see, select which colors the text and hyperlinks use, and choose how many pixels the box occupies on the screen.

   As always, pay special attention to the Size settings. You can either set the width of the widget manually or choose to have it autoresize (which may not work on your site, depending on the other design elements you have chosen).

   You can also choose to display the tweets of another user — although you should make sure that the user's account isn't private and allows you to display their updates.

   If you go back to the main widgets page, Twitter will also allow you to create a widget that displays tweets based on predetermined search terms that you specify, your all-time favorite tweets, or even a list of your favorite Twitter users.

5. **When you're happy with the settings, click the button that generates the code you need and embed it in your site.**

If you use a WordPress Mobile Pack plug-in to optimize your site for mobile devices, the Profile Widget may fail to show up. In that case, go to your WordPress Dashboard page. Under Appearance, click Mobile Theme. A page opens showing the settings for the WordPress Mobile Pack. About halfway down is a box next to the Remove Media setting. After you make sure the box is deselected and save the changes, a JavaScript widget like this Twitter feed runs on your mobile web page. Of course, all kinds of *other* scripts are then allowed to run on your page, so test your WordPress blog thoroughly to make sure you haven't unwittingly enabled an option that slows page load times to a crawl. For more on optimizing your blog for WordPress, see Chapter 13.

Figure 14-5: You can include a Twitter feed on your mobile site.

Getting Discovered with StumbleUpon

www.stumbleupon.com/badges/landing

StumbleUpon (see Figure 14-6), a social bookmarking site, has outlasted much of its competition. Only a few years ago, the Internet was seemingly overflowing with services, such as Blink and Backflip, that promised to allow users to show off fun new sites they had found or to rely on the wisdom of the crowd to find the latest, hottest Internet meme of the moment. For a while, the lists of *chiclets* (tiny icons representing these social bookmarking sites) were growing so extensive that they were longer than many of the blog posts they accompanied. But a funny thing happened on the way to universal oneness: Users started rebelling against all the chaos, and many of these sites withered away.

StumbleUpon, as one of the survivors, has built a strong inventory of tools for site designers to share their content with an installed user base of more than 10 million. Experts say that because of the way StumbleUpon consistently reaches into its database to recommend sites to its users, having users submit and like a page contributes more to long-term traffic than the brief spikes you gain from other sharing services.

You have to sign up for the service (don't worry — it's free), and then you can either create a standard badge to display on your site or, if you're comfortable with using JavaScript, you can custom-create a StumbleUpon badge. Some useful JSON source code for you to experiment with is provided at http://www.stumbleupon.com/help/badge-api-documentation/.

TIP

To truly leverage the social part of a social bookmarking site such as StumbleUpon, you must do more than include this badge on your website. You have to engage with the other users on StumbleUpon by chatting with them about the links they like, voting on their submissions, and generally participating in the community.

Figure 14-6: Promote your site with StumbleUpon.

Building Passport Stamps with Gowalla

`http://gowalla.com/api/docs/iphone`

The Gowalla app for the iPhone/iPad is the first of three location-based services we feature in this chapter. Mobile experts have long been predicting a radical change in the way users surf the web, because using mobile devices with built-in GPS functionality enables a whole new level of relevance to come to the experience. That is, when the web knows where you're located, it can tailor the content that appears on your screen to that data, such as showing you search results for Thai restaurants located within driving distance.

Gowalla encourages its users to earn prizes for checking in at various locations (as shown in Figure 14-7) while also sharing their opinions and pictures with their friends or other users. A business can buy a custom Passport Stamp for its location as long as a year in advance, to coincide with special promotions. The stamps, which cost between $200 and $2,500, offer businesses a cool incentive for users to visit their locations and use their mobile phones to check in.

However, Gowalla functionality isn't limited to the users of its app. A site designer can give users a way to check in to Gowalla by inserting a hyperlink to the feature they want their audience to use when checking in. For example, if you want your site users to add you as a friend and check out places you think are cool, you would have on your site a link that looks like this:

```
<a href="gowalla://users/YOUR USERNAME">Add me as a friend on
        Gowalla to explore some of the places I love</a>
```

You can also link to items such as the user's Passport (to highlight the number of badges they have earned) or to the specific URL for the spot where you want them to check in.

These links cause the user's iPhone/iPad to launch the Gowalla app; if it isn't installed, the link simply fails to work.

The 3G version of the iPad has GPS functionality built in. The Wi-Fi-only version of the iPad can still deliver some location-aware data to these services, but it does so primarily by using WiFi triangulation through the Skyhook API, to track the location of the WiFi hotspots the iPad is using to access the web. For more on the Skyhook API, see `http://www.skyhookwireless.com/howitworks`.

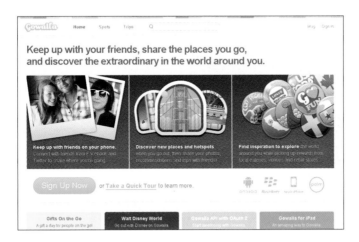

Figure 14-7: Add location-based services in Gowalla.

Using Extensions to Build Foursquare into Your Site

`http://foursquare.com/apps`

The location-based service we describe in this section is the one whose game-like interface has been copied by the competition. *Foursquare* has shot to the front of the pack with its combination of antic humor and growing usefulness. Users compete with their friends to see who can check in most often, and they're rewarded with weekly bragging rights on public leaderboards that show who visited the most places and earned the most points.

Many mobile websites have already integrated Foursquare (see Figure 14-8). Navigate to the Foursquare apps gallery, and click the Websites tab to see examples of mobile websites using the GPS and personal data generated by Foursquare on their sites. One example is Citynumbers.com (`www.city numbers.com`), which shows what the most popular events, concerts, or restaurants are in Amsterdam, according to how many users are checking in (and saying favorable things) using Foursquare. Other mobile websites let you see where in your city the highest number of users are congregating (`http://foursquare.com/app/misotrendy`), the hottest event (`http://foursquare.com/app/nitefly`), or the location where your friends in the area want to meet for lunch, based on a group vote (`http://foursquare.com/app/lunchwalla`).

The code snippets that you can cut and paste into your site are found at `http://groups.google.com/group/foursquare-api/web/api-documentation`. You need to understand a little JavaScript if you want to customize these snippets. We recommend that you check out the gallery of plug-ins for Foursquare as well at `http://foursquare.com/apps/?cat=Plugins` because they may save you the time it takes to develop your own functionality.

Figure 14-8: Foursquare is a great example of a location-based service.

Setting Up a Game with SCVNGR

`http://scvngr.com/build/challenges`

The location-based service *SCVNGR* looks like what a cartoon character yells through gritted teeth at a flock of buzzards. SCVNGR (see Figure 14-9), as its name hints at, helps you organize scavenger hunts, where a combination of online tools and GPS check-ins lets users build up points and win real prizes. After you register (SCVNGR is free), you can use its simple tools to build three basic features:

- **Challenges:** The designer picks a spot using GPS and dares players to try to be the first to arrive and check in using their phone.

- **Rewards:** A user who earns enough points at a place can win whatever reward (such as a discount or free item) the designer offers.

- **Treks:** Just like a traditional scavenger hunt, a designer sets up a course to follow, offering clues to lead players to the next check-in point.

You can link to any SCVNGR place page from your mobile website, so your mobile users can find the games you've set up and the rewards they can win. Because the place pages also include a list of users who have played, you can see the kind of response you're getting. Clever sports marketing coordinators are setting up SCVNGR hunts on the day of a big game, to give the sports fans in attendance a fun event to do outside the stadium (and to lead them to the expensive pavilions erected by corporate sponsors).

Figure 14-9: Set up your own scavenger hunt with SCVNGR.

Linking to Answers on LinkedIn

`www.linkedin.com`

The professional social networking site LinkedIn has become the grown-up answer to Facebook and MySpace and other, more casual sites. Unlike sites targeted toward teenagers and their drive to accumulate as many friends as possible, the LinkedIn guiding philosophy is that users are cautioned against linking to anyone they don't know in real life and are willing to vouch for. The key ingredient in LinkedIn's success is the *virtual introduction,* where you use a virtual version of "I know a guy who knows a guy" to help you reach out to business professionals to try to do business.

Think of the "Six degrees of separation from Kevin Bacon" game that was popular a few years ago, and add the possibility of making real money. However, LinkedIn fiercely weeds out spammers and trolls: If you go there looking to relentlessly plug something sleazy, the site will ban you in a heartbeat.

One of the most valuable, but most overlooked, tools in LinkedIn is its Answers function, where the social networking service attempts to engage its users in an international form of crowdsourcing. The LinkedIn users can pose questions in a wide variety of categories and vote on which answer is the best.

For professionals looking to build their profiles (and employability), the Answers section is a good place to start to connect with other users and to spout off on topics near and dear to their hearts. The resulting discussions of topics make good content for a profile site and can be displayed on your mobile website by using an RSS feed.

Start by going to the Answers Home page at `www.linkedin.com/ answers?trk=tab_answers` and either answering a question yourself or browsing the categories. When you find a category that you believe has relevant and potentially interesting discussions occurring, such as International or Technology, click the drop-down menu under the Subscribe to New Questions In heading to see the RSS link. Copy the link and then paste it on your website to receive continuous updates on the interesting discussions you participate in or that help to add (free!) valuable content to your site.

15

Ten Ways to Market Your Site

In This Chapter

▶ Search engine optimization

▶ SMS messages

▶ QR codes

▶ Mobile coupons

▶ Image recognition advertising

▶ Facebook

▶ Rich media

▶ Online recommendations

▶ Social bookmarking

▶ Media strategy

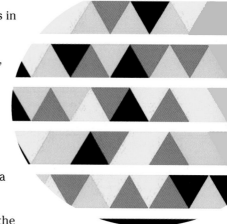

*T*he mobile web brings some exciting innovations in promotion, but also brings many challenges.

Advertising on mobile devices seems, at first glance, to be a losing game. The screen is a tiny fraction of a proper flat-screen TV, the connection to the Internet is far more tenuous than using a cable modem or DSL line, and typing on the itty-bitty keyboard is comfortable only for leprechauns. The larger size of the iPad solves some of these challenges, although its screen is still smaller and the keyboard still trickier to use than those you find on a laptop or desktop computer.

Nevertheless, even on the more diminutive iPhone, the mobile web offers these important advantages:

✔ **People carry their mobile phones with them wherever they go.**
Studies show that people who forget and leave their phones behind in
restaurants usually realize the error within an hour or two; however,
most people realize in about *a day* that they've left behind their wallets
containing their IDs, cash, and credit cards. This situation demonstrates
how integral mobile phones are in people's lives.

✔ **The mobile phone offers one of the rare times in modern life when
you have the undivided attention of your audience.** Think of the environment that most advertising gets tossed into — to sink or swim. The
average teenager flips through TV channels with music blaring from
iPod earbuds, a laptop open to Facebook while instant messaging, glossy
magazines open on the bed, and a video game console blasting aliens.
Good luck breaking through that level of chaos.

In contrast, the same teenager riding the bus to school *cocoons* with
the media — that is, the teenager sits down, pulls out a mobile phone
or media player, puts headphones on, and plays music or videos.
Researchers say that even in busy and crowded environments, where
visitors to your site may be distracted, having the media player in the
teen's hand creates a special state of connection and concentration.

✔ **People trust content delivered via their mobile devices.** According to
research by several mobile marketing experts, the trust is built up from
hearing your mom's voice come out of the device, for example, or relying on it to reach 911 when you witness a car accident.

That trust translates into a much better chance that your marketing
message actually gets through. But don't just take that at face value;
early research shows that, when done properly and integrated with
other media, mobile advertising yields a return on investment that's surprising even seasoned advertising executives.

✔ **Mobile devices increasingly have GPS built in.** Using GPS, your mobile
phone knows where you are (that's why it can tell you where to go when
you get lost). GPS also lets advertisers take advantage of location data
to display ads that are more relevant — when an advertising message
reaches a potential customer in a particular location, you can do things
like promote your coffee shop to anyone within a city block of your front
door.

Targeting your ads to appear where and when your customers need
them transforms the ads from intrusive spam that everyone grumbles
about into a useful service that solves a need. For instance, you might be
glad to know:

• Where the nearest tire repair shop is when your car blows a tire on
the way to work

• Who can help you remove a red wine stain from a cashmere
sweater before the stain sets in

- Where you can find the nearest place to refill your allergy medication before you wind up in the hospital

Of course, location-based targeting raises all kinds of privacy concerns, which is why so many mobile advertising practitioners talk about *opt-in* marketing campaigns, which require that consumers agree to receive advertising sent to their mobile phones.

Making Your Site Search Engine Friendly

After you go to all the trouble to make your website work well on the iPhone and iPad, don't forget to make it search engine friendly as well. Although many of the same rules of search engine optimization (SEO) apply, you need to understand a few key differences and special additions, as well as a few things you shouldn't do on your mobile site, if you want to be included in mobile search engines, such as Google's, shown in Figure 15-1.

Figure 15-1: Most major search engines offer mobile-optimized search options, but Google has one of the most advanced mobile search services.

Scoring high in search engine results is complicated because millions of sites vie for the top spots and search engines use complex formulas to determine which website should match any given keyword search. The formulas that search engines use to prioritize websites are guarded more carefully than Coca-Cola guards its recipe. And, if that doesn't make it complicated enough, most search engines change their formulas regularly. (How regularly is also secret.)

The reason for all this secrecy is that the people who run sites such as Google and Bing want to deliver the best results when someone conducts a search — not just a list of the sites that reflect a smart web marketer's ability to trick its way into the top position. Because a great deal of money can be made at the top, web marketers spend countless hours testing how search engines work, to come up with their best guesses about the criteria that search engines are using and how best to move their sites up the list.

The result is sort of a cat-and-mouse game, with search engines changing the rules to thwart the most calculated efforts of specialists in SEO and with people who specialize in SEO charging big bucks to figure out the secret formula that can put someone on top.

For the most part, search engines score sites based on the words and images on web pages and on how well their content matches the keywords that are searched. For example, if you own a B&B (a bed-and-breakfast) in Point Reyes Station, California, you should include *at least* the name *Point Reyes Station* on your website because the term *B&B* has many competitors and people searching for lodging in the area are likely to include the town's name in their search. Additionally, just searching for B&B might also turn up drink recipes for a cocktail made out of brandy and Benedictine liqueur.

A helpful way to determine how best to make your own site search engine friendly is to search for the keywords that you want to lead people to your site and then study the websites that match those words already. Often, the best way to move your website up the ranks in search results is to emulate the strategies of other sites that are already doing well.

Achieving the best placement, especially for popular keywords, is a full-time job, but here are a few do's and don'ts for making your site search engine friendly:

- ✔ **Do add a meta tag that identifies your site as mobile friendly.** Search engines, such as Google, are much more likely to find your mobile site, and deliver it to mobile devices, if you include this piece of code in the head region at the top of your page code. Just enter the following line of code, exactly as it appears, anywhere between the <head> and </head> tags at the top of your web page:

```
<meta name="HandheldFriendly" content="True" />
```

- ✔ **Do make sure your code is valid.** This advice is even more important on the mobile web than it is on the desktop web. Take the time to have online validators evaluate your site, such as the ones at the World Wide Web Consortium (W3C), and make sure your code is up to snuff. (You can find more on testing and using code validators in Chapter 11.)

✔ **Do invite other sites to link to you.** Most web marketers and information architects agree that Google rewards people who attract the highest number of links to their sites, especially if those sites already have good rankings themselves. The theory makes sense: If lots of other websites consider your site good enough to send their visitors to it, your site probably has something of value to offer.

✔ **Do develop a list of keywords and write a good description for your site.** The trick to writing a good website description is making it concise (most SEO experts recommend no more than 75 words), packing it with your most important keywords and phrasing it to read like a sentence. Include this description toward the top of your home page in the *meta description tag,* a special tag that can be used to add information just for search engines.

✔ **Do include your most important keywords in the title of your web page and in the name of the file.** The title doesn't appear in the body of a web page; the title appears at the top of the browser window. You can add or edit the title of a page in Dreamweaver by changing the text in the Title field at the top of the workspace. Similarly, including keywords in the filename of every page in your website can also boost rankings.

✔ **Do include keywords in the headlines on your web page.** Most search engines place higher priority on keywords that appear in the headlines on a page, but only if you use heading tags to style those headlines. Heading tags, which include <h1> (the biggest) through <h6> (the smallest), identify text as headlines in a way that search engines easily recognize. These tags haven't changed from XHTML to HTML5, so complying with this guideline is easy.

✔ **Do register your mobile site with search engines.** Mobile search engines, such as Yahoo!, as shown in Figure 15-2, feature mobile sites, but only if they know that you're there and have designed a site for the mobile web.

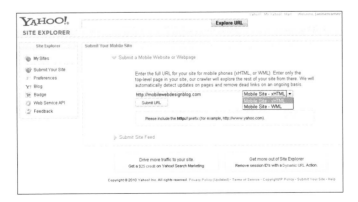

Figure 15-2: Submit your mobile URL to Yahoo! and other mobile search engines to help visitors find you more easily.

- ✒ **Don't stuff in extra keywords.** Although keyword stuffing is a popular strategy in the world of SEO, it's increasingly frowned on by search engines. Plus, it's downright self-sabotaging on the mobile web, where every word counts and adding extra words can cost you valuable download time.

- ✒ **Don't expect instant (or permanent) results.** Even if you do everything right in the search engine search game, you might still have to wait for the results of your efforts to be recognized. Some search engines can take weeks or months to reflect changes to web pages on the Internet. Search engines, such as Google, generally update the most popular sites very quickly while lagging weeks or months behind in updating less-visited sites.

A great place to learn more about how search engines work and how to achieve the best ranking is at `www.searchenginewatch.com`.

Reaching Out with SMS Messages

The length of Short Message Service (SMS), or *text,* messages is limited to 160 characters, so your advertising message has to be short and sweet. These messages can contain links to Web sites or *click-to-call* messages: You click the SMS so that your phone places a call. SMS campaigns are much simpler to deal with than common short code (CSC) campaigns. (Common short codes typically call on people to send, or *text,* a specific word to a five-digit number to elicit a specific action, such as donating ten dollars to Haiti earthquake relief, voting for the next winner of *American Idol,* or entering a contest to win a free home makeover.)

Companies such as the ones in the following list have lots of information on their websites about what you need to do if you want to run a large-scale SMS messaging campaign to market your site:

- ✒ **Clickatell:** (`www.clickatell.com`) Clickatell claims to be the first online SMS *gateway* — the first company to allow users to send SMS messages to mobile devices from desktop computers. It sends SMS messages to devices in more than 220 countries and territories around the world and also sells common short codes in six countries, including the United States.

- ✒ **txtwire:** (`www.txtwire.com`) Originally created specifically to take advantage of mobile marketing, txtwire has branched out to also provide emergency-alert services for schools and local government. A smaller company than others on this list, it seems to be more open to working with small businesses.

- ✒ **TxtImpact:** (`www.smsgatewaypro.com`) This diversified company offers SMS applications to let people vote, enter contests, play trivia games, and do much more. It also sells shared CSCs (ones that run only while your marketing campaign is running) as well as dedicated CSCs that would belong only to you.

✔ **iLoop Mobile:** (www.iloopmobile.com) The company has slick templates for SMS marketing campaigns and aims its product offerings at large advertising agencies. Though not an SMS gateway, iLoop Mobile works with bulk SMS providers and bundles technical services with its professional consulting work in a way that may be attractive to people who want only a one-stop solution.

Make sure you understand what you're signing up for before you start your campaign or else you can wind up with a much more expensive bill than you expect. Though most reputable companies charge 5 cents or less per text message sent, the rates these companies charge for advertising campaigns can vary wildly; some want as much as 50 cents *per customer* for every text message they send.

If you want to get your feet wet, the social media company Brightkite (http://brightkite.com) has rolled out a free service that enables you to send bulk SMS messages to as many as 25 people at a time. Brightkite (see Figure 15-3) was originally conceived of as a kind of location-based Twitter — a place where people can quickly and easily upload their locations and their activities. Then their friends can track them and see whether they're nearby for serendipitous meet-ups. Like many other social networking sites, Brightkite has expanded its range of functions; in its case, Brightkite's services now include sending mass text messages and allowing the people who receive those text messages to then send text messages to each other (and you). This capability may be enough for a small business to stay in touch with its most loyal customers.

Figure 15-3: Brightkite offers a free group SMS service.

Connecting with 2D Barcodes

2D barcodes and *mobile tags* are visual codes that can be scanned using any mobile phone or device equipped with a camera, an Internet connection, and an app that can read barcodes or tags.

2D barcodes and tags come in different shapes, brands, and colors, but they're all part of a fast-evolving area of advertising. They're showing up on billboards, buses, business cards, newspaper and magazine ads, and the contact pages of websites. In theory, you can use a 2D barcode on any object you can print in a decent resolution. (We're thinking of making postage stamps next.)

As shown in Figure 15-4, some 2D barcodes (such as the QR code in the top of the figure) look a little like a scrambled black-and-white checkerboard. Others, like the Microsoft tag at the bottom of Figure 15-4, are more colorful. The QR code and the Microsoft tag in this figure serve the same purpose — to make it easy for visitors to save contact information to their phones by scanning it with the phones' built-in cameras.

Scan this QR Code to save Mark's contact info

Scan this Microsoft tag to save Mark's contact info

If you're wondering why we used both types of barcode in this part of the Jelly Rancher contact page (featured in Chapter 7), it's because each barcode requires its own software, and we want to make things as easy as possible for our visitors, no matter what 2D barcode reader they happen to have on their phones. We have them all, and we recommend you download all of the apps on the list of popular barcode software that follows.

The good news for web designers — and anyone else who wants to put 2D barcodes on hats and business cards — is that they are remarkably easy (and free) to make.

Figure 15-4: In the Jelly Rancher website featured in Chapter 7, we included the two most popular types of 2D barcodes.

There are a growing number of companies creating software for generating and scanning 2D barcodes. Here are a few of the most popular:

Microsoft Tags: Anyone with an Internet connection can create these colorful tags for mobile devices for free on the Microsoft Tag site (see Figure 15-5), which makes them an increasingly popular addition to everything from business cards to bumper stickers.

On the Microsoft Tag site, you can even customize the codes with your own photos in the background. To read the tags, you need the Microsoft Tag Reader application, which is available for the iPhone, iPad2, and most Android, BlackBerry, and Windows mobile devices. Find the most up-to-date details about tag support at `http://tag.microsoft.com`.

Figure 15-5: You can scan Microsoft tags with the iPhone or iPad2 or many other devices.

Scan this QR Code for details

Figure 15-6: QR codes are easy to create, but powerful enough to contain more than a thousand characters of information.

QR codes (Quick Response codes): QR codes, such as the one shown in Figure 15-6, are limited to black and white. But because they were the first, and have long been the most popular, 2D barcodes, they are increasingly featured in ads in magazines and newspapers, and we've even seen them on billboards and the sides of buildings.

The term *QR code* may seem almost synonymous with *2D barcode* because the use of QR codes is free of any license fees, there are dozens of websites and services that make it easy to create QR codes (like the one shown in Figure 15-6), and most mobile devices include a camera capable of reading them. If you have an iPhone and you have the Google app, you already have a QR code reader because it's built in. Just click the small camera in the Google app and point the camera on your iPhone or iPad at the QR code to activate it.

Use an online service to create a QR code. Here are a few to get you started:

KAYWA: The service at `http://qrcode.kaywa.com`, generates all the code you need. Just enter your information and click the Generate! button and you can create a QR code that links to a URL, sends a text message, calls a phone number, or sends an SMS.

Chrome Extensions: Search this site at `https://chrome.google.com/extensions` and you find several QR code extensions, including the QR Code Generator, by Oscar Fröberg. You can also find QR code extensions for Firefox.

SnapTag: With this software, you can design barcodes around a logo or graphic. SnapTag, developed by Spyderlynk (see Figure 15-7), is challenging the clumsy black-and-white barcode design of the old days (a few weeks ago) and making it possible to create barcodes that make an impression on humans as well as on code readers. The information is encoded in the breaks in the lines in the circle around the logo at the center of the tag.

Figure 15-7: Spyderlynk's SnapTag technology allows you to use your corporate logo or an interesting picture as part of your code.

No matter which service you use to create a barcode or tag, you can create codes with a variety of options, including:

✔ A text message is sent, such as a special offer: "Save 20% if you buy in the next 10 minutes."

- ✔ A menu opens, giving visitors the option to save contact information to their devices.

- ✔ A video begins in the video player automatically.

- ✔ The Safari web browser opens a linked website.

The list of ways to use barcodes continues to grow. Here are a few examples to illustrate ways these codes are already being used:

- ✔ In San Francisco, Scanbuy partnered with Citysearch to produce QR codes that were placed in the windows of 580 restaurants. Customers with the ScanLife software on their phones can point their phone's cameras at the code in the window. As soon as the software recognizes the code, the phone displays a Citysearch review and information about available food and drinks.

- ✔ Not to be outdone, Antenna Audio has QR codes at tourist attractions in San Francisco. Users can point their phones' cameras at the codes and are treated to an audio tour of the site and an explanation of its history.

- ✔ Newspapers, such as the *Pittsburgh Post-Gazette,* run QR codes alongside concert reviews and sports stories. When readers point their phone cameras at the code, their phones open a page where readers can buy and download songs that the reviewed band played or browse jerseys of teams that played in the game.

- ✔ Another highly successful use of QR codes belongs to the magazine *Get Married.* It uses the Microsoft Tag engine, which makes it possible to create color QR codes instead of the mostly black-and-white codes. Another advantage of using Microsoft tags is that you can turn almost any picture into a QR code, making the codes far more visually appealing. *Get Married* now includes Microsoft Tag QR codes in nearly every ad in its print and online editions.

Using Mobile Coupons

The capability of the mobile web to deliver a coupon to the user exactly when and where it will have the most impact creates an immediate and personalized call to action that highlights one of the most powerful advantages you can gain in any advertising campaign — instant gratification. Imagine reaching out to a customer with a discount or special offer to tempt them while they walk past your place of business. Or sending a coupon good for a free concert T-shirt to the teenager in the audience who is the first to SMS-message the correct answer to a trivia question displayed on the big screen.

When customers use a printed coupon, you can gather only limited information about them, such as in which general zip code you distributed the coupon (assuming that your customers didn't share their coupons with someone from across town).

When you use mobile coupons, you can track exactly who was sent a coupon, how long until it was redeemed, and all kinds of other demographic information that can help you make your marketing and sales efforts more efficient.

The next wave of mobile coupons is likely to be driven by the growing inclusion of GPS functionality in HTML5 on the iPad and iPhone. Already, startups such as mobiQpons and Yowza!! show coupons based on the user's proximity to stores. Yowza!! even allows users to share coupons with their friends by using social networking, thus tying their coupons to the most popular use of the mobile Web today — updating Facebook and Twitter.

Mobile coupons come with one major snag: Because the coupon barcode appears on a phone's LCD screen, many older, laser barcode readers can't process the information. For just this reason, Target Corporation recently spent tens of millions of dollars to replace all scanners at its cash registers around the United States.

To make using coupons as easy as possible, many mobile coupon companies are rolling out small, point-of-sale terminals that can be used to verify coupons. Others are offering alternatives, such as setting up toll-free numbers for merchants to call to verify and track coupons.

You can try a free mobile coupon service, at MixMobi, shown in Figure 15-8, to see whether it gets traction and whether your customers like it. MixMobi lets you try its mobile coupon service for 14 days (or 5,000 page views, whichever comes first).

Figure 15-8: You can create a free mobile coupon to test the service at MixMobi.

Sharing Offers via Image Recognition

The exciting innovation of image recognition in advertising lets users take pictures of any object with their phones' camera — say, the label on a bottle of wine or the cover of a book — and find more information about the object by being directed automatically to a related website.

Men's Health and *Rolling Stone* were the first print publications to take advantage of this new way of extending the reach of traditional advertising. Image recognition is attractive for publishers because they can offer advertisers a chance to tie together their print and online ad campaigns seamlessly.

Advertising based on image recognition faces some initially daunting challenges in the broad mobile market because many cellphone cameras produce blurry, dim images and sending those images can be expensive or complicated. However, the iPhone's superior camera quality and ease of use make it a natural option for this new way of extending your brand.

Among the companies making inroads with image recognition ads are

- **Amazon:** If your product is listed on the Amazon.com site, you're already recognizable in the Amazon app. Amazon tests its own image recognition engine and claims that even if a user takes a picture of an object that's not on the site, such as a dog, the app responds by showing ads for related products, such as dog food or flea medication.

- **GetFugu:** The mobile start-up company GetFugu recently launched its *See It* technology, which allows users to point their phone camera at any modern corporate logo or sign, take a picture, and then be directed to that brand's website. The app also includes voice and GPS search functions.

  GetFugu claims that its technology has made the logo recognition process almost 90 percent accurate and that it can discern among such similar items as the Apple logo, the AT&T logo, and the *Death Star* from *Star Wars*.

- **Google Goggles:** This app has gotten a lot of press because of its "wow factor." Using Google Goggles (see Figure 15-9), you can point your phone camera at almost any object and see more information about it. Point the camera at a label on a wine bottle, for example, and you'll likely be directed to the winery or a wine distributor. Point your phone camera at a building or another landmark and you see information about its architect, the history of its location, or other details. You can even take a picture of someone's business card and Goggles automatically enters the information into your contact database. This technology seems destined to become increasingly popular for all kinds of uses.

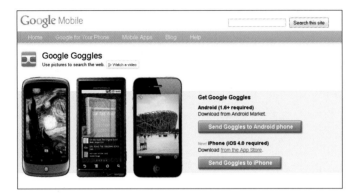

Figure 15-9: Google Goggles makes it possible to search for information by taking a photo of any object, including buildings.

Exploring Rich Media Ads

If you're not including video, animation, and other interactive features in your iPhone and iPad designs, you're missing out on the most innovative aspect of these new devices. *Rich media* is the catchall phrase of the year — an attempt to give a name to all the ways you can create multimedia content and make it interactive.

Among the best services for delivering rich media ads to the iPhone is the AdMob Interactive Video Mobile Ad Unit. Google's acquisition of this service is a clear sign that Google sees a big future in the mobile video advertising market. The considerable resources and expertise of Google mean that the AdMob ad product (see Figure 15-10) will probably get a wide market rollout.

Research by the Nielsen Company predicts that mobile video will grow at the rate of 137 percent per year and that it will comprise the single largest segment of global mobile data usage by 2013. Because advertising travels where the eyeballs are, most major ad agencies are feverishly working to prepare their creative directors and staff to take advantage of this shift.

Before you get carried away with video on your iPhone/iPad sites, remember that the bandwidth limitations that come with the mobile web still plague many iPhone users. Even with 3G (and 4G) networks, video can really slow things down. If the connection is broken (a risk on any mobile connection), your visitors may not return to a page that takes too long to download.

Figure 15-10: The AdMob platform, now owned by Google, delivers video ads to the iPhone and other mobile devices.

Reaching Facebook's 500 Million Users

With an Oscar-nominated movie and more than 500 million users, the social-networking site that started out as Mark Zuckerberg's attempt to make Harvard's yearbook more interactive online has become a global phenomenon. How pervasive is Facebook these days? According to a study by researchers for the United Nations, more people in Indonesia knew what Facebook was than knew what the word *Internet* meant. To these new users, Facebook *is* the Internet. It's what they use. They don't realize that Facebook lives as just a part of the Internet.

Meanwhile, after the revolutions in the Middle East, parents in places like Cairo, Egypt, are naming their children Facebook. And according to the American Academy of Matrimonial Lawyers, Facebook is now the primary source of evidence in divorce cases. It is increasingly the tool people use to organize meetings, brag about their accomplishments, or — of most interest in this chapter — promote their products and services.

According to Facebook's own statistics, people who use Facebook on their iPhone/iPads are 200 percent more active in viewing and sharing content, and they are also 300 percent more likely to engage with a site financially (either by buying something or recommending to a friend that they make a purchase) when they interact with that site through a Facebook link on their mobile device.

The good news for web designers is that a recent study by Covario's Social Media Insight tracking tool found that creativity trumps money on Facebook. Just throwing money at a marketing and advertising campaign does not return results that are as good as having a compelling message (or website).

In Chapter 14, we showed how to add the Facebook Like button to your site. But you should not only empower your users to share your content with their friends — you should also seek out and participate in the communities related to your business. That means spending the time to do searches for Facebook Groups, Fan Pages, and Events (to help you understand these features, we have created a guide on our DigitalFamily.com site at `http://www.digitalfamily.com/social-media/Facebook-Fan-Pages-vs-Groups.html`). Your first step should be to set up what social media marketing experts call a "listening post." Learn what your prospective users are talking about before you start jumping in to try to sway them in your direction. If nothing else, you'll find valuable insight into what the problems and concerns of your users are, and what they wish someone would do to help them out.

Leveraging Online Word of Mouth

One of the biggest shifts brought about by the rise of the Internet, and the empowerment of any average computer user to reach a potentially global audience, has been the increase in the power of what used to be known as *word-of-mouth* marketing. Before the web gave us all the power to be magazine publishers (or radio DJs, or TV producers), our opinions were limited to the people in our immediate vicinity. Sure, if we really felt strongly about something, we could write letters to the editor, or graffiti our opinions on bathroom walls, but realistically, we mostly shared our thoughts with a pretty small group of people.

These days, typing a couple of sentences into the comment section on a blog and clicking OK means that an opal miner in the Australian outback and a jewelry designer in Milan can instantly learn whether the fruit of their labor is likely to be a popular Mother's Day present this year. Research by McKinsey & Company shows that opinions shared by what are perceived to be "ordinary people" are responsible for almost 50 percent of all purchasing decisions.

It's simple. We trust what people like us — that is, people who are not highly paid celebrities appearing in slick TV commercials — say about their experiences. While it's true that Facebook (which has worked hard to optimize its site for the mobile web; see Figure 15-11) is currently the most popular venue for the free exchange of opinions, you can use many other sites out there to get the word out about your site and/or your product.

Here are some of the most popular social networking sites and what you can expect to find there:

✔ **Yelp:** (www.yelp.com) This site started out as an e-mail recommendation service, morphed into a place where foodies could talk about their latest gastronomical adventures, and now serves as a directory of local businesses as diverse as veterinarians, accountants, and yoga instructors. A good review on Yelp can help drive traffic to your mobile website; a bad one means you should either respond on Yelp (if it's unfair) or fix what's wrong,

✔ **LinkedIn:** (www.linkedin.com) This is *the* site for professional connections and online business networking. If you're online to develop business contacts with other professionals, especially if you're job hunting or trying to attract new business clients, this is a powerful place to promote yourself and your website. Unlike Facebook and MySpace, LinkedIn is all business.

✔ **MySpace:** (www.myspace.com) One of the all-time most popular social networking sites, MySpace makes it easy to create a profile site, add music, write a blog, and post

Figure 15-11: Social media sites, such as Facebook, were quick to adapt their designs to the mobile web.

as many photos as you want to share with the world. Although the site once dominated the social networking landscape on the Internet, at the time of this writing, it was rapidly falling behind its biggest competitor, Facebook. Still, its huge online audience is a popular place for musicians, performers, and many others to promote themselves and their websites.

✔ **Ecademy** (www.ecademy.com): Similar to LinkedIn, professionals at the Ecademy site network, seek new clients, hunt for jobs, and recruit employees. What makes Ecademy different is that it's much more international, with an especially strong audience in Europe and Asia.

✔ **Ning:** (www.ning.com) You can create your own social networking site at Ning and invite your friends and colleagues to create profiles there, in your own exclusive social network environment.

When you make it easy for people to share information about your product, you make it much more likely that your satisfied users will say nice things about you.

Getting Ranked on Social Bookmarking Sites

Social bookmarking sites rank the popularity of web pages by the number of votes they get. The result is that these sites are excellent resources for people who want to keep up with what's popular online. Most offer special software that makes it easy for anyone to vote on a site.

Getting your site listed on social bookmarking sites is a highly effective way to increase traffic. Dozens of these sites and services exist, with more sure to come, and they feature catchy and unusual names, such as Digg (http://digg.com), delicious (http://delicious.com), and StumbleUpon (www.stumbleupon.com, and reddit (www.reddit.com). In Chapter 14, we showed how to create your own customized StumbleUpon badge; while it's now the market leader in social bookmarking, we encourage you to experiment with the other popular sites and services. After all, the more inbound links you get from popular sites, the better page ranking you get in search engine results (sometimes known as "Google Juice").

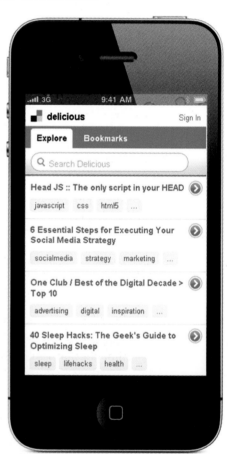

Although delicious is designed to store and share bookmarks, and features a mobile version (see Figure 15-12), it's a great place to promote your site. An often-overlooked feature of delicious is the ability to share your links with your friends. It's helpful because you can not only promote your latest creations but also use their links as a way of finding out what the latest, hottest, funniest trend on the web is all about.

Figure 15-12: Delicious is a popular social bookmarking site.

While you can submit your own pages on any of these sites, they generally frown on it, and if you do it too frequently, you can be banned. Besides, your one little vote doesn't make much difference anyway. A better method is to add to your site a button from each of these services that helps your visitors easily vote for you. If you're a blogger, you can add a button every time you post. You can get the buttons ("chiclets") for free and add them to your pages by simply inserting a little code you generate on the social networking site.

Marketing a Website to the Media

The iPhone and iPad are hot topics in the media these days. When you finish designing your site for these new media devices, don't forget to promote them to traditional media outlets.

Attracting media attention to your mobile website is not unlike attracting it to any other business. The trick is to tell a good story and attract the attention of someone who can write about it in a publication that your target audience reads. If you're looking for press coverage, be sure to include a Press section on your website with contact information, story ideas, and any other press coverage you've received.

Don't wait for journalists to come to you! Never pester a reporter with a barrage of e-mail, press releases, or phone calls, but realize that a well-timed or well-pitched message can catch the attention of a reporter *and* have the desired result — your web address in the press. One good way to find journalists who might be interested in your site is to visit related sites and study their Press sections to find out who has been writing about them. Note not only the publication but also the writer. Then send a note directly to that person with a message that starts like this:

> Dear *fabulous journalist* <insert *that person's name,* of course>:
>
> I enjoyed reading the article you wrote on the XYZ Company and thought that you might be interested in what we're doing.

Keep your message brief, and try to include a news hook and story idea that go beyond just promoting your business. The fact that your site works on an iPhone/iPad is exciting, but make sure that you have more of a news hook than just the accessibility of your site on these devices. For example, rather than tell a reporter that you have the best B&B site in northern California, pitch a story about the best hikes in the area and how visitors can use your interactive maps on their iPhones as they hike. With any luck, the article on interesting hikes will include a quote from you and a mention of your B&B's mobile website.

Index

• *Z* •